THOU MY BEST THOUGHT

How to Understand and Know God

Todd Tjepkema

ISBN 978-1-64515-979-7 (paperback)
ISBN 978-1-64515-980-3 (digital)

Christian Faith Publishing, Inc.
832 Park Avenue
Meadville, PA 16335
www.christianfaithpublishing.com

Printed in the United States of America

ENDORSEMENTS

"*Thought-provoking* and *convicting*, these are the first two words that come to mind after reading Todd Tjepkema's first book, *Thou My Best Thought*. This book will challenge preconceived notions on how we should approach the Christian life and sanctification. It is less a how-to book but more a description of Todd's own journey as he navigates family, friends, worship, and ministry all in the pursuit of helping others and struggling with his own questions. Todd brings a fresh approach, laced with humor and common sense, to what can be complicated issues and questions that we all face. I came away thinking I wish I had read this book years ago. Todd has a way of relating spiritual truths in a simple, easy to understand way that edifies and encourages."

—Dan Bewley, Administrative Pastor, Canton, Michigan

"If you want someone to sit across from you on an armchair who will open up the Scriptures in a heartwarming manner, this is the book for you. The author uses personal family stories as well as thought-provoking illustrations to add insight to his substantive biblical research into life-changing ways to live a joyful Christian life. His personal journey through a variety of church theologies as well as various approaches to how-to lists on living the Christian life have challenged him to offer this book, resulting in a well-balanced, practical, relational focus on friendship with Jesus that will appeal to the twenty-first-century reader."

—Mark J. Tjepkema, a biased appraisal by his dad,
Board Certified Chaplin, Ret.

"I really loved it. I enjoyed every chapter and especially the first five. The book was a blessing, Todd, and as I was reading, I could think of about three people that I would love to share it with. I think it represents your thoughts and what you taught the last few years, and I think it is worth sharing. I rarely read this type of book because frankly, they either are too frothy or I already know most of the ideas shared or they are just plain boring :). I wasn't bored one bit. In fact, I used it as a devotional base as I read through it, and I loved it. Your ideas are sound, and I like the approach to how to really know who God is. I love your writing style. It is easy to read and easy to understand for anyone who reads it."

—Sandy Fullmer, Bible College Professor
International Baptist College and Seminary

"It has been such an honor to read your book. I have enjoyed it so much and learned so much as well. I love your real-world examples. And I love how you talk about the natural elements of life explaining the supernatural. I felt like I was right alongside of you learning important truths."

—Tiffini Sproul, Biblical Counselor

"Pastor Todd, thank you for asking me to preview and comment on your book. It has been a blessing to me. I have not seen a book of similar content; I am thankful your teaching will be in written word. God used your teaching of His principles to begin the saving of my soul. The information flows well, and the illustrations/examples are powerful and thought-provoking. As I read, I find myself joyful. Does that make sense? I'm not having difficulty understanding, the words and examples are like having a conversation with a friend (a wise friend)."

—Ruth Lynch, Bible Student

To my best friend, Yeshua ha-Mashiach (Jesus Christ), may these words glorify You and cause all to understand and know You better.

Thus says the Lord:
"Let not the wise man glory in his wisdom,
Let not the mighty man glory in his might,
Nor let the rich man glory in his riches;
But let him who glories glory in this,
That he understands and knows Me,
That I am the LORD, exercising
lovingkindness, judgment, and
righteousness in the earth.
For in these I delight." says the Lord.

—Jeremiah 9:23–24

The Lord Jesus does not desire that we should merely seek to make believers out of sinners but wants us to make disciples out of saints. Preaching results in believers, but only by teaching the saints can we make them disciples.

—M.R. DeHaan

Contents

Foreword

I marveled when I saw it. A Bible verse I had known for years jumped off the page and spoke to me in a fresh and profound way. Jesus increased in wisdom and stature and in favor with God and men (Luke 2:52). It had never occurred to me that Jesus also had to grow in His understanding and knowledge of God. When I saw that, as if for the first time, I was stirred in my spirit with the thought, *If He had to increase in knowledge about God, how much more do I!*

Yes, Jesus was fully God and never ceased to be God when He came to earth, but one critical point we often miss is that He willingly laid aside His divine prerogatives to be born of a virgin in the incarnation. He chose to function as a man on earth, not as God. The Scriptures are abundantly clear on that point (e.g. Philippians 2:5–8). That being the case, consider the ramifications. His brain was not preprogrammed with God-knowledge. Like any other human, He had to learn about God and grow in communion with the Heavenly Father.

Even at the age of twelve, Jesus was filled with a passion for knowing God. We see this in the brief account given in Luke's Gospel. When his parents had departed for home after Passover festivities in Jerusalem, the boy Jesus was not in the caravan. He lingered in the temple to listen to the rabbis teach about Jehovah and to ask questions. When his parents finally caught up with Him a few days later, they were astonished to see his level of understanding at such a young age along with His dedication to learn more.

Jesus hungered and thirsted after righteousness. He told his earthly parents, I must be about my Father's business. Some of the modern Bible versions translate: I must be in my Father's house. The biblical books of Hebrews and Revelation teach that the earthly temple was merely a shadow or reflection of the heavenly temple—the place of God's dwelling and communion with man. Thus, what better place for Jesus to learn about God than the holy temple of Jehovah?

Think of the profound application for New-Testament saints. Our bodies are described as temples of the Holy Spirit (1 Corinthians 6:19–20). Thus, God is all the more accessible and communion with Him is even more personal in this age of grace. We have no excuse! God promises to dwell with each of us, in our individual temples, when we love Him and keep His Word (John 14:23). This is a conditional promise of fellowship when we meet His conditions, extending above and beyond the unconditional promise of Holy Spirit indwelling that occurs at regeneration. He further promises that when we seek Him, we will find Him if we will search diligently (Jeremiah 29:13).

Todd Tjepkema takes up the baton and runs with these truths in his excellent book, *Thou My Best Thought*. He walks us through his own pilgrimage—both in personal life and as a ministerial counselor—sharing practical insights as to how he learned the secret of real change: growing in knowledge of God while believing Him to do His sanctifying work in our lives. Some authors write of knowing God as if it were an end in itself. However, that is stopping short. Tjepkema takes knowing God to its logical and biblical conclusion, demonstrating how it should lead to practical, progressive sanctification, and conformity to the image of Christ.

How well do you know God? Is it possible to know too much about Him or have too much fellowship with Him? Of course not! I doubt any believer would be so audacious as to assume they already know all there is to know about Him. Yet sometimes, we act as know-it-alls by not taking time to know Him in a deeper, fuller way. Furthermore, do you believe God? That is, do you depend upon His Word, His grace, for enablement in all things? Therein lies the secret of spiritual victory.

Knowing God and believing Him are foundational to living for Him and glorifying Him. In fact, as Tjepkema points out, your reward at the bema is contingent upon it. The heart cry of the Apostle Paul was, "That I may know Him!" This book will help you learn how to know Him and how to depend upon Him. If that is your desire, then I would urge you to sit back and enjoy this insightful book. The author will take you on a journey that will repeatedly point you back to the Scriptures and challenge you to greater spiritual heights.

James Hollandsworth
Author, *The End of the Pilgrimage*
Pastor, Tricity Baptist Church, North Carolina

Acknowledgments

To my wonderful wife, Barbara, and our children Geoff and Liz, Fluffy and Emily, Tim and Robert, a great big hug and thank you for your many encouragements to keep going with this long process. Also thank you for your many examples of love for me to draw on for illustrations.

To my dear friend and fellow laborer in the Gospel, Pastor James Hollandsworth, another big thank you. God used the teachings of James on Christ's kingdom to both change my life and bring great joy in my walk with our Lord. I couldn't have done this without you, buddy!

To our special friends Pastor Dan and Beth Bewley, many hugs and kisses for your many years of friendship. Thank you to Dan for his words of encouragement upon completion of the book. And an even bigger thank you to Beth—if she hadn't spent so much time proofing the book, nobody would be able to read it.

Finally, thank you to the following friends for willingly reviewing this book before publication and giving valuable input both theological and grammatical. I greatly appreciate your wisdom and insight, and I am honored by your friendship.

Taylor McCloskey
Ruth Lynch
Tim Kufrin
Sandy Fullmer
Tiffini Sproul

Introduction

What is your purpose in life? What motivates you to do what you do? What gets you out of bed each morning? There are many answers to these questions. Some say their purpose in life is to be happy. While others may say their purpose is to serve others, giving of one's self, or loving others. One guy said he thought our purpose in life was to survive because that is what you see in all animals. In this book, we are going to explore the question of our purpose. Therefore, I would like you to write down, at the top of this page, your purpose in life. Is it to make lots of money, to have a great career, raise a family, retire early, whatever you think it is? Be completely honest with yourself, don't try and guess what the most spiritual answer is. No one else will see your answer; but for your benefit only, write down your purpose in life. Then throughout the book, we will talk more about it, and at the end of the book, I will ask you again to see if it has changed in any way. The reason I ask you this is because a few years ago, I lost my purpose in life.

Have you ever wondered where God is or doubted if He even exists? Have you cried out in pain, wondering why He seems not to be answering your pleas? Of course, those with no faith or differing faiths probably think these things quite often. The scary thing is when those thoughts come from us who believe that Jesus Christ is the Son of God and the Savior of the world. And even crazier when a pastor of fifteen years begins to have those doubts.

That is the beginning of my story and the reason for this book. In 2008, after being a discipleship and counseling pastor for approximately fifteen years and a believer in Jesus Christ for nearly thirty-five years, I doubted whether God cared about me. I was under a lot of stress at that time, and hardly a day went by that I didn't consider just quitting the ministry and finding a regular job. At that time, the church where I served as assistant pastor was going through a multimillion-dollar-building program. And being a ministry with a preschool, K5-twelfth-grade academy, college, and missions board, this was no small task. We were trying to sell the property that the church had occupied for thirty years and build multiple new buildings on our new property. It was very stressful for all involved.

But that wasn't the root problem—it was just the added stress that brought out the real issues in my life. The root of the problem was that after some fifteen years of discipling and counseling my fellow believers, I was becoming discouraged by the lack of positive results in their lives. The problem wasn't listening to everyone's problems as many think would be the tough part of counseling. The real struggle was when people would come back the next week, and there hadn't been any change for them. In the early years of my ministry, I believed that I could help others overcome their problems, even the stubborn ones. And if they didn't change, then it was because I had not yet learned the right words to persuade them. Therefore, I was working very hard to learn more from God's Word so I could help people find relief from their troubles.

Reasons abounded for this resistance to change. For many, it was a lack of motivation to change. They were hoping for some magic pill that would take away all the pain so they wouldn't have to do the hard work it takes to change. For others, it was that the biblical advice I was giving them didn't seem to work. I found that for a lot of people, it didn't matter what I said, they weren't changing. In fact, it is common among biblical counselors to expect only around 20 percent of the people being counseled to experience significant change. It was starting to feel like a waste of time, thus, my desire to quit. Along with that, I was struggling with the lack of biblical change in my own life. I too was wondering where that "Peace of God which surpasses all understanding" (Philippians 4:7) was that the Bible promises. I began to think that there had to be something better. God and His Word should have better results than 20 percent. I must be missing something.

It was then that I cried out to the Lord, "If You are there, I need to know!" And praise God! He answered that prayer. I found that He is true to His promise that if we seek Him, we will find Him. The problem was not that He wasn't there but that I hadn't learned how to seek Him properly. That is what this book is all about—it is my testimony of how I came to understand and know my God better. Of course, He is an infinite God, and I am nowhere close to knowing Him completely. That is why He provides to all those who believe in Him an eternity with Him, for that is how long it will take to know Him. But even with a small growth in my knowledge of Him, I am now experiencing the love, joy, peace, and contentment that God has promised to all who will follow Him.

I will share throughout this book more of the details of God's faithfulness in my life. However, I wished to share just a little, to begin with, to let you know that this book is not an in-depth theological study of sanctification. My goal for this book is to make it practical for the average believers who want to have a more intimate and personal relationship with their God. While some of what I will share may sound new, I desire to keep it simple. Like Paul said to the early believers in Corinth, "But I fear, lest somehow, as the serpent deceived Eve by his craftiness, so your minds may be corrupted from the simplicity that is in Christ" (2 Corinthians 11:3).

I too fear that today's believers, especially in America, have gotten away from the simplicity in Christ. That doesn't mean that Jesus is simple nor that knowing Him will necessarily be simple. Here the Greek word translated *simplicity* means bountiful, singular in focus, and with all sincerity. Paul is saying that the secret to the abundant life in Jesus Christ is to have a bountiful, singular focus on Jesus Christ with all sincerity. Not only did Jesus come to give us new life, but He also provided an opportunity for an abundant life in Him (John 10:10) if our focus remains on Him. Focusing on Christ is a theme throughout Paul's writings. To the Philippians, he told them to *be anxious for nothing* but to turn their worries over to God and meditate on Him (Philippians 4:4–9). And to the Colossians, Paul told them not to focus on the things of this earth but to *look on the things above* (Colossians 3:2).

It is kind of like a young man who falls in love with a young lady. She is the most beautiful woman he has ever seen, and he is so infatuated with her that he can't think of anything else. All this young man wants is to be with her, talk with her, hold her, and stare into her eyes. If you are married, you hopefully remember these feelings. Our God wants us to fall so in love with Him that the things of this life grow strangely dim in the light of His glory and grace. The secret to the abundant life is loving the Lord our God with all our heart, soul, and mind. That is why loving God is the greatest commandment.

Finally I have also learned, through this crisis of faith, that many have had the same experience. I discovered that believers throughout history, men and women, have had similar experiences of doubt. It is as if God brings all of us to this barrier of faith like a huge wall. And we must choose if we are going to give up and rest up against the wall. Or will we do whatever it takes to break through that wall and continue our search for Him? I liken it to the Israelites as they stood before the Promised Land with a decision to either trust God and go into the Promised Land or fear the giant problems of life and refuse to go forward. The Israelites learned that if they only took that first step of faith, that God was right there to part the waters and that their fears were misguided. We too will find out that there is a door in the wall, and Jesus is on the other side knocking. All we must do is open the door.

"Behold, I stand at the door and knock. If anyone hears My voice and opens the door, I will come in to him and dine with him, and he with Me" (Revelation 3:20).

Revelation 3:20 is often used in the context of unbelievers trusting Christ for salvation. But in the context of this verse in Revelation, Jesus is talking to lukewarm believers. These believers had become complacent with their wealth and thought they needed nothing. Sounds like America, right? So God comes along and because He so greatly desires an intimate relationship with His children, He allows crises in their lives. These crises are to remind us that there are bigger issues in this life than self.

Do the circumstances in your life look like unconquerable giants? Maybe you too are at that barrier of faith in your life? Do you wonder if God is out there or if He really cares for you? Are you wondering about God's promises of joy, peace, and contentment? Or maybe you want to avoid that crisis of faith and seek God now before it happens? Then this book is for you. However, this book is not about how to have temporal peace or how to get rid of all the struggles of life. It is about having a deeper understanding and love for your God so that no matter the circumstances God allows in your life, you can find joy, peace, and contentment in Him. You were created to have an intimate relationship with Jesus Christ, to be His bride for all eternity. There is no deeper human relationship than that of a husband and wife.

CHAPTER 1

God's Bride

> For I am jealous for you with godly jealousy. For I have betrothed you to one husband, that I may present you as a chaste virgin to Christ.
>
> —2 Corinthians 11:2

Once upon a time, before galaxies even existed, a king went looking for a bride for his son. Sounds like a fairy tale, but this is no fictional tale. Long before any human ever wrote a fairy tale, God began the greatest love story ever told. It is a true story with a happy ending. It is very much like a medieval-prince-in-shining-armor kind of story. The king has created a kingdom that he wants to leave to his son. The kingdom is perfect and all ready to go; the only thing missing is a bride for his son. The king desires someone worthy to rule and reign with his son and live happily ever after.

Understanding that God did not create us to be His slaves but to be the bride for His Son was the missing piece to the puzzle for me. It was why I was not experiencing the joy of the Christian life. I think it is what is missing in a lot of Christians' lives. We tend to see a separation in our relationship with God as if He is the King, but we are just the peasants in the kingdom. Mostly we run our own lives, working for the King, and providing our crops for the good of the kingdom. Then occasionally (every Sunday), we see the King go by, and we praise, worship, and glorify Him. Sure there are those that are closer to the King—the ones that work in the castle. Those are the full-time Christian workers and the pastors. The missionaries are those knights that go on a quest and slay the dragons in faraway countries. We fail to understand that the Prince of the Kingdom wishes us to be His bride.

The Joyful Christian Life

In my earlier Christian life, I was just working for the Lord and had missed the fact that God wanted a deeper relationship than that. No wonder I was miserable—I saw God as my boss. Even though God is a good boss, the relationship between a boss and worker is nothing compared to a relationship between a husband and wife. God uses the picture of marriage to explain the Christian life. The relationship between a man and a woman is very similar to the relationship God desires with us.

Before moving on, let me insert this little side thought. As a marriage counselor for over twenty-five years, I know that many couples do not have a loving marriage. Also there are those who have not been married. As I present marriage as an example of the relationship God desires with us, we must see it in the light of a perfect marriage. Even though God uses the natural to explain the supernatural, we must remember that God is the perfect expression of the person He represents. He is the perfect husband, the perfect friend, and the perfect father. We may need to imagine what a perfect marriage would look like to fully understand the comparison God is illustrating.

The secret to the joyful Christian life is an intimate, personal fellowship with Jesus Christ. It is not through serving Him, glorifying, worshiping, or obeying Him. Don't get me wrong; those are all important aspects of the Christian life. We will look at them closer when we look at the purpose of life in chapter 4. But none of those qualities happen, at least as authentic as God expects, before we first have an intimate fellowship with God. For we cannot serve, glorify, worship, or obey that which we do not know. Sometimes we believers are so busy with what we are doing that we miss out on *who* we should be knowing, kind of like the father who works eighty hours a week to provide for his family but misses out on spending time with his family.

> "And it shall be, in that day," says the Lord, "That you will call Me 'My Husband,' And no longer call Me 'My Master.'" (Hosea 2:16)

> I will betroth you to Me forever; yes, I will betroth you to Me In righteousness and justice, in lovingkindness and mercy; I will betroth you to Me in faithfulness, and you shall know the Lord. (Hosea 2:19–20)

> For, I am jealous for you with godly jealousy. For I have betrothed you to one husband, that I may present *you as* a chaste virgin to Christ. (2 Corinthians 11:2)

God uses this illustration of marriage throughout the Bible. In Genesis, we see that the only thing God says is not good about His creation is that man is alone (Genesis 2:18). The first institution developed by God was not government, religion, or the church—it was marriage (Genesis 2:24). It was the only institution started before the Fall. The family is God's original design for evangelism. God's original idea was not a bus ministry, knocking on doors, making phone calls, or inviting friends to evangelistic meetings. Nor was God's initial idea the church or the Israelites to reach the world. He planned that each father and mother would have such a close relationship with Him that their children would desire the same, and their children, and their children. Unfortunately that didn't work so well, but that doesn't mean that God doesn't still want to work through the marriage relationship.

God calls Israel His bride and accuses them of chasing after harlots when they were unfaithful. God even divorced Israel for a while (Jeremiah 3:8) but later remarried her. Of course in the New Testament, the church is identified as the bride of Christ who Jesus wants to present without spot or wrinkle (Ephesians 5:27). In the Gospels, there are numerous illustrations of the bridegroom and the wedding feast. Jesus's second coming parallels the wedding traditions of His time which would make sense as Jesus will be returning someday for His bride.

Jewish Wedding Traditions

The Jewish traditions during Jesus's time for courtship and marriage were quite a bit different than they are today. When Jewish children were young, the boys and girls were allowed to play together. But when they came of age, twelve years old, they were no longer allowed to intermingle. The young girl, a virgin, was not allowed to talk to any male except those in her immediate family. Often the young lady would marry a young man a few years older. For it took a man some time to prove that he could care for a bride. A young man wishing to marry might have in mind a young girl known from childhood, but he couldn't just ask her out for coffee. He was not allowed to talk to her because she was still a virgin and under her father's protection. They couldn't even text each other. If a man wanted to get married back then, he would have to go to her father's house and negotiate a marriage arrangement.

The young man would take with him presents for the father and the rest of the family. The presents would represent his wealth and his worthiness to marry the young lady. The young man would then ask the father for his daughter. In earlier Jewish history, the young lady often had no say in the arrangement and had to marry whomever her father chose for her. However, in Jesus's time, the young lady more often had some say in whom she would agree to marry. Then the father and the future groom would make a binding agreement of betrothal.

This betrothal agreement was like our engagement time, but it was far more binding. The couple was considered married though they did not yet live together, and it took a divorce to break the agreement. This is the situation Mary and Joseph were in when she found out she was pregnant with Jesus. Legally Joseph could have had her stoned for what looked like her impurity, but the angel interceded. Therefore, the betrothal period was a very serious time. While there was no specific length of time for the betrothal, it usually lasted a year.

During that year, many important things happened for the young couple. One of which was that the couple could now talk to each other but under strict supervision, usually by the other women in the family. At least they could get to know each other some before spending the rest of their lives together. Second, it was the man's responsibility to go and prepare a home for his future bride. Often this was accomplished by adding a room to his parents' house. Most of the young Jewish men of Jesus's time would not have been able to afford their own home. The bride's responsibility was to remain pure, prepare her wedding garment, and watch for the groom's return.

When the specified time was up and everything was ready, the groom would go to the bride's house to claim her and take her to his house. It was a tradition at that time for the groom to surprise the bride with his coming, and often, it happened at midnight. While the bride didn't know for sure when the groom would come, it was her responsibility to be ready at any time. Still she would have an idea as the specified time got closer and perhaps on her way to gather water each day, she could see that the room was almost finished.

The groom would lead a large crowd of his friends and family to the bride's house; then the bride's friends and family would follow them all back to the groom's father's house. At that time, the groom would present the bride to his father; for because she was a virgin, this would perhaps be the first time the father would meet the bride. Technically she was presented for his approval, although I doubt many brides were rejected. For all fathers are the same, they are picky about who marries their daughters but overjoyed that someone will now take care of their sons (smile).

Then came a great wedding feast that usually lasted for an entire week. There would be lots of eating, drinking, and celebrating. Many gifts would be given to the young couple, and they would have gifts for each other. After seven days of feasting, they would have the marriage supper and a few ceremonial actions that would complete the marriage. Now the couple was officially married, and they would retire to their home/room. Thus, they would live happily ever after.

Our Betrothal

Did you notice all the parallels with Jesus's second coming? Jesus came to our Father's house (earth) to ask for our hand in marriage. He gave the greatest gift of love to prove His worthiness—His life. Now unlike Jewish tradition, in this marriage, we do have a say whether we want to accept the proposal, for not everyone wants to accept the offer of the King of heaven. It makes no sense that some wouldn't want a relationship with the Creator of all heaven and earth. But in this case, our Father will not force us to accept the marriage. But for us who do, we are now in the betrothal period. Jesus has returned to his house to prepare a place for us.

> Let not your heart be troubled; you believe in God, believe also in Me. In My Father's house are many mansions; if *it were* not *so,* I would have told you. I go to prepare a place for you. And if I go and prepare a place for you, I will come again and receive you to Myself; that where I am, *there* you may be also. (John 14:1–3)

The word translated *mansions* in verse. 2 can also be translated *rooms* which makes more sense that there would be rooms, not mansions in the Father's house. Either way, Jesus has gone to prepare a place for us and someday, He will return for us. Our responsibility is to prepare the wedding garment. In the Scriptures, this represents practical righteousness; our souls are to be without spot or wrinkle (Ephesians 5:27). We are to remain pure and faithful to Jesus. We are not to cheat on Him by chasing after idols (1 John 5:21). Although we don't chase after carved images anymore, our idols can be self, work, family, power, fame, etc., anything that comes before Jesus in our priorities.

> I counsel you to buy from Me gold refined in the fire, that you may be rich; and white garments, that you may be clothed, *that* the shame of your nakedness may not be revealed; and anoint your eyes with eye salve, that you may see. (Revelation 3:18)

> Behold, I am coming as a thief. Blessed *is* he who watches, and keeps his garments, lest he walk naked and they see his shame. (Revelation 16:15)

> And to her it was granted to be arrayed in fine linen, clean and bright, for the fine linen is the righteous acts of the saints. (Revelation 19:8)

We are also to be looking for Jesus to return; there is even a crown for those who look for Him (2 Timothy 4:8). Looking for His return is not staring up into the heavens. Like the faithful servant in Matthew 24:45–51, looking for the master's return, he is faithfully going about his duties. The illustration is warning us about being surprised at Jesus's return that we don't want the Master to come back finding us doing something we shouldn't. We should be living every day like this is the day Christ comes for us. If we knew these were the last hours of our earthly life, what would we want to be doing?

Of course, this is our time to get to know the Groom better. This is the time for us to start perfecting our walk with Him. This is the time to do what we will be doing for all eternity—abiding in Jesus Christ. Abiding means to live with; this is where the illustration is slightly different from the Jewish traditions. We start living with Jesus immediately and don't have to wait until after the marriage supper to get to know Him better. While we too do not know the exact time of Jesus's return, we do know it is getting close.

A Bride without Spot or Wrinkle

The Groom's return for His bride represents the coming rapture of the church. We will meet Jesus in the clouds, and He will take us away from our house. He will take us to His Father's house where He will present us to Him. I do think there will be a judgment at that time; it is called the judgment seat of Christ (Romans 14:10; 1 Corinthians 3:11–15; 2 Corinthians 5:9–11). It will not be a judgment of salvation—whether we are saved or not. It will be a judgment of our works—whether we remained faithful.

> For no other foundation can anyone lay than that which is laid, which is Jesus Christ. Now if anyone builds on this foundation *with* gold, silver, precious stones, wood, hay, straw, each one's work will become clear; for the Day will declare it, because it will be revealed by fire; and the fire will test each one's work, of what sort it is. If anyone's work which he has built on *it* endures, he will receive a reward. If anyone's work is burned, he will suffer loss; but he himself will be saved, yet so as through fire. (1 Corinthians 3:11–15)

This is not a judgment of who will or will not be in the kingdom but a judgment of how white our garments are. Jesus will be asking us, "What did you do with the new life I gave you?" Some will have gold, silver, and precious stones to present; but unfortunately, some may have very little to present. These will be like the unfaithful servant of Matthew 24 who looked to his welfare rather than looking for Christ's return. I have more on this judgment in chapter 9.

After the judgment comes the wedding feast. Typically the Jewish wedding feast lasted for an entire week. I don't think that it is merely coincidence that the seven years of the tribulation are referred to as Daniel's seventieth week (Daniel 9:27). While the earth is going through the seven years of tribulation, we will be feasting with our Lord. While many good scholars disagree when exactly we will receive the rewards and crowns promised in the New Testament, I believe it may occur during these seven years. That would parallel the giving of gifts during the Jewish wedding feast. However, those are future things, so no one can be absolutely sure.

Wedding Gifts

Speaking of rewards, in Revelation 2–3, Jesus talks about rewards for overcomers, those who are found faithful. There are many different ideas about these rewards. Again because they are future events, no one can be sure exactly what they refer to. Therefore, I could be wrong about my interpretation, yet these rewards sound curiously like wedding gifts during a wedding festival. Could they be part of the gifts to the bride during the festival week?

"He who has an ear, let him hear what the Spirit says to the churches. To him who overcomes I will *give to eat from the tree of life*, which is in the midst of the Paradise of God" (Revelation 2:7, emphasis added).

"He who has an ear, let him hear what the Spirit says to the churches. He who overcomes *shall not be hurt by the second death*" (Revelation 2:11, emphasis added).

"He who has an ear, let him hear what the Spirit says to the churches. To him who overcomes I will give some of the *hidden manna to eat*. And I will give him *a white stone*, and on the stone *a new name* written which no one knows except him who receives *it* (Revelation 2:17, emphasis added).

"And he who overcomes, and keeps My works until the end, to him I will give *power over the nations*" (Revelation 2:26, emphasis added).

"He who overcomes shall be *clothed in white garments*, and I *will not blot out his name from the Book of Life*; but I will *confess his name* before My Father and before His angels" (Revelation 3:5, emphasis added).

He who overcomes, I will *make him a pillar in the temple* of My God, and he shall go out no more. And I will *write on him the name of My God* and the name of the city of My God, the New Jerusalem, which comes down out of heaven from My God. And *I will write on him My new name*" (Revelation 3:12, emphasis added).

"To him who overcomes I will grant to *sit with Me on My throne*, as I also overcame and sat down with My Father on His throne" (Revelation 3:21, emphasis added).

In 2:7 and 2:17, we see that the overcomers will eat of the *tree of life* and the *hidden manna*. Well, of course, what else would be served at the wedding feast of God's Son? Later in Revelation, John tells us that the *tree of life* produces twelve different fruits—one for each month. I wonder if we will get to try each one at the feast?

In 3:5, it talks about receiving *white garments*. We have already seen this represents the righteousness of the saints. But these seem to be given to us rather than what we might have been wearing. I wonder if Jesus will give us new white garments to replace our own, maybe representing His righteousness for ours? Then in 2:17, it talks about a *white stone*. Could this be something like an engagement ring? I had to give my wife a white stone to get her to marry me (smile). Also 2:17 and 3:12 talk about the overcomer receiving a *new name*. When does a young lady get a new name? When she gets married.

The overcomer will be a pillar in the temple, according to 3:12. That makes me think of the "mom" being the pillar of the home. She is the one on which the home is built. What about *going out no more*? I wonder if this might reflect the idea of the Prince leaving the castle and going out into the kingdom to find His Bride? Then He brings her back to the castle to live with Him forever. She would never have to go out again to work in the fields; He would provide everything she will ever need.

Then I believe we have some references to the bride ruling and reigning with Jesus. In 2:26, we have the overcomer having *power over the nations* and in 3:21 *sitting* on *the throne* with Christ. Also later in Revelation, John talks about Jesus receiving rule over all the nations. It would make sense that His second-in-command, His queen, would also have that power.

Finally in 2:11 and 3:5, we have John talking about the overcomer not being *hurt by the second death*, or their *name blotted out from the Book of Life*. There are many thoughts on what these both mean, and can a believer even be hurt by the second death or blotted out of the Book of Life? I do not pretend to even come close to understanding what the Holy Spirit is referring to here. Greater minds than mine do not even agree. However, being a married man, the first thing that pops into my head is that when I married my wife, there was this, though unverbalized, promise that nothing would ever hurt her again. That is as far as it depends upon me, and I am a pretty big guy, often well-armed (smile). But my duty as a husband was to protect her and even die for her. I wonder if these passages are Jesus's way of saying to His bride, "Nothing will ever hurt you again?"

Now after the seven years of tribulation, most scholars do believe that is when the marriage supper of the Lamb will occur (Revelation19:7–9). After which Jesus will return to earth with His bride and cast Satan into the bottomless pit. Then Jesus will rule and reign in His kingdom for 1,000 years with His bride (Revelation 20:4) where they will live happily ever after.

Never allow your heart to question the love of God. Settle it on the front end of your desiring to know Him and experience Him, that He loves you. He created you for that love relstionship. He has been pursuing you in that love relationship. Every dealing He has with you is an expression of His love for you. God would cease to be God if He expressed Himself in any thing other than *perfect love!* Your relationship with God right now reveals what you believe about Him. It is spiritually impossible for you to believe one way and practice another. If you really believe that God is *love*, you will also accept the fact that His will is always *best.*[1]

Jesus's Mighty Men

Wasn't that a great love story? Nevertheless, when I first learned this about Jesus, I must admit, it was kind of weird talking about myself as the bride of Christ. Part of that uncomfortable feeling is caused by Satan's corruption of human relationships. We know from the Scripture that God is a spirit and is neither male nor female. Both males and females were created in His image. Still here are a couple of other illustrations from the Scriptures of the intimacy of the relationship God desires with us. In John 15:15, Jesus told His disciples that He no longer would call them servant but friend. The best-friend relationship also represents the type of relationship Jesus desires. A guy's relationship with his best friend is often deeper than a lady's relationship with her best friend. It is like God knew that men could relate better to a best-friend relationship.

This is because ladies grow in relationships by talking to one another, it is a face-to-face relationship. But a lady may not have many opportunities to develop that kind of relationship with another lady especially if she is busy raising a family. That is why she wants to talk to her husband all the time (smile). Men though, develop relationships shoulder to shoulder, by working and playing together. Men then often have more opportunities to develop friend relationships, spending eight hours a day working together or four hours playing golf together. That is why a man doesn't want to talk to his wife; he just wants to be with her (smile) When it comes to the male-female differences in relationships, often they are not right or wrong, just different.

A man's friendship can be especially deep when they fight together. That is, when they serve together in the armed forces. That is why most guys like war stories so much; it is not about violence and death. It is about the honor of fighting with their buddy and sometimes dying for him. No greater love has a man than he lay down his life for a friend (John 15:13). War movies are kind of like chick flicks for men (smile).

The Scriptures left for us an example of this in the story of King David. David is a picture of Christ. He was anointed king but then didn't take the throne for many years. As King Saul was chasing David around the wilderness, David had a group of mighty men who follow him. They remained loyal to David throughout his tough times. It was from this group of mighty men that David chose those who would fill the important positions of his kingdom. They were chosen because they remained faithful to David. Jesus Christ has been anointed King but does not yet sit on His throne. When He comes back to rule over His Kingdom, He will choose those who have remained faithful to rule and reign with Him.

Thus, great joy can come into our lives if we choose to believe Jesus is looking for a few good men (and women) to follow Him, to remain faithful to Him during this time of wilderness wandering, to believe that someday, He will return and establish His kingdom.

> For I am already being poured out as a drink offering, and the time of my departure is at hand. I have fought the good fight, I have finished the race, I have kept the faith. Finally, there is laid up for me the crown of righteousness, which the Lord, the righteous Judge, will give to me on that Day, and not to me only but also to all who have loved His appearing. (Timothy 4:6–8)

Happy Is the Man Who Finds Her

Another illustration of a deep relationship with Jesus is found in Proverbs.

King Solomon is advising his son, for he wants him to find God's wisdom for life. Solomon, according to Scriptures, was the wisest man ever to live, so he could deeply relate to the need for wisdom. In his writings, Solomon feminizes wisdom, calling wisdom a her. He illustrates wisdom as a good woman and evil as a harlot who is trying to steal away the heart of his son.

Proverbs 2:6 says, "For the Lord gives wisdom." Wisdom is not something we learn by accumulating lots of knowledge or many years of life. Wisdom is God Himself; wisdom is not something God has added to Himself. It is His very essence; He is wisdom. Thus, when Solomon encourages his son to pursue wisdom, he is encouraging him to pursue God Himself. It is only in a deeply intimate relationship with God that we receive wisdom. So guys, we are to pursue Jesus like we would pursue a good woman.

> My son, if you receive my words, and treasure my commands within you, So that you incline your ear to wisdom, *and* apply your heart to understanding; Yes, if you cry out for discernment, *and* lift up your voice for understanding, If you seek her as silver, and search for her as *for* hidden treasures; Then you will understand

> the fear of the LORD, and find the knowledge of God. (Proverbs 2:1–5)
>
> Happy *is* the man *who* finds wisdom, and the man *who* gains understanding; For her proceeds *are* better than the profits of silver, and her gain than fine gold. She *is* more precious than rubies, and all the things you may desire cannot compare with her. Length of days *is* in her right hand, in her left hand riches and honor. Her ways *are* ways of pleasantness, and all her paths *are* peace. She *is* a tree of life to those who take hold of her, and happy *are all* who retain her. (Proverbs 3:13–18)
>
> Get wisdom! Get understanding! Do not forget, nor turn away from the words of my mouth. Do not forsake her, and she will preserve you; love her, and she will keep you. Wisdom *is* the principal thing; *therefore* get wisdom. And in all your getting, get understanding. Exalt her, and she will promote you; she will bring you honor, when you embrace her. She will place on your head an ornament of grace; a crown of glory she will deliver to you. (Proverbs 4:5–9)

A Perfect Father

Now there may be those out there who have never been married or ever had a good friend. They may be struggling with relating to these illustrations. God has an answer for you too—He is your heavenly Father. Even if some didn't know their parents or they had horrible parents, God is the perfect Father. He will always be there for us. He has unlimited wisdom, and His advice is never wrong. He can provide in any circumstances. His power to protect is beyond measure. His love, oh His love! It is beyond measure; it is deeper than the deepest sea, higher than the highest mountain. It is larger than the universe.

Some people settle for a superficial relationship with God. Others hunger for an increasingly deeper walk with Him. They want to experience God in all His glory. God is prepared to satisfy our longing for an intimate relationship with Him.[2]

That desire in our souls to need someone to love us was placed there by God Himself. It is a hole so large that other humans, career, power, money, or fame will never fill. It is a God-sized hole that only God can fill. He is everyone's Father whether they like it or not; He gave birth to us all. Therefore, every single one of us has access to everything that He is. There is no excuse for us not to have peace, joy, contentment, and love in our lives. There is nothing bigger than God. Thus, there is nothing big enough to prevent joy in our lives.

"Do you thus deal with the Lord, O foolish and unwise people? *Is* He not your Father, *who* bought you? Has He not made you and established you?" (Deuteronomy 32:6).

"For unto us a Child is born, unto us a Son is given; And the government will be upon His shoulder. And His name will be called Wonderful, Counselor, Mighty God, Everlasting Father, Prince of Peace" (Isaiah 9:6).

"Look at the birds of the air, for they neither sow nor reap nor gather into barns; yet your heavenly Father feeds them. Are you not of more value than they?" (Matthew 6:26).

"If you then, being evil, know how to give good gifts to your children, how much more will your Father who is in heaven give good things to those who ask Him!" (Matthew 7:11).

"Jesus answered and said to him, 'If anyone loves Me, he will keep My word; and My Father will love him, and We will come to him and make Our home with him'" (John 14:23).

"I will be a Father to you, and you shall be My sons and daughters, Says the Lord Almighty" (2 Corinthians 6:18).

> But when the fullness of the time had come, God sent forth His Son, born of a woman, born under the law, to redeem those who were under

> the law, that we might receive the adoption as sons. And because you are sons, God has sent forth the Spirit of His Son into your hearts, crying out, "Abba, Father!" Therefore you are no longer a slave but a son, and if a son, then an heir of God through Christ. (Galatians 4:4–7)

This is it! This was what my heart was searching for in my time of doubt. The secret to the abundant life in Jesus Christ is in knowing Him. Joy in this life comes only by having an intimate love relationship with Jesus Christ. This will be the foundational truth that the rest of this book is founded on. God desires a personal love relationship with each of us which looks like the husband/wife, father/child, and best-friend relationships. If that is not your desire, then this book is not for you. But if you desire to know and understand God that you too might have this deep relationship with Him, then read on!

---

1. Henry T. Blackaby and Claude V. King, Experiencing God: How to Live the Full Adventure of Knowing and Doing the Will of God (Nashville: Broadman & Holman Publishers, 1994), 18.
2. Richard Blackaby, M.Div., PhD, general editor, The Blackaby Study Bible: Personal Encounters with God Through His Word (Nashville: Nelson Bibles, 2006), 108.

CHAPTER 2

God's Way of Change

Yet indeed I also count all things loss for the excellence of the knowledge of Christ Jesus my Lord, for whom I have suffered the loss of all things, and count them as rubbish, that I may gain Christ. —Philippians 3:8

Thou My Best Thought is the title I chose for this book; you may recognize it as a line from the old hymn "Be Thou My Vision." The hymn was translated from an old Irish poem by Eleanor Hull in 1912. It is one of my favorite hymns, and the Irish folk tune makes it a favorite of many. This line, "Thou my best thought," has become my theme of discovering a closer walk with God. Life revolves around what we think or, more specifically, what we believe. It is not what we feel or what we do that comes first.

For example, we don't start off being angry for no reason and then hitting someone. Nor do we hit someone for no reason. There is always a thought that precedes those feelings and/or actions. We are angry because we believe that person insulted us, disrespected us, or took advantage of us. Anger is brought on by a thought that something is not fair; some expectation that is not met. Now sure, we may wake up grumpy and angry, maybe from not enough sleep; however, that anger will rear its ugly head because of some negative thought. How do I know anger is more than a feeling? Because if someone showed up at our door with ten million dollars, our anger would quickly go away. Feelings and actions are all controlled by our thoughts.

> "Let this *mind* be in you which was also in Christ Jesus" (Philippians 2:5, emphasis added).
>
> "And do not be conformed to this world, but be transformed by the renewing of your *mind*, that you may prove what is that good and acceptable and perfect will of God" (Romans 12:2, emphasis added).

That is not to say we must get rid of our feelings or that our feelings aren't important. All good gifts come from the Lord, and our feelings are a gift from God. There are many positive feelings such as love, joy, and peace, but our feelings are a poor guide for our lives. When that knucklehead cuts us off in traffic, we are going to feel angry. What we think/believe about that feeling will determine whether or not we act like Christ. If we are self-focused, we are probably going to think, *How dare that guy drive like that and risk my life. What an idiot*! And then, maybe we speed up and cut him off, feeling we have the right to retaliate. However, if we are Christ-focused, we may think, *How sad, that guy is probably stressed out and isn't enjoying life. He needs the peace of God. I will pray for him.*

It is not our feelings that get us into trouble with God—it is our thoughts. The Apostle Paul said in Ephesians 4:26, "Be angry, and do not sin." Paul is not telling us to be angry; what he is saying is when we are angry, do not choose to sin. Yes, we choose how we will react to our feelings. Sometimes we react badly as a habit, and it doesn't feel like we are choosing our response. But just because the bad habit happens so quickly, that doesn't mean we can't slow down and choose a better response.

"Be still, and know that I *am* God; I will be exalted among the nations, I will be exalted in the earth!" (Psalms 46:10)

God would never hold us responsible for something that we could do. Therefore, the struggles in human lives are not based on the circumstances of life but on what we choose to believe about those circumstances. We can either believe we are in control of the circumstances of life and therefore we must change them, or we can believe God is sovereign and nothing happens to us outside of His will. The circumstances of our lives are allowed by God, and He has promised they are for our good. If we are trying to control those circumstances and prevent them, then we are preventing God's good for us.

"And we know that all things work together for good to those who love God, to those who are the called according to His purpose" (Romans 8:28).

By Faith Alone

All this is to lead us to the very important point that greatly affects our joy in the Lord. While we rightly believe that salvation is by faith alone, we tend to believe that sanctification is through our hard work. We believers in Jesus Christ know for certain that our salvation is by grace alone, through faith alone, in Christ alone and not by good works which we have done. It is the battle cry of the Reformation, *sola fide,* which is Latin for "faith alone."

This misunderstanding that sanctification is by our hard work has stolen away the joy from our life with Christ. *Sanctification* means to be set apart and made holy, to mature. It is the process of the Holy Spirit working in the life of the believers to help us grow in our faith, to become more like Jesus Christ. Jesus made it clear that to be saved for all eternity, we must be born again; therefore, sanctification is the same as a child growing up to adulthood. God often uses the natural to explain the supernatural. Accordingly the spiritual life is very much like our natural lives. Parents give birth to children; they help them grow to maturity, and in thirty to forty years (smile), they move out and start their own family. As Christians, we are born again (justification) when we believe in Jesus Christ. We hopefully mature for the rest of our natural lives (sanctification) by walking in faith. Then someday when we are mature, we will move on (glorification) and be rewarded for our faith by becoming the bride of Christ.

The first thing we find then, about faith, is that it is an assent to, and an acceptance of, truth simply upon the word of someone else without proof or any other evidence. It is believing what I cannot see, hear, feel, taste, smell, or understand. Faith is accepting the word of another just because we believe what he says is true. It, therefore, comes down to this simple fact—that faith is confidence in another.[1]

The Bible tells us that sanctification is also by faith alone. "The just shall live by faith" (Romans 1:17; Galatians 3:11; Hebrews 10:38). And although we say it is by *faith*, our actions say that we actually believe maturity is through our hard work. After someone comes to Christ for salvation, we then begin telling them all the things they must do like get baptized, read the Bible, and join the church. I am not saying those actions are not necessary so don't throw away the book. I will come back to them later and show their proper place in the process. However, I have been in the ministry of discipleship for twenty-five-plus years, and I have yet to see a discipleship program that isn't a list of things to do. But trying to do these things in our strength with our self-effort leads to self-righteousness. Unfortunately in most discipleship material, there is very little, if anything, on how this mature living is by faith. The lists aren't necessarily wrong; the problem is how we get there. Of course, I have not seen every discipleship program written; therefore, if one is found that is more faith-based than duty-based, praise the Lord! It is probably worth hanging on to and following.

The back of the discipleship workbook used in a former church stated that if you follow these steps (Bible reading, prayer, giving, etc.), you will have joy in your Christian life. That statement caught my attention as I was learning more about a right relationship with God. I thought to myself, *That's not right. Joy, at least real joy in Jesus Christ, doesn't come from doing those things. Real joy only comes from Jesus Himself.* I know a lot of Christians that try to follow these discipleship lists, and they sure don't have any joy in their lives. And besides, wouldn't people in false religions also be doing the same thing, reading their version of Scripture, praying to what they thought was a god, and giving to whatever organization they had? Wouldn't they be feeling joy too? Of course, the natural response to those questions would be, no, they do not experience joy because they do not believe in the true God. That's the whole point! What we do is important, but what we believe is far more important!

Man's Way of Change (Obedience Based)

Look at the formula below. I had our math teacher in the academy, Mrs. Taylor McCloskey, help me with it. I call it the Christian Growth Formula. When someone accepts Jesus as their Savior, they naturally want to know what to do next. So we tell them about maturing as a believer and give them a list of things to do. Again the problem is not so much the list as it is, but that we have misunderstood how to do the list. I call it Man's Way because it has missed God's Way.

$$\frac{M}{H}+\frac{10\%TM\left[3C+2B+1P+D_{r}O+(PO)^{2^{2}}\right]}{7-6}+\frac{1A\left(G+\frac{1}{5}\right)}{P}+O\left(\frac{H_{2}O+S^{W}+Min+m\sqrt{v}}{-sin-ABW}\right)=\frac{I}{C}$$

M/H	Me cooperating with the Holy Spirit; we are a 50-50 partnership
10%TM	10 percent of my time and money
3C	Three church services a week
2B	Two times reading the Bible
1P	One prayer meeting
DO	Attend church whenever the "doors are open"
PO^{22}	Poo-poo squared/working in the nursery
7-6	one day a week for God
1A	"One another" can't forget to serve each another
G	Giving
1/SP	Half as much *serving*; it is easier to give to the poor than serve them the poor
O	Obedience in all things; O outside the brackets equals times everything

H2O	Add water baptism
S^W	Add soul winning
+Min	Add a ministry
$m\sqrt{v}$	Add memorizing verses
-sin	Subtract sin
-ABW	Subtract anger/bitterness/wrath
=I/C	"I Change," work hard enough/change into a better Christian.

Does that look simple? Does that look easy? In the foreword, I talked about a need to get back to the *simplicity that is in Christ.* And what does faith have to do with it? In fact, more things could be added to this formula. I haven't even put in the activities considered unallowable like no drinking, no drugs, no sex before marriage, no going to the movies, no pants on women, no long hair on men, and no tattoos on anyone. Sounds complicated, right? Let me simplify it: Me obeying + my self-diligence = I change.

Notice that the simplified formula is *me, myself,* and *I.* That is why Man's Way doesn't work; this method of discipleship is all about self-effort. For if I could change/sanctify myself by doing these things, then I would be tempted to say, "Look what I have done." Unfortunately this is what many Christians do—they judge their righteousness and others' by how well they keep this list. Also if I could do all this myself, Christ didn't have to die, for He died to take away our sins. If we could take care of them ourselves, then He didn't need to die.

At the beginning of the Christian life, we are concerned without doing and not with our being, we are distressed more by what we have done than by what we are. We think that if only we could rectify certain things, we would be good Christians; therefore, we set out to change our actions. We try to please the Lord, but we find that something within us does not want to please Him. And the more we try to rectify matters externally, the more we realize how deep-seated the problem really is.[2]

This wrong formula was the first lesson God had for me as I was seeking Him. In my counseling training and ministry, I had gotten caught up in everything being about obedience to God's Word. This is not hard to do, for the Bible talks a lot about obedience, some 750 verses. I know, I looked them up. When someone would come to me for advice, I would think to myself, *Now where is this person not obeying God*? I would then tell them which commandments they were failing at and tell them to go home and change them. It is true that obedience to God is critical to overcoming the struggles of life, but the problem lies in how to get to that obedience without it being self-effort and, thus, self-righteousness.

> Oh, foolish Galatians [*Americans*]! Who has cast an evil spell on you? For the meaning of Jesus Christ's death was made as clear to you as if you had seen a picture of his death on the cross. Let me ask you this one question: Did you receive the Holy Spirit by obeying the law of Moses? Of course not! You received the Spirit because you believed the message you heard about Christ. How foolish can you be? After starting your new lives in the Spirit, why are you now trying to become *perfect* [*mature*] by your own *human effort*? (Galatians 3:1–3, NLT, emphasis added)

Richard Longenecker in his commentary on Galatians said this about Galatians 3:3:

> So, the strategy of the Judaizers was not to deny the importance of faith in Christ for salvation, but to affirm the necessity for Gentiles to accept at least the minimal requirements of the Mosaic Law for filling out their commitment to God and perfecting their Christian lives. It was not, therefore, an overt advocacy of legalism per

> se, but a call for Gentile believers to accept a lifestyle of Jewish nomism.
>
> As such, it combined faith in Christ for initial acceptance before God and a nomistic lifestyle for true holiness, thereby claiming to work out in full the meaning of righteousness. Paul, however, was not content to allow any supplement to the work of Christ, either for one's initial acceptance before God or for one's life as a Christian. For Paul, the gospel of Christ crucified so completely rules out any other supposed means of being righteous before God that he finds it utterly incomprehensible for anyone who had once embraced such a gospel ever to think of supplementing it in any way.[3]

Judaizers were a group of false teachers that Paul was warning the Galatians about. Nomism is trying to adhere to a set of laws or rules as a person's primary exercise of their religion. This rule-keeping to obtain paradise is a key indicator of a false religion. Although the Judaizers were not adding good works to salvation, they were trying to add self-effort to sanctification. Therefore, Paul was passionately fighting against them and anyone who would cheapen the sacrifice of Jesus Christ. From the very beginning of the church, there have been those who wish to make maturing in Christ about keeping the rules. Again it is not that the rules are wrong but telling people to change their behavior doesn't change their behavior.

When my wife, Barbara, had our four children and we brought them home from the hospital, we didn't present them with a list of things to do to mature. We didn't say to those infants, "Okay, we gave you life, now it is time for you to mature. You need to stop that crying, learn to walk, get your clothes on, feed yourself, and go to school. Oh, and don't forget to learn to drive, you can't expect your mother and me to be driving all over the place." Of course, that would be ridiculous, yet that is pretty much what we do to infant believers. What did we naturally do with our infant children? We loved them, nurtured them, fed them, picked them up when they fell down, and taught them how to drive.

We Cannot Change Ourselves

In my generation, Nancy Reagan, President Ronald Reagan's wife, promoted her war on drugs with her catchphrase, "Just Say No." She told millions of school kids to say no to drugs. So how is that working? Have we gotten rid of all the drugs? No, of course not. I am sure her campaign had some effect on a few, but it did not get rid of the drug problem. From the beginning of time, humanity has been trying to change behavior by telling it what to change. If that were going to work, certainly it would have happened by now?

In the believers' lives, we can put off, for a time, some of our sinful nature. And in our strength, we can put on some of the habits of a maturing life. Many pastors and counselors point to chapters 4–6 of Ephesians as a model of what to do to mature in Christ.

> But you have not so learned Christ, if indeed you have heard Him and have been taught by Him, as the truth is in Jesus: that you *put off*, concerning your former conduct, the old man which grows corrupt according to the deceitful lusts, and be renewed in the spirit of your mind, and that you *put on* the new man which was created according to God, in true righteousness and holiness. (Ephesians 4:20–24, emphasis added)

But when we *put off* and *put on* behavior in our strength, we are only managing sin; we are not overcoming sin. What most leaders miss when teaching these passages is verse 23. Between the *put off* and *put on,* Paul says, "Be renewed in the spirit of your mind." Before the list of good behaviors in Ephesians chapters 4–6, Paul has been explaining in chapters 1–3 the character of Christ. It is only by the renewing of our mind that real change comes. As Paul says in his prayer for the Ephesians (3:14–21), first we must know the love of

Christ. Then and only then will we be complete in Him. Only after we have changed our minds about Jesus Christ can the Holy Spirit make lasting change in us.

> For this reason I bow my knees to the Father of our Lord Jesus Christ, from whom the whole family in heaven and earth is named, that He would grant you, according to the riches of His glory, to be strengthened with might through His Spirit in the inner man, that Christ may dwell in your hearts through faith; that you, being rooted and grounded in love, may be able to comprehend with all the saints what *is* the width and length and depth and height—to know the love of Christ which passes knowledge; that you may be filled with all the fullness of God. Now to Him who is able to do exceedingly abundantly above all that we ask or think, according to the power that works in us, to Him *be* glory in the church by Christ Jesus to all generations, forever and ever. Amen. (Ephesians 3:14–21)

It was through these truths that the Lord led me deeper in my search for Him. It would not be through my works of righteousness that I would change. God was showing me that lasting change comes from an intimate knowledge of Him. And that change would be by Him and Him alone. If I could change myself or others, then I would get all the glory. But my God is a jealous God, and He will not share His glory with anyone.

Galatians contains five reasons why we cannot change ourselves nor can we change others.

1) *Foolish*: It is foolish for us to try and change ourselves (Galatians 3:1–3).
2) *Vain*: Jesus died in vain if we could change ourselves (Galatians 2:16–21).

3) *Redeemed*: It was Jesus's death that redeemed us from the curse of the law; we could not redeem ourselves (Galatians 3:10–13).
4) *Promise*: God would be going back on His promise to bless the Gentiles in Christ Jesus if we could change ourselves (Galatians 3:14–18).
5) *Boast*: We are not to boast in what we have done but are to boast in the cross of Jesus Christ (Galatians 6:13–16).

Then the Lord took me to Philippians chapter 3. Here Paul is being very transparent and sharing with the readers the list of his righteous accomplishments.

> Though I also might have confidence in the flesh. If anyone else thinks he may have confidence in the flesh, I more so: circumcised the eighth day, of the stock of Israel, of the tribe of Benjamin, a Hebrew of the Hebrews; concerning the law, Pharisee; concerning zeal, persecuting the church; concerning the righteousness which is in the law, blameless. (Philippians 3:4–6)

Paul is saying if anyone could accomplish pleasing God with his life, he could. Just look at all the righteous things he had done. In our own time, it might sound something like this: I was baptized when I was four years old, I grew up in the church, I went to church every time the doors were open. I read through my Bible every year and give 10 percent of my wages to the church. I am a Baptist of the Baptists, a deacon in good standing, and I have separated myself from the evil of this world. Sounds pretty good, right? Especially that part about being at church whenever the doors are open. However, Paul goes on to say this:

> But what things were gain to me, these I have counted loss for Christ. Yet indeed I also count all things loss for the excellence of the

> knowledge of Christ Jesus my Lord, for whom I have suffered the loss of all things, and count them as rubbish, that I may gain Christ and be found in Him, not having my own righteousness, which is from the law, but that which is through faith in Christ, the righteousness which is from God by faith. (Philippians 3:7–9)

From these words, I realized that I had been doing it all wrong for many years. And therefore, I had been encouraging others in the wrong way of maturing. I had been trying to mature myself by working really, really hard to please God by keeping His commandments. And every time I failed, I would tell myself that the reason I failed was that I wasn't trying hard enough. Notice the personal pronouns in those thoughts: *I* failed, *I* would have to work harder. It was our previous formula: me, myself, and I.

God was able to show me His formula for change, the formula that revolved around Him, not me. And like previously mentioned, it is simple, a singular focus upon Jesus Christ. Nothing is simpler than A+B=C.

God's Way of Change (Faith-Based)

Attributes + belief = change (A+B=C). God's formula is about knowing God's attributes and understanding who He is plus choosing to believe that what He says about Himself is true. Then God can make lasting change in my heart. So then, I am not just managing sin, but God has removed my desire for that sin, and lasting change occurs. It is God that conforms me to the image of His Son, not merely my good works. It is like when King David cried out to God when repenting for his sin with Bathsheba. "Create in me a clean heart, O God" (Psalms 51:10). Only God can create a new heart in me!

I expanded on the formula just a little to make it clearer: knowledge of God + belief in God = changed by God. This is the most important principle in the entire book. For it is around this formula that everything else revolves. It starts with knowing God—who He is, what He is like, what He loves, and what He hates. But it is not knowing all the facts that change us. There are many immature Christians in our churches today who know a lot of facts about God but are still immature. Change comes when we add to that knowledge belief in God. It is when we choose to believe that what God says about Himself is true; then God can create in us a new heart.

Oh sure, we say we believe all those facts about God. We say we believe He is loving, holy, sovereign, all-powerful, etc. But our actions reflect our true belief. For example, if we believe that God is sovereign, all-powerful, and loving, then why do we keep worrying about the circumstances of life? If truly nothing happens to us outside of the will of God and all things work for our good, why are we stressed out?

In the formula, one cannot be utilized without the other and still have change. We can't have belief without knowledge; then we would believe in any ole thing. And we can't have knowledge without belief, that would be only head knowledge. There are a lot of people in this world that know something about the God of the Bible and Jesus Christ, but they are not saved.

God used this same formula of A+B=C to save/justify us. Somewhere, sometime, someone gave us some knowledge about God. Knowledge like there is a God and we can live forever with Him in paradise. But sin entered this world and destroyed that relationship. However, there is good news—God sent His Son to die for us so that relationship could be restored. Did that knowledge alone save us? No! Just knowing those facts doesn't save anyone. It is when we choose to believe those facts that God can save us. And when we choose to believe Him, He makes the most important change of all. He imputes to us His Son's righteousness, and we become acceptable to Him for all eternity.

One of the facts we learn about God is that He is unchanging. And that is true in this case. The same way He saved us, knowledge of God + belief in God = changed by God, is the same way He is going to bring us to maturity. After salvation, God has some more knowledge about Himself that He wants us to know. In fact, there is so much more knowledge; we will never know all of it, for He is infinite. That is why heaven is for eternity—that is how long it will take to know God. Even though we will never know everything about God, if we choose to continue to believe this ongoing revelation of Him, then He can continue to change us into the image of His Son.

You'd better get used to it down here because the knowledge of God is the focus of heaven. Let me tell you something about heaven. Only one thing happens there: people get to know God. You will spend eternity in heaven getting to know God. You may say, "How boring." I say no, how exciting. You see, there's only one difference between earth and heaven. Heaven holds the perfect knowledge of God while knowledge of God keeps getting interrupted down here. For example, you have to go to sleep. So for eight hours, you are not conscious of God. Or you have problems that distract you from God. In heaven, God takes away all the negatives so that you have uninterrupted knowledge of Him.[4]

Obedience, the By-Product of Faith

Some may still be wondering, *What happened to obedience?* While obedience from self-effort does not produce maturity, obedience to God's Word is still very important. Obedience is still the key to experiencing the peace of God. But like I said before, how we get to obedience is where many Christians have missed it. In the Man's-Way formula, obedience comes first; it is believed to be the *product* of righteousness. That is if I obey, I become more righteous. Or if I work hard at obeying God, then I will grow in favor with Him and He will love me more.

In the God's-Way formula, obedience comes last. Obedience is the *by-product* of already having a loving relationship with God. In other words, I have learned how much He loves me (knowledge of God) and learned that there is nothing I can do to earn more of God's love. I already have all of it; there is no more to earn. When I choose to believe this about my God (belief in God), then God creates in me a new loving heart (changed by God). And with this new heart,

I can obey the two greatest commandments: love the Lord my God with all my heart, soul, and mind, and love my neighbor as myself.

When you come to know God by experience, you will be convinced of His love. When you are convinced of His love, you can believe Him and trust Him. When you trust Him, you can obey Him. When you love Him, you have no problem obeying Him.[5]

One Sunday as I was listening to the sermon, the pastor quoted Psalm 118:1, "Oh, give thanks to the Lord, for He is good! For His mercy endures forever." I didn't hear an audible voice, but it was as if the Holy Spirit said to me, "Todd, how would you teach this verse?" I thought, *If I were giving a chapel message to some young people, I would tell them that they must be thankful.* For I learned in Bible college that you should always have a proposition that started with "You must..." So I would tell those young people, "You must be thankful." They should be thankful for their God, for their moms and dads, for their Christian school teachers, for their principal, for their pastor, for their brother and sister, and their cat and dog. And then I would either guilt them into doing better or positively encourage them to be obedient to God's Word. And of course, I would have an illustration or a poem about being thankful. That's how I would have normally taught it, by concentrating on the command be thankful. Then the Holy Spirit impressed on me, "No, Todd, teach them that I am good and how My mercy endures forever, then they will be thankful."

Understanding and Believing Who God Is and How Real Change Happens in the Believers' Lives

Too many of our sermons are about what we are supposed to do and not enough about what we need to know about our God. We are teaching do theology (keeping lists) instead of know theology. I call the prior "dodo theology" for it too was right there in Philippians 3; Paul said that all that he had done in his strength was as rubbish, dung. But he set that aside for the excellence of the knowledge of Christ, to know Him and the power of His resurrection, knowing Christ. If we want to see real change in our churches, we are going to need more sermons on the perfections of God. Paul, in his letters, left us a wonderful example. Most of his letters start with who God is and end with what believing that knowledge will look like—the fruit of the Spirit, not our fruits.

Of course, when that change does happen, we don't obey God perfectly; that continues to be part of the maturing process. Because we still live in a sin-filled world and we are not yet absent from the presence of sin, there remains a struggle between the old and new natures. So yes, as we mature, we will still stumble occasionally. Like a child learning to walk, the child still falls every so often. Even adults fall occasionally; but hopefully as we mature, we fall less and less.

However, having a new heart of love does make it easier to obey God's commands. When we love Him deeply, we naturally want to do the things that please Him and not do the things that disappoint Him. It is just like my relationship with my wife. When I am loving her, it is very easy to do those things that please her. Because of my love, I want to please her, so much so that it doesn't feel like a duty, it's just the right thing to do. In counseling couples that are struggling with their marriage, I can give them a whole lot of suggestions on how to treat each other better. But if they have chosen to no longer love one another, all the tips in the world will have no effect. But if I can get them to choose to love each other again, I don't have to tell them how to treat each other; they do the right thing because of love.

A+B=C in Scripture

Let me say it one more time to help it sink in (it will not be the last). Knowledge of God + belief in God = changed by God. Notice the main object is *God.* Maybe others have never heard it put this way, I know I hadn't even after being in the business of discipleship for over twenty-five years. While I did make up how this formula is expressed, it came right from the Scriptures. I found it first in those passages in Philippians.

> Yet indeed I also count all things loss for the *excellence of the knowledge of Christ Jesus my Lord*, for whom I have suffered the loss of all things, and count them as rubbish, that I may gain Christ and be found in Him, not having my own righteousness, which is from the law, but that which *is through faith in Christ*, the *righteousness which is from God* by faith. (Philippians 3:8–9, emphasis added)

This passage in the Amplified Bible is worth noting:

> Yes, furthermore, I count everything as loss compared to the possession of the priceless privilege (the overwhelming preciousness, the surpassing worth, and supreme advantage) *of knowing Christ Jesus my Lord and of progressively becoming more deeply and intimately acquainted with Him [of perceiving and recognizing and understanding Him more fully and clearly]*. For His sake I have lost everything and consider it all to be mere rubbish (refuse, dregs), in order that I may win (gain) Christ (the Anointed One), And that I may [actually] be found and known as in Him, not having any [self-achieved] righteousness that can be called my own, based on my obedience to the Law's demands (ritualistic uprightness and supposed right standing with God thus acquired), but possessing that [genuine righteousness] *which comes through faith in Christ* (the Anointed One), the [truly] right standing with God, which *comes from God* by [saving] faith. (Philippians 3:8–9, AMP, emphasis added)

Isn't that glorious? "K*nowing Christ Jesus my Lord and of progressively becoming more deeply and intimately acquainted with Him* *[of perceiving and recognizing and understanding Him more fully and clearly.]"* As I will explain in more detail in chapter 4, our very purpose in life is to know our God. Here is the secret to the abundant life in Christ Jesus (John 10:10). To know Him deeper and deeper each day, to love Him with all our heart, soul, and mind. Yes, we are also to glorify, worship, serve, and obey Him, but that all begins with knowing Him. For we cannot glorify what we don't know; also we cannot serve, worship, or obey what we don't first know.

As I began to understand this A+B=C formula, I started seeing it throughout Scripture. Here are a few more examples.

> In Him you also *trusted* [B], after *you heard the word of truth* [A], the gospel of your salvation; in whom also *having believed* [B], you were *sealed with the Holy Spirit of promise* [C]" (Ephesians 1:13, emphasis added).

> For this reason I bow my knees to the father of our Lord Jesus Christ, from whom the whole family in heaven and earth is named, that He would grant you, according to the riches of His glory, to be *strengthened with might through His Spirit in the inner man* [C], that Christ may dwell in your hearts *through faith* [B]; that you, being rooted and grounded in love, may be able to *comprehend* [A] with all the saints what is the width and length and depth and height— to know the love of Christ which passes *knowledge* [A]; that you may be *filled with all the fullness of God* [C]. (Ephesians 3:14–19, emphasis added)

> Simon Peter, a bondservant and apostle of Jesus Christ, *To those who have obtained like precious faith* [B] with us *by the righteousness of our God and Savior Jesus Christ* [C]: Grace and peace be multiplied to you in the *knowledge of God and*

> *of Jesus our Lord* [A], as *His divine power has given to us all things that pertain to life and godliness* [C], through *the knowledge of Him* [A] who called us by glory and virtue, by which have *been given to us exceedingly great and precious promises* [C], that through these you may be partakers of the divine nature, having escaped the corruption that is in the world through lust. (2 Peter 1:1–4, emphasis added)

And of course, A+B=C is found in the Old Testament too, for our God's ways are unchanging—first in the negative sense as a warning and then as a glorious promise.

> Then they will call on me, *but I will not answer* [C]; they will seek me diligently, but they will not find me. Because they *hated knowledge* [A] and *did not choose the fear of the Lord, they would have none of my counsel* [B] and despised my every rebuke. (Proverbs 1:28–30, emphasis added)

> *Trust in the Lord* [B] with all your heart, and lean not on your own understanding; In all your ways *acknowledge Him* [A], and *He shall direct your paths* [C] Do not be wise in your own eyes; fear the Lord and depart from evil. (Proverbs 3:5–7, emphasis added)

Glory in This

The Hebrew word translated *acknowledge* above is the same word translated *know* in Jeremiah.

> Thus says the Lord: "Let not the wise man glory in his wisdom, let not the mighty man

> glory in his might, nor let the rich man glory in his riches; but let him who glories glory in this, that he understands and *knows* Me, that I am the Lord, exercising lovingkindness, judgment, and righteousness in the earth. For in these I delight." says the Lord. (Jeremiah 9:23–24, emphasis added)

It is from these verses that I got the subtitle for this book, *How to Know and Understand God.* To understand and know God has become the purpose statement for my life. I was about forty-five years old when the Lord started showing me these truths or I should say when I started seeing them, for they had been there all along. At that time, I prayed to the Lord, "Father, please forgive me. I spent the last forty-five years primarily focusing on everything other than you, Lord. If you give me another forty-five years or so, I will make my priority to get to know you better."

Spending more time with God doesn't mean that God doesn't want us to enjoy the other aspects of life like family, friends, career, sports, hobbies, and even ministry. But with all those things, we can spend too much time doing, and they can have negative effects on our lives. We can spend too much time at work or ministry and our family will suffer. We can spend too much time with our family and our kids may become spoiled. However, I am not sure we can spend too much time getting to know our God. I do think there was one man who spent too much time with God; his name was Enoch. Enoch walked with the Lord for 350 years, and then one day, God just took him home to heaven. If that is the consequences of spending too much time with God, I want to be the second person to spend too much time with Him.

Sure there have been monks and hermits that have supposedly given up everything to spend all their time with God. I don't know any hermits personally, and I can't look into their hearts to see if they found God or not. But becoming a monk is not what I am talking about. For I believe if we are seeking after God, He will bring balance to our lives, giving His wisdom on what does and does not need to be done each day. When we are spending significant time with Him, we can hear His still, soft voice tell us things like "You have spent enough time at work, you need to go home and be with your family" or "Turn off that TV and go say hello to your neighbor." We have trouble balancing all the duties of life because we are trying to do it in our wisdom. I once heard that busy stands for *B*urdened *U*nder *S*atan's *Y*oke. We glorify busy people; we think they are succeeding in life. They probably aren't because they probably aren't spending much time with their God.

My wife and I have four grown children. When they were younger, they all watched those kid programs on TV, the ones where other kids their age are going through the problems of life. Interesting that their parents were hardly ever around, and they solved all their problems by themselves. But as I look back at those shows, it dawned on me that the goals of these kids all fell into three major categories. They all wanted to be rich by becoming a professional athlete, an entertainer (singing or acting), or the nerd who starts an online business.

Doesn't that sound like the three categories of Jeremiah 9:23? The glory and riches that come from the *wisdom* to invent the next greatest online app that can be sold for millions, and they can retire at twenty-seven. Or they want the fame and glory that comes from the *might* of professional athletes. Or they wanted the worshiping fans from the *riches* and notoriety of entertainment. And it is not only the young people that desire these things. It is their parents too who wish they had the fame and glory. But if they can't get it themselves, maybe their child can. Christians also fall for these temptations. Isn't Satan deceptive? Instead of persecuting the Christians in America, he gives them whatever is their heart's desire which pulls them away from growing in their relationship with God. Satan cannot steal away a believer's salvation, but he can distract that believer with earthly wisdom, might, and riches so that he is no longer salt and light to the rest of the world and is not drawing the unsaved into a loving relationship with God.

Finally in considering God's change formula, the *knowledge* of God is the only part of your life this book can help. The *belief* in

God part only you can do. I can't believe for you; others can't do it for you—even God will not force you to believe. You must choose whether you will believe the knowledge you receive. Then the *change* by God part only God can do. There is an old proverb that says that what man has made, man can fix, but what God has made, only God can fix. Knowing and believing in God is the only way He can fix you.

What God does to us is even more than a fix, He redeems us and makes us new. Like a broken vase, God doesn't just glue us back together and if we look hard, we can still see the cracks. No, He makes a brand-new vase to be used for His glory. As we saw in King David's confession, he asked God to create in him a new heart. In numerous places, David talked about loving God with his whole heart (Psalms 9:1; 111:1, 119:2, 34, 69, 138:1). But this seems to contradict what Jeremiah said about the heart, that it is "deceitful above all things and desperately wicked" (Jeremiah 17:9). The word *whole* does not only communicate completeness of all of our heart, but it also communicates healing and newness. To experience the abundant life of Jesus Christ, we must believe we have wicked, sinful hearts and ask God to give us a new, whole heart.

Therefore, if anyone *is* in Christ, *he is* a new creation. "Old things have passed away; behold, all things have become new" (2 Corinthians 5:17).

---

1. M.R. DeHaan, Studies in Hebrews, (Grand Rapids: Kregel Publications, 1996), 150.
2. Watchman Nee, Sentinel (Randal) Kulp, compiler, Secrets to Spiritual Power: From the Writings of Watchman Nee (New Kensington, Pennsylvania: Whitaker House, 1999), 21.
3. Richard Longenecker, World Biblical Commentary, Vol. 41, Galatians (Dallas: Word Books Publishers, 1990), 106.
4. Tony Evans, Our God is Awesome: Encountering the Greatness of Our God (Chicago: Moody Press, 1994), 26ff.
5. Blackaby and King, 20.

CHAPTER 3

God's Relationships

> For I desire mercy and not sacrifice, And the knowledge of God more than burnt offerings.
>
> —Hosea 6:6

Someone once asked Michelangelo how he made such beautiful sculptures. Supposedly he said, "I simply remove what is not supposed to be there." In Michelangelo's mind, when he looked at that big chunk of marble, he saw the image of David inside. This way of thinking is how God sees us when He is changing us into the image of His Son. When we come to God at salvation, what He sees is an unformed chunk of marble. And sure, it has some beauty in its original creation, but that is nothing compared to what He wants to form it into. He sees within the marble the image of His Son and all He needs to do is remove the parts of us that are getting in the way. At first the big chunks, then the fine details, and finally the polishing.

Why is God "conforming us into the image of His Son?" (Romans 8:29). It is because Jesus Christ was the perfect example of humanity and the Christian life. When I interned with a Christian counselor, he would often say, "There has been only one normal human being on this earth, all the rest of us are abnormal." Of course, he was talking about Jesus Christ. Part of Jesus's purpose in coming to earth was to be an example of how we should live. Jesus could have just come and died for our sins and still accomplished our salvation.

But the Holy Spirit recorded for us His three years of ministry so that we could learn how to live totally dependent on Him. Jesus perfectly did the will of His Father; Jesus perfectly loved Him, perfectly worshiped Him, and perfectly glorified Him. So it makes *perfect* sense that God would be changing us into the perfect image of His Son.

"For to this you were called, because Christ also suffered for us, leaving us an example, that you should follow His steps" (1 Peter 2:21).

"For consider Him who endured such hostility from sinners against Himself, lest you become weary and discouraged in your souls. [4]You have not yet resisted to bloodshed, striving against sin" (Hebrews 12:3–4).

"He who says he abides in Him ought himself also to walk just as He walked" (1 John 2:6).

Just like a chunk of marble, we don't have a lot to do with that change. All the marble has to do is remain in the presence of the master and yield to the change. For all the change is done by the master's hands, not the marble itself. The illustration that God uses in the Scriptures is the potter and the clay.

> But indeed, O man, who are you to reply against God? Will the thing formed say to him who formed *it,* "Why have you made me like this?" Does not the potter have power over the clay, from the same lump to make one vessel for honor and another for dishonor? *What* if God, wanting to show *His* wrath and to make His power known, endured with much longsuffering the vessels of wrath prepared for destruction, and that He might make known the riches of His glory on the vessels of mercy, which He had prepared beforehand for glory, *even* us whom He called, not of the Jews only, but also of the Gentiles? (Romans 9:20–24)

> Surely you have things turned around! Shall the potter be esteemed as the clay; For shall the

> thing made say of him who made it, "He did not make me?" Or shall the thing formed say of him who formed it, "He has no understanding? (Isaiah 29:16)

God changing us into the image of His Son will be by Him alone, for He must get all the glory. As I said at the close of the previous chapter, what God has made, only God can fix. Even as little children, we didn't have a lot to do with our bodies maturing; we simply let nature take its course. But we are not inanimate objects like the marble or the clay; God created us with a free will. Therefore, we can choose to run away from the Master's hands. While God is the only one who can create lasting change in us, we can, like little children, hinder our natural growth with malnutrition. We have the free will to resist the changes of God. The Bible calls it grieving the Holy Spirit when we hinder God's maturing process. God will not force His change upon us, for this would not be true love on His part nor true love on our part.

Love Can Be Rejected

For us to truly love God, we must also have the option to hate Him. I know that sounds extreme, but it is the principle of love. Love cannot be forced, demanded, or compelled. If we do not have the option to hate God, then we are being forced to love Him. Forced love is not real love. When my children were younger and much smaller than me, I could have forced them to say, "I love you, Dad." But that wouldn't be real love if I force them to say it. On the other hand, there is nothing sweeter to a parents' heart than to hear their child, unprompted, say, "I love you."

Once we become a child of God, we can never stop being His child. Just like my children, even if I were to disown them (which a loving father would never do). Genetically they will always be my children. But we sometimes can be disobedient children and thus, hinder the change He is trying to accomplish in us. There are many Scriptures in the New Testament that are wrongly interpreted as being a comparison between the saved and the unsaved. More often, these verses are a comparison between the obedient child and the disobedient one. And too often, we miss out on God's warnings and direction for our change into the image of His Son. Therefore, it is important for us to know where, when, and how we are grieving the Holy Spirit and preventing God's change in our lives.

The Love/Hate Relationship of Change

The word *change* is an interesting word. Probably no other word in the human language is both loved and hated as much as the word *change*. We all hate the thought of change in our lives. Our sin nature makes us all great lawyers, and we easily justify the weaknesses in our lives. We are good at coming up with excuses for our sin and why we don't need to change. After all, you can't teach old dogs new tricks. My Bible college teacher used to respond to that excuse with, "We are not talking about old dogs, and we aren't talking about tricks."

However, the old saying everyone hates change is not quite correct. We love change when we are talking about others. Oh, how clearly we see the change needed in others especially when that change in them would make our life better. We are happy to point out how our spouse, child, boss, neighbor, friend, pastor, fellow believer, etc. should change. We are all about changing the rest of the world, and therefore love change when it happens to them. We see it in politics all the time; each party is all about bringing about change. If we would vote for them, we could see real change. Unfortunately just like in politics, in humans too, very seldom does actual change happen.

When I am counseling couples with marriage problems, I always hear things like, "If she would just do (fill in the blank), our marriage would be better." Or "If he would just do (blank), I would love him more." The biggest problem I have with marriage counseling is getting the couples to stop focusing on what the other person needs changed and to focus on what God wants to change him or her personally. In fact, if the couple cannot get past the notion that the other person needs changing first, the success rate for that marriage is about 0 percent. Consequently very little of marriage counseling effects lasting change; they are always waiting for the other person to change first. However, the inverse is true. If the couple can focus on what they individually need to change, there is almost a 100-percent-success rate. The same is true of us with our God. If we can stop blaming everyone and everything else and yield to the change God wishes for us, a deep relationship develops, and we can experience the abundant life Jesus promised.

So one of the major hindrances to our change as believers is we treat God the same as those struggling couples treat each other. We believe that if only God would change, life would be fine. If He would change His demands on our lives, if He would change the people He put in our lives or the circumstances of life, then all would be good. If only we had a better job, a better car, a better house, more money, more time, etc., then we would be happy. Yet when we complain about the people and circumstances that God has allowed in our lives, we are complaining about God Himself. Consequently we are also complaining about the very mechanism that God is using to conform us to the image of His Son.

> And we know that all things work together for good to *those who love* God, to those who are the called according to *His* purpose. For whom He foreknew, He also predestined *to be* conformed to the image of His Son, that He might be the firstborn among many brethren. (Romans 8:28–29, emphasis added)

God didn't promise that all things would *feel* good, just that all things would be *for our* good. And in the context of the next verse, that *good* would be Him conforming us to the image of His Son. But also notice there is a condition in verse 28, "to those who love God." The unsaved do not believe in God and do not love Him. Nonetheless, we who do believe in Him can, at times, not love Him. Like the Apostle John wrote, "Jesus said, "*If* you love Me, keep My commandments" (John 14:15, emphasis added).

> Jesus answered and said to him, "*If* anyone loves Me, he will keep My word; and My Father will love him, and We will come to him and make Our home with him. He who *does not love Me* does not keep My words; and the word which you hear is not Mine but the Father's who sent Me. (John 14:23–24, emphasis added)

> *If* someone says, "I love God," and hates his brother, he is a liar; for he who does not love his brother whom he has seen, *how can he love God* whom he has not seen? And this commandment we have from Him: that he who loves God *must* love his brother also. (1 John 4:20–21, emphasis added)

In the passages from the Gospel of John, Jesus is talking to His disciples. And in 1 John, the apostle is talking to the brethren in Christ. All these passages are talking to believers. And as we know from practical experience, believers can occasionally be disobedient. Therefore, when we are not obeying God like complaining about the circumstances of life, we do not love Him. And if we do not love Him, then He cannot use those circumstances to change us.

> Do all things without complaining and disputing, that you may become blameless and harmless, children of God without fault in the midst of a crooked and perverse generation, among whom you shine as lights in the world, holding fast the word of life, so that I may rejoice in the day of Christ that I have not run in vain or labored in vain. (Philippians 2:14–16)

When we realize we have a problem, we have already fixed about 80 percent of the problem. Understanding that we can hinder the change that God wishes to do in us goes a long way in allowing God to make that change. We need to see life as God's plan and purpose to make a change in us for our good and not fight against that change by trying to control those circumstances. Most people see themselves as the authors of their stories. They feel they are writing their stories through the decisions they make. Few of us recognize that God is the Author. What's the difference? When I am the author, I think I need to be in control, and I must fight against the hard times. But as a believer, I gave up the right to be my own author. God is the Author of my life; He is writing my story. He is using those hard times for my good. I am merely the reader, and I can sit back and enjoy the story, saying, "I wonder how God is going to get me out of this one?"

> For I through the law died to the law that I might live to God. I have been crucified with Christ; it is no longer I who live, but Christ lives in me; and the *life* which I now live in the flesh I live by faith in the Son of God, who loved me and gave Himself for me. I do not set aside the grace of God; for if righteousness *comes* through the law, then Christ died in vain. (Galatians 2:19–21)

When I was a kid, I watched on TV that old Batman show with Adam West. It didn't take long to realize that no matter how dire the circumstances, Batman and Robin always escaped the bad guy's trap. Why then did I keep on watching it? The reason was the wonder of finding out how Batman would get out of this one. We all know the end to our own stories—good will conquer evil. We have been promised an eternity in paradise. What's the worst thing that could happen to me today? I could die and spend eternity with my Lord with no more pain, no more sorrow and only joy. Why am I worrying? Let's sit back and enjoy God's story of our lives. God created all mankind with the ability to enjoy a good story. The earliest form of entertainment was storytelling. The creation story in Genesis 1 was the first story ever told. The Israelites sat around the fire telling that story to their children for thousands of years. I think God created us with this desire for a good story to remind us He is our Author.

Therefore, we learned in chapter 2 that one of the things that hinder our change is not understanding how lasting change happens, Man's Formula vs. God's Formula. At the beginning of this chapter, we looked at how we can hinder His change by choosing not to follow His ways. To finish off this chapter, we will look at how we can help facilitate that change rather than hinder it.

As God was taking me through this process of knowing Him, my first question was: How? How do I get to know you, Lord? And to be honest, I had no idea. My original method was to be obedient to His Word. God had shot that one down, and I had no idea where to go next. Therefore, I thought, *I can at least start with writing down the things I do know about God.* I got a notebook and started collecting things about God's character. That was very helpful, and I write more about that notebook in chapter 4 when I explain how to create a biography of God.

The Natural Explains the Supernatural

As we saw in chapter 1, God uses the natural to explain the supernatural. God wants us to understand that He uses human relationships as a model of the spiritual relationship He desires with us. Throughout Scripture, God uses as illustrations the natural things of life to help our finite minds understand a little bit of His infinite mind. We will never understand fully the love God has for us, yet we can understand it somewhat when God sacrificed His only Son for our sins. Our minds can wrap around the idea of how much love it would take to allow our son to die for others.

One of the most important natural examples God uses is our human relationships. We are the children of God, we are the bride of Christ, and Jesus calls us friend. In those human relationships, God is explaining how He wishes our relationship would be with Him. Because we are so familiar with these human relationships, we sometimes take them for granted and don't realize that God had a real purpose in creating these relationships. God wasn't just sitting around one day when all of a sudden, it dawned on Him that the marriage relationship was just like the relationship He desired with His creation. No, He created these human relationships with a divine purpose.

For God didn't have to create the marriage relationship, the parent/child relationship, nor the best-friend relationship. When he created animals, He proved that humans didn't need these types of relationships to flourish. God didn't have to create the marriage relationship to populate the earth. There are asexual animals that don't need a mate to reproduce. Nor do many animals have the same mate for life. Also animals have many different parenting methods. I personally like the papa grizzly bear. When he has kids, he leaves them with the mama bear to raise, and he goes off alone to a life of eating and sleeping. Then there is the sea turtle that lays her eggs and swims away, letting the children take care of themselves. While some animals run in packs, there are just as many that prefer the solitary life with no friends asking to borrow money or help them move. God could have created humans any way He wanted and still fulfilled His plans for the earth. Secularists point to these animal characteristics, such as multiple mates, to justify their destruction of the family. But God's plans for humanity are much greater than just populating a planet.

We must realize that these human relationships are God-given examples for our benefit. When we do, then knowing and understanding God becomes quite easy. All we must do is imagine what a perfect marriage relationship looks like, and we have an idea of the intimacy God desires of us which was kind of a duh moment for me. If knowing Jesus Christ is our main purpose in life, then it would make sense that God would show us how to do it. The problem has been that we haven't realized how important the picture of human relationships is to understanding God. I have already mentioned the top three relationships: the marriage, the parent/child, and the best friend. But the Bible lists many more: The Teacher and His disciples, the Counselor, the great Physician, our Lord and King, our Savior, our Creator, our High Priest, our Refuge, and our Strength to name a few.

It doesn't take a seminary degree to understand what these names and titles are communicating. They take on the simple meaning that each would have in natural life. A shepherd cares for and protects his sheep. A counselor gives guidance and direction. A physician heals. A Savior saves, etc. There are four-hundred -plus different names and titles for the Trinity in the Scriptures. And as far as I know, every positive adjective in the English language is used to describe our God: loving, caring, kind, merciful, long-suffering, protecting, and on and on. God has a lot He wishes to share with His creation about Himself.

Again I mentioned in chapter 1 that when we are comparing human relationships with divine relationships, we must remember that God is the perfect example of that human relationship. God is the perfect spouse, father, friend, counselor, teacher, pastor, etc. Another caution is that when we are studying the perfections of God, we must be careful not to get caught up in just one or two of them. If we focus on the love and mercy of God, we may miss out on the judgment and chastisement of God. And if we focus just on the holiness of God, we may miss out on His forgiveness and grace. This focus on one or two characteristics of God is how many false theologies and beliefs get started like legalism and license. It is important for us to study all the perfections of God so that we will have a well-balanced view of who He is and to avoid false teachings.

Therefore, getting to know God is very much like getting to know any other human being. When we get to know other humans, we find out they are all different. Hence, each of our relationships with God will be a little different. That is because God loves variety. Look at God's creation and the variety there is in it. I love woodworking and learning about the trees God has created. There are about 220,000 different species of trees. That is a small number compared to the 6-billion-plus different humans there are in the world, and no two relationships are exactly the same, kind of like snowflakes (smile). Sure some will be similar. Like I shared earlier, we have four children, and yes, I love them all the same. But our relationship with each other is very different. They each have their likes and dislikes, they have different interests, and they have different activities they like to do with their old dad.

One Size Does Not Fit All

One of the disservices we in Christian leadership have unwittingly done is trying to make a relationship with God a one-size-fits-all program. We write books on how to have a devotion time with God and inadvertently imply this is how everyone should spend their devotion time. Most likely, that program worked well for the author. Still it is unlikely to have the same effect on everyone else. God made us all different with different personalities and abilities. The number of ways to have a devotion time with God is equal to the number of people in the world. Therefore, when well-meaning writers come up with devotion plans, they usually discourage people rather than encourage them to spend more time with their God. That is because it is not a personal fit for them, and they often don't enjoy it as much as the writer did.

These devotion programs that were written for a broad audience are like me giving the same marriage relationship advice to every couple that comes to my office. Or it would be like my son telling me he is ready to get married and wanting to know how to find a wife. So I tell him, "This is what you do. You eat lunch in the Motorola cafeteria at Fifty-Second Street and McDowell and keep an eye out for pretty girls. Then when you see one, you go sit down with her and introduce yourself. And if she talks to you, then you invite her out to lunch, and everything will work out from there." That's how I met my wife. Wouldn't it be foolish of me to say all that to my son? Is the same plan I used going to work for him? Not likely especially since that Motorola plant is no longer there. All of us who believe in Jesus Christ got saved the same way—by faith in Him; nonetheless, each of our journeys to that faith is different. But that is how we treat getting to know God through devotion programs. We say, "This is how I spend time with God, and this is how you should spend time with Him." Which I am trying very hard not to do with this book but to provide us with the basics so we all can find God individually.

Therefore, the first practical advice I can give for our journey to knowing God better is to find out what we each like to do with God. The devotion books aren't bad; they are just limited. We can still read them, keep what sounds interesting, and ignore the rest. Ask others what they like to do with their time alone with God. Try a lot of different things. When we enjoy what we are doing, it sure makes it easier to keep on doing it. Also be willing to change your devotions as new interests come along. As we grow older, our likes and dislikes change. Have fun with God! If I am a loving husband, I am not going to demand that my wife spend time with me doing things she hates to do.

Many people have the gift of music; I do not. I wish I could play an instrument. I would use my devotion time like King David who played his harp unto the Lord. But I was created to be an audience. Hey, if nobody was in the audience, there wouldn't be anyone to listen. But I do like to listen to good music when I am alone with God. Sometimes all I will do for my devotion is sit back, close my eyes, and listen to the words of the songs. If the house is empty, I might even sing along. We can get creative with our time. We don't have to stay inside; we can go for a walk with the Lord. We can listen to the Bible rather than read it especially if we have a long commute to work. We can turn off the TV and watch a sermon online. Some like to write more than others; they could start a journal, write out their prayers, or write a letter to God.

Also there is nothing holy about the time of the day we are alone with God. Not everyone is a morning person. Right now, I am writing this and it is nearly midnight, that is because all my family has gone to bed, and it is quiet in the house. I can't do it early in the morning. Besides all the family being up, I don't think so well in the morning. For me, having my devotion time in the morning is not my best time, and I always want to give God my best.

That is the only qualification I would give on time alone with God. When we meet with Him, we should want to give Him our best. Don't give Him the leftovers of the day. Too many Christians only have their devotion time if they have gotten everything else done for the day. I wrote a saying in the front of my Bible. I am not sure where I got it from, but it says, "I have all the time I need today to do what God wants me to do." I know that God wants to spend time alone with me today, thus, if I don't have time to do that, then I am doing something that He doesn't want me to do. That doesn't necessarily mean what I am doing with my time is wrong or evil. When I have a bookshelf full of good books, to add an even better book, I may have to remove a good one.

We all experience joy when hanging out with the people we love, doing the things we love together. If we do what we like with the Lord, we are more likely to enjoy it and stick with it. Understand, God did not intend our devotion time to be a boring duty. Like spending time with a good friend, God wants our time alone with Him to be joyful and desirable. An interesting Bible study is to look at all the times the Bible talks about the joy of the Lord. Seven times in the Gospel of John, Jesus talks about our joy being full. And John makes joy the very purpose of his little book, 1 John, "And these things we write to you that your joy may be full" (1 John 1:4). Thus, we should not let anyone steal our joy by making us feel bad that according to them, we are not doing our devotions right.

The Four T's of Relationships

Now after talking about how much God loves variety, there are some aspects of relationship building that will be the same for all of us. In the example of my son finding a wife, his experience will be very different than mine, but there are some important similarities. He does have to get out there and meet someone; he can't just sit in the house and hope she rings the doorbell. Also he needs to talk to the girl and get to know her; he can't just walk up to a random girl and say, "Hey, let's get married." Although I have heard of some Christian colleges' relationships that were close to that (smile). But I digress.

As the Lord was teaching me these things about Himself and relationships, I realized that getting to know God was the same as getting to know my wife. And while it took some time to fine-tune this application, I eventually came up with the four Ts of relationships: time, talk, trust, and talent. They are the parts of every relationship that need to be the same. They are vital in developing loving and lasting human relationships and vital to developing our relationship with God. They are critical for knowing God.

Time

Spending a lot of time with someone is the only way to build a deep relationship. Cabbage matures in only a few weeks, but it takes an oak tree hundreds of years. Which type of relationship is most desirable—one that provides benefit for a few hours or one that can benefit an entire lifetime? Significant relationships don't happen in short amounts of time. Our deepest relationships are usually the ones we have spent the most time on. I remember reading an article many years ago that said the average American dad only spends thirty minutes a day with their child and only three of those minutes in meaningful conversation. No wonder our young people are struggling so much.

You cannot know God on the run any more than you can know any other person that way. Personal relationships are not built "efficiently." They take enormous amounts of time devoted to interaction with the other person.[1]

Any relationship, if it is going to grow, needs private space, time together *without an agenda* where you can get to know each other. This creates an environment where closeness happens, where we can begin to understand each other's heart. You don't create intimacy—you make room for it. This is true whether you are talking about your spouse, your friend, or God. You need space to be together. Efficiency, multitasking, and busyness all kill intimacy. In short, you can't get to know God on the fly.[2]

Yet how little interest the heirs of salvation show in their inheritance. They hardly have time to read the book of precious promises. If they only knew what it contained, they would stop everything to find out and enjoy His provisions. It will take an eternity for us to discover the wealth which He has left us.[3]

After meeting the young lady that would become my wife in the Motorola cafeteria, we started spending time together. We would have lunch together. We would go on dates and sometimes spend the whole day together. It was through all this time together that we fell in love with each other. But if I had told Barbara when we first met, "You know, Barb, I am an important person here at Motorola and quite often, I have to work long hours. Also I have a lot of things I like to do after work. I coach Little League with my roommate, Chris, and I play a lot of golf. But since you are so cute, I would like to get to know you better. However, I probably can only give you about fifteen minutes a day." That wouldn't have gone over too well, right? She would have said I was crazy and found someone else to date. Christians today are lucky if they spend fifteen minutes a day with their God. They read their daily devotional book, spend a few minutes in prayer, and off they go to do their thing. And they wonder why they don't have much of a relationship with their God.

Besides doing marriage counseling, I have done a lot of premarital counseling. One of the questions I ask all the young couples is, "Where are you going for your honeymoon?" The answer usually is a week here or there, sometimes ten days and even occasionally, two weeks. I say to them, "That's fantastic! Whoever invented the honeymoon was brilliant. It is the perfect way to start your new relationship." I go on to tell them, "After you let Mom know you made it there safely, then turn off your phones and spend the whole time getting to know one another. Stare into each other's eyes, take long walks on the beach, and of course, be intimate with each other." I then explain to them how this time alone is a great foundation to build on and how important it will be to do the same throughout their marriage. And even though it will be tough, especially if the Lord blesses them with children, it is vital for their marriage that the two of them get away and be alone together throughout their marriage.

Then comes the million-dollar question. "If spending a week or so alone together is an important start to your relationship and it is important to continue to keep your relationship together (pause for effect), have you ever spent a week alone with God?"

Their reactions are the same as most everyone's, "I have never thought of that." I go on to explain to them that if time alone is important to a relationship that will last fifty to sixty years, how much more important is it to a relationship that will last fifty to sixty bazillion years and is only getting started? Yes, the quality of our relationships is directly proportional to how long we spend with that person. Sure there could be some negative examples in the natural realm like having a terrible boss. But that is not true of our God.

Therefore, a practical action we can add to our lives is more time alone with our God. We can spend four to five hours playing golf, an entire day shopping, but we find it strange to even consider more than an hour or so alone with God. I have added more time to my devotional life and wow! What a blessing! But it can be hard at first, we must stick with it. One time, I had two days at a friend's cabin to spend alone with God, but I had a hard time getting started. After unpacking and settling in, I opened my Bible with every intention to read for a few hours. About fifteen minutes later, I fell asleep. When I woke from my little nap, I tried again—this time, I fell asleep after about thirty minutes. What I found out was that it took me almost an entire day to quiet my soul from the stresses of life before I could concentrate on God. Doctors tell us that until the stress in our lives is removed, we often don't know we are under stress. People going on vacation often find that for the first couple of days, they have a hard time doing anything—all they want to do is sleep. This desire to sleep is a sign of stress.

Consequently we may want to start slowly, maybe a couple of hours or half a day alone with God. Then work up to a day or two. Ultimately I recommend at least one whole day, four times a year, once a quarter, and an extended period of maybe three to five days, once a year. If we apply the principle of the tithe to our time, then 10 percent of our day would be about 2.4 hours. That is what I shoot for now.

If doing it all at one time sounds impossible, try an hour in the morning, a half-hour around lunchtime, and an hour in the evening. My biblical counseling mentor would read his Bible after every meal. For breakfast, he would read four chapters in the Old Testament, for lunch he would read five Psalms and the Proverb for the day. Then for dinner, he would read four chapters in the New Testament. Doing that, he would read through the Old Testament once a year, the New Testament four times a year, and Psalms and Proverbs once a month. That is about the perfect proportion of God's Word for us, and a great reminder that man does not live by bread alone.

But if life is stressful, I recommended a devotion time of a minimum of two hours to unwind. Spend some time listening to music to relax; when things are more focused, then spend time studying, again giving God our best. Of course, there is no extra grace in a certain amount of time, no magic in the one-week example. Don't fall back into a sense of duty in your time alone with God. Remember, this is about getting to know God more than it is about a set amount of time. Also we mustn't let Satan discourage us if our time is not consistent every day. Sometimes there are emergencies in life, and we can't get to that time alone with God. I don't get to spend the same amount of time with my wife each day. That time ebbs and flows according to our schedules. But I better not go very long without being with her.

Spending time alone with God is a "must happen" in the relationship but how that time is spent is open for variety. Each human couple enjoys doing different things when alone together. Some enjoy going for long walks while others enjoy going out to dinner. Some may enjoy the crowd when going to the theater, and others prefer the peace of their own home. I have a good friend who thinks the best vacation is going to a big city to go to all the restaurants, museums, and other sights. But my wife and I think the best vacation is a cabin somewhere in the woods and to stay there the whole time reading books and taking hikes.

One last thing before we move on, I have spent a lot of time on *Time* because it is so important, and it is where we believers are the weakest. Also we tend to think church attendance and ministry count as time with God. Ministry does not count as spending time alone with God nor does going to church. Both are good and important things for believers to do, but there is more. Ministry and church attendance are like group dating God—it can be a useful thing, but it is not intimacy. When our children started getting interested in the opposite sex, we would let them group date. That was because we didn't want them to have the temptations of being alone together. But we also wanted them to get used to the opposite sex, to interact, to talk with and learn how to respect one another, for we didn't want them to live with us forever. When they got older and were ready for marriage, we encouraged them to be alone with their prospective mate to get to know each other better. That was important for them in determining if that other person was God's will for their lives.

When I first got into ministry, I was already married. And I found out the hard way that spending time with my wife at church events didn't count as being with her. I remember when she pointed out that going to the church's Valentine's banquet while having fun being around good friends was not the meaning of Valentine's Day. I scored a few points for going to the banquet but when I got a babysitter and we went out alone for dinner, I scored major points. Just like I told those premarital couples, you will technically spend a lot of time together, but the valuable time is the time alone.

God is similar to my wife; He loves our service and fellowship with other believers. It is clear from Scripture that fellowship with our fellow believers is very important. But we were first and foremost created for an intimate relationship with Him. Like I tell my kids, "I love you greatly, but I plan to live the rest of my life with your mom. She gets priority." When we get to heaven, I do think we will enjoy one another, but Heaven is for us to be with God. And while this is divine imagination on my part, if Jesus is omnipresent, couldn't He be walking through the forest with me while soaring through the galaxy with you? Again God is using the natural to explain the supernatural. It is important to look for it; God has made it quite easy to understand Him.

Talk

Every marriage counselor in the world says that the key to a good marriage is communication. I have found that whatever couples can't talk about, they will fight about no matter what the subject—money, sex, goals, feelings, the kids, etc. If when I met my wife we spent a lot of time together but we didn't talk to each other, the relationship wouldn't have gone anywhere. Of course when we were dating, we did the opposite; we talked almost all the time. Now those were the dark ages before emails, texting, and Facebook. We spent most of our time talking on the phone, and we did it sometimes for hours. Yes, we did that silly thing young lovers do—"You hang up first." "No, you hang up first." Back then, we didn't have to worry about using up our minutes. It was through those conversations that we learned about each other, and it was from that knowledge that we decided to spend the rest of our lives together.

When it comes to God, the primary forms of communication are His Word and prayer. He communicates to us through the Bible, and we communicate to Him through prayer. I believe that because God gave us two ears and one mouth, we are supposed to listen twice as much as we speak. In the Gospels, Jesus said numerous times, "If anyone has ears, let him hear." Jesus was not talking about hearing with the outer ear but hearing with the inner ear. He was talking about taking His Words into our hearts and believing in them, really hearing Him. Kind of like when my wife asks me, "Are you listening?" She knows I may technically be hearing the words she is saying, but I am not listening with understanding. A listening ear is one way we communicate love. Interesting that in the Old Testament, the phrase that shows up is God saying, "They have ears but do not hear."

Listening to God speak is another *must happen* in the relationship. But again, there is a lot of room for variety. Listening to God's Word preached each week is a good place to start. But listening to preaching is kind of like going out to dinner; every so often it is a privilege to have someone else prepare the meal. But to stay healthy, we must feed ourselves most of the time. There are five major ways of taking in God's Word: listening, reading, memorizing, studying, and meditating. Again the important part is finding what we enjoy. Some people enjoy memorizing Scripture. I am not one of them, but it can be very beneficial. Some strange people (smile) like to study God's Word in the original Greek and Hebrew.

And of course, there is the tried and true, read-your-Bible-through-in-a-year program. Let me give a couple of words of encouragement on that. Reading through your Bible in a year is very beneficial; every believer should do it at least once in a lifetime, but many people fail. Genesis is the most read book of the Bible because of all the people who try to read through the Bible but then quit sometime in February when they hit Leviticus or Deuteronomy. There is nothing magical about getting through the Bible in a year. If we stop somewhere along the way, we shouldn't wait until next January to start again so we can tell everyone we read the whole Bible in a year. We should instead start again where we left off. The important part is getting to know our God, and if it takes two to three years to get all the way through the Bible, then so be it. It is important to enjoy the journey and not let the journey steal the joy of finding God.

I prefer the Elmer-Fudd program of Bible reading (those under the age of forty may have to Google Bugs Bunny and Elmer Fudd). But for us older folk, we know Elmer Fudd was always wabbit hunting. That is how I enjoy God's Word. I read until a "rabbit" (an interesting thought) pops up. Then I "chase" (hunt) that rabbit through the Scriptures. I like to study God's Word more topically rather than book by book. That comes from being a counselor; people have problems topically, not in the context of a chapter or an entire book. Also I naturally like to collect things: baseball cards, marbles, and old pocket knives. I used to have a hard time being consistent in my Bible reading. But when I started collecting verses on the character of God, I found I could do that for hours. Collecting verses about God was easy to stick with because it fit my personality. Spending hours in God's Word might be hard to imagine, but it is such a blessing!

Before we move on to the third T, let me say a little bit about prayer. There are so many good books on prayer that I won't go into much detail here. And just like Bible reading, there are many options for prayer. Prayer is simply talking to God just like we talk to anyone else; nevertheless, prayer should remain reverent, for we are talking to God. It doesn't mean we have to be on our knees with our head bowed and our eyes closed. We can still be reverent with our eyes open, looking up to heaven as we talk to Him. We can talk to Him as we walk through the park, as we drive to work, or as we run on the treadmill.

One of the hang-ups I had for many years, that kept me from praying more, was the idea why pray when God already knows everything? Again this is where God using the natural to explain the supernatural helped me see prayer in a whole new light. God reminded me of my good friend Daniel Dan and I worked together for many years, and we would often have lunch together. I enjoyed those lunches immensely, not only because Dan was a good friend but because he was funny. He always had a funny story or observation to lighten our stressful day. In fact, there were a few times that I might not have gone back to work if I hadn't had lunch with Daniel Well, after about a year or so, I had heard all of Dan's stories. But I didn't mind hearing them again because he was my good friend. Even though I knew the end of the story, I still loved to hear him talk.

That is when I realized that even though I am not telling God anything new, like a good friend or a loving parent, He loves to listen to me talk. It was a realization of God's love for me that encouraged me to pray more. Prayer is not about needs, it is about love. We must stop treating God like a giant ATM in the sky who is only there to fulfill our daily needs and discover we have in God a loving spouse, parent, and friend that wants to talk.

Trust

No relationship gets very far if there is no trust in one another. Not to brag but when I was younger, I was a lot better-looking, and I dated a fair number of girls. What made Barb different than all the rest? It was by getting to know her through talking and listening and spending time together that I decided to trust her with my heart. That is what love is all about—trust. We can be attracted to numerous people, but the one we have the deepest relationship with is the one we trust.

Trust is truly a God thing. This is where the natural illustration breaks down just a little. Nowhere in Scripture are we commanded to trust one another. We are only commanded to trust in the Lord. We are commanded to love one another and if we can find another human we can trust in, then we have found a good thing. But nowhere in Scripture are we told to trust in humans. Because no matter how much we love one another, we humans will always let each other down, for we are not perfect. Because we still have our sin nature, we cannot be trusted. Most of the time, we don't intend to be untrustworthy, but our selfish nature pops through every so often. When God said, "Trust in the LORD with all your heart" (Proverbs 3:5), *all* means all. There is no part of our heart leftover to trust in one another; we are to put all our trust in God.

That doesn't mean that human relationships are not important and that we can't love one another. And it doesn't let us off the hook to be as trustworthy as we can. Barb has trusted me with her heart and with God's help, I should do all that I can not to break it. But she would be foolish to expect that I never will. Trust is a reminder that we were created for God's good pleasure. We will be His bride, no one else's—for all eternity. And while He wants us to enjoy the human relationships He provided for us, He also wants us to remember that we were created for Him. From a human point of view, that may sound selfish on God's part. But when You are the Creator of all the universe, You get to decide what to do with Your creation.

Trust is the most important aspect of a growing relationship with our God. We must decide to trust God in who He says He is and what He expects from us. Remember when I said I wanted to be like Enoch and spend too much time with God? Well, look at what the writer of Hebrews said about Enoch:

> By faith Enoch was taken away so that he did not see death, *"and was not found, because God had taken him";* for before he was taken he had this testimony, that he pleased God. *But without faith it is impossible to please Him,* for he who comes to God must believe that He is, and *that* He is a rewarder of those who diligently seek Him. (Hebrews 11:5–6, emphasis added)

Without faith (trust) *it is impossible to please God.* Trusting God is both the easiest and the hardest thing for us believers to do. Trusting is simply deciding in our minds that what God says is true. It is just that easy—it is just deciding. But on the other hand, it is the hardest thing for us to do, for it takes setting aside our selfish, sinful nature and deciding not to do things our way but to humble ourselves and decide for God's way. It is the greatest example that Jesus left behind for us when He said, "Not My will, but Your will be done." That is trust!

Talent

Speaking of pleasing God, we now come to the last T—talent. I had to stretch a little to get this one. But *talent* refers to those things that we do. How we treat one another determines the growth of the relationship. Here is where putting off the old man and putting on the new man comes into our relationship with God.

But first, back to the courtship of my wife. One of my first jobs out of high school was at this drafting shop in downtown Phoenix. I had wanted to be a draftsman ever since learning some drawing techniques in a third-grade art class. I perfected my skills by drawing in church when I was supposed to be listening to my dad preach but don't tell him. Anyway that little drafting shop was full of young college-age guys just like me. And since none of us were married, we all hung out together outside of work. Well, like most young men, we liked to make fun of each other. Men show they like you by being mean to you—it is a guy thing. When I was dating my future wife, I would make fun of her too. I think she put up with it because she was nice. After we got married, I found out that she didn't appreciate my skill of teasing her. Ever noticed women don't think the same way we men do?

To please my wife, I had to *put off* that habit of making fun of her, although it still slips out occasionally. But the other thing I found out was that she likes flowers. I never bought flowers for my buddies at the drafting shop; it probably would have gotten me beaten up. To please my wife, I *put on* buying her flowers, although

I don't always remember to do that. Anyway if I hadn't changed my behavior, our relationship wouldn't have lasted very long.

It should be obvious that how we treat one another greatly affects the depth of the relationship. For our relationship with God, it is important for us to put off our sin which saddens Him and put on the change of Christ-like behavior that pleases Him. As a believer, our sin no longer condemns us to an eternity apart from God, but our sin does hinder our fellowship with Him. Sin for the believer is like throwing rocks in a creek. The creek is the flow of fellowship coming from the Lord to our hearts. That flow of fellowship from God's fountain never changes, but the rocks of our sin hinder that flow. At first, we might not notice too much of a difference; but if we keep throwing in those rocks, the fellowship slows down to a mere trickle. When we "confess our sins" (1 John 1:9), God scoops out all those rocks and restores the full flow of fellowship.

As I finish up this chapter, did you notice something about those four Ts? That's right; they follow God's change formula for your life, knowledge of God + belief in God = change by God. *Time* and *talk* accomplish the knowledge of God. *Trust* is the belief-in-God part. And *talent* is the changed-by-God part. Therefore, a practical way for you to get started in a deeper relationship with God is by spending more alone time with Him, talking and listening to Him, choosing to believe His truth, and yielding to the change He is making in you.

---

1. Jim Berg, God Is More Than Enough: Foundations for a Quiet Soul (Greenville, South Carolina: Journeyforth, 2010), 158.
2. Paul Miller, A Praying Life: Connecting with God in a Distracting World (Colorado Springs: NavPress, 2009), 46.
3. M.R. DeHaan, Studies in Hebrews (Grand Rapids: Kregel Publications, 1996), 131.

CHAPTER 4

God's Purpose for Us

And this is eternal life, that they may know You, the only true God, and Jesus Christ whom You have sent.

—John 17:3

When I was in high school, we had aptitude tests to help determine a career interest. There were not only tests in English and math comprehension but also tests in dexterity and mechanical aptitude. Little washers and nuts had to be threaded on a small screw. Completed sets would be counted after two minutes. After all the tests were completed, we were called into the school counselor's office in pairs to review the results. The counselor told me I had done great and would do well at most anything. Well, I had known from the third grade that I wanted to be a draftsman. The counselor asked if I was taking the drafting classes the school offered and if I knew where I wanted to go to college to which I responded, "Yes."

The counselor then turned to the other student who was with me and told him he had done well too. The counselor then asked him what he was interested in doing for a career. The student said he wanted to be a professional baseball player. I did a double take; being an athlete myself and living in a small town in Oregon, I knew most all the athletes in the school. I couldn't remember seeing this student in any sport. The counselor looked a little taken aback too. But he continued to ask him more questions. "So, you like to play baseball? Have you played a lot?"

To which the kid answered, "Yes," and that he had played some Little League.

The counselor then said, "So, you are on the school team? How are you doing?

To which the kid said, "No, I am not on the team." Now these days, kids can do well in club sports without playing high-school ball. But this was the late '70s in a small town in Oregon—there were no other teams. I couldn't tell if this guy was being honest or joking; he seemed like a regular student.

I am sure the counselor was dumbfounded too; I don't think he knew what to say. He muttered something about maybe you should try out for the team and then something about how hard it is to get into professional sports to which the kid just answered, "Okay." Having nothing else to say, the counselor let us go. I am pretty sure that kid never played professional baseball. Again a small town in Oregon, I probably would have heard about it.

Why did I tell this story? I want to talk about the purpose of life in this chapter. We all, whether we realize it or not, are driven by what we believe is our purpose in life. I knew I wanted to be a draftsman, so I worked at it. I took every drafting class the school had; I even took the advanced class twice. In about sixth grade, I found out draftsmen print everything on their drawings. Therefore, to practice my lettering, I stopped writing in cursive and printed all my papers. To this day, the only thing I can write in cursive is my signature. But that other guy hadn't done much to achieve his goal. If he really wanted to be a professional baseball player, he didn't seem to be going in that direction.

Our perceived purpose in life is very important! It guides us, it leads us and is at the root of our life decisions. If we think our purpose in life is to eat, drink, and be merry for tomorrow we die, then we probably spend most of our time partying and having fun and, as little time as possible, having a career to make lots of money. But if our purpose is to be rich and powerful so that we can have anything we want, we are probably working eighty hours a week and hardly ever seeing our family and friends. If a person wants to be a professional athlete, he practices eight hours a day. If he wants to be a movie star, he moves to Hollywood.

Our purpose even affects our attitude and how we treat one another. For most men, their primary goal in a family is peace. After fighting the battles of life all day long, they want to come home to their peaceful castle. So they may yell at the kids for making too much noise. For women, their primary goal is oneness in the family. They want all the people in the family to get along and therefore to deal with problems. So she may nag everyone, wanting to talk all the time about the lack of connection she is feeling. He wants peace; she wants to talk—not right or wrong, just different goals. But these differences often cause conflict especially if they are self-centered. Our perceived purpose also influences our most important relationship—the one with God. If we think life primarily belongs to us, then we only visit God on Sundays. But God has a different purpose for us.

To Know God

For Hebrews, to know something was to experience it. Biblically for a man and woman to "know" each other was to engage in sexual relations. Knowing God meant the people had more than mere factual knowledge about Him. It meant they experienced Him personally (Hosea 2:16). They received His love and care. The Old Testament prophets often condemned God's people for seeking to know pagan idols more than they sought to walk with and love the true God (Hosea 4:6; 6:6).[1]

I strongly believe that knowing God is the God-given purpose for our lives. Understanding that purpose and choosing to believe it will have a huge effect on our joy, peace, and contentment. Let's first start with what I mean by knowing God. Some Christians may disagree with me. Some Christians believe that their purpose is to glorify God while others believe it is to be happy. Both are important, and some may continue to disagree with me after I have explained it. But that's okay if they differ; I think we will all still be going to heaven. However, I don't wish for them to disagree because they have a false understanding of what I mean by knowing God.

Knowing God is the intimate love relationship I have with Him that when based on faith alone results in my sanctification and His glorification.

Knowing God is part of all three aspects of our faith: justification, sanctification, and glorification. Our knowledge of Him grows exponentially through those three phases. At our initial salvation, justification, we are introduced to God and it is the beginning of our knowledge of Him like being introduced to a stranger. We *should* then spend the rest of our natural lives growing in that knowledge of Him; this is called walking with the Lord or sanctification. Finally after this life, we will spend eternity walking with Him, growing in our knowledge of Him. Throughout our eternal life, we are to grow in the knowledge of God.

> Simon Peter, a bondservant and apostle of Jesus Christ, to those who have obtained like precious faith with us by the righteousness of our God and Savior Jesus Christ Grace and peace be multiplied to you in the *knowledge of* God and of Jesus our Lord, as His divine power has given to us *all things that pertain to life and godliness*, through the *knowledge of Him* who called us by glory and virtue, by which have been given to us *exceedingly great and precious promises*, that through these you may be *partakers of the divine nature*, having escaped the corruption *that is* in the world through lust. (2 Peter 1:1–4, emphasis added)

Probably the biggest misunderstanding when I talk about knowing God is that people believe it means just knowing the facts about God. I don't fault them for that; we all know Christians that know a lot about God. They know all the stories, they know all the standard theology, and they know all the rules. But they have very little joy or contentment in their lives. So of course, knowing God doesn't sound like the answer to most. But knowing God is so much more than just knowing some information about God.

Knowing God is Not Just Knowing the Facts

There are millions of people who know about God and have heard some of the stories in the Bible. Many false religions know some things about Jesus Christ. But none of that knowledge saves them. Just like I pointed out when we were talking about the change formula, for our salvation, just knowing about God didn't save us. Salvation came when we chose to believe in that knowledge of God.

Knowing God is Believing

Continuing to believe God (1 John 5:13) is often the step that is missing for most Christians; this is what is keeping them from enjoying God. They believe in God for salvation, but the rest of their faith is weak. We must continue to believe in what God says about Himself to truly know Him. As we study God's Word, it is only when we believe what we are studying that God can affect change.

We were saved on that day that we first believed in the Lord Jesus Christ. But we continue to need Jesus Christ to save us every day. I am not talking about salvation from eternal condemnation, but the everyday saving from the influences of sin. I will go more in-depth in chapter 5 when we talk about the trichotomy of faith. But briefly, there are three tenses of salvation. In the past, I was saved from eternal condemnation. In the future, I will be saved from the very presence of sin. But right now, in the present, I am being saved from the power of sin and its continuing consequences in everyday life just as the author of Hebrews speaks to us in chapter 12 when speaking about the chastisement/discipline of God's children. Therefore, knowing God is an ongoing belief in God. John said:

> These things I have written to you who believe in the name of the Son of God, that you

> may know that you have eternal life, and that you may *continue to* believe in the name of the Son of God. (1 John 5:13, emphasis added)

In fact, John's writings follow this truth. While there is some overlap, the Gospel of John is primarily about our initial salvation. The books of 1 2, and 3 John are primarily about our present salvation—how we should live now. Revelation is primarily about our future salvation. Therefore, to be saved, we must believe in Jesus Christ. To continue to be saved, changed into the image of Christ, we must continue to believe in Him. That continued belief is choosing to believe in the ongoing truth that we learn about God, for example, His sovereignty, omniscience, love, holiness, etc.

One of the more important things to know and believe is that God loves us and desires a relationship with us. Here is an example: When we love someone, we can't stop thinking about them. Remember as a young person, that first crush? We all had them and remember how we couldn't stop picturing the other person in our mind and how we wanted to be around them all the time?

> How precious also are Your thoughts to me, O God! How great is the sum of them! *If* I should count them, they would be more in number than the sand; When I awake, I am still with You. (Psalms 139:17–18)

This thought from Psalm 139 has been precious to me for many years. Having lived all over the United States, I have been to a lot of beaches, sand dunes, deserts, and even the Great Lakes. There is a lot of sand in the United States let alone the whole world. God has had thoughts of us for every one of those grains of sand, wow! One time when I was wondering out loud about how many grains of sand there may be, my teenage son said to me, "Just google it, Dad." I always forget we can find out anything online. So I did.

What I found out was that some researchers from the University of Hawaii, being well-versed in beach stuff, did an estimate on how many grains of sand there are on the world's beaches. They figured out the average size of a grain of sand and multiplied that by all the world's beaches and deserts. They came up with seven quintillion, five hundred quadrillion grains of sand. That is 7.5×10^{18} or 7.5 with 18 zeros. That's a lot of thoughts of you and me.

It is a number almost too large to comprehend. But to help us get close, our national debt at the time of writing this is shy of twenty-two trillion dollars or 2.2×10^{12}. In other words, if we took 22 trillion and divided it by eighty years, divided by 365 days a year, and divided it by 24 hours a day, a person would have to spend a little over 31 million dollars an hour or 8,720 dollars a second for 80 years to spend our national debt. That's the bad news. The good news is if God thought of us the same number of times as our national debt, He would be thinking of us 8,720 times a second.

However, the University of Hawaii's number is much larger than our national debt, 2.2×10^{12}. When we go from twelve zeroes to thirteen, we are not doubling the number but increasing it by a factor of ten. So even though twelve to eighteen zeros don't sound like a lot, it is a huge difference. But it gets even better. The University of Hawaii only calculated the beaches and deserts. The earth is only one-third land, the other two-third is water, and what is at the bottom of all those oceans, seas, and lakes? Grains of sand! So the number of grains of sand for the entire earth is even larger. To change the illustration slightly, the estimate is that there are 7×10^{27} atoms in an average human of 150 pounds. Therefore, it is likely that God has had thoughts of us for at least every atom in our bodies. Also that means that God loves some of us more than others (smile).

The sad thing is that if we thought about God twice a day, every day, for eighty years, which would be a good average since many days, we don't think of God at all, that number would be 58,400 or about a handful of sand.

We are modern people, and modern people, though they cherish great thoughts of themselves, have as a rule small thoughts of God.[2]

This is where most of us go astray. Our thoughts of God are not great enough; we fail to reckon with the reality of His limitless wisdom and power. Because we ourselves are limited and weak, we imagine that at some points, God is too and find it hard to believe that He is not. We think of God as too much like what we are.[3]

Knowing God is Being Changed by God

We do not know God if His character hasn't rubbed off on us. If we haven't become like Christ in our personal lives, it probably means we don't have much of a relationship with God. If the "fruit of the Spirit (Galatians 5:22–23), love, joy, peace, longsuffering, self-control" is not prevalent in our lives, we may not be walking with Him or at least not walking very closely. Now we must be careful not to make up some arbitrary measure of who is walking with the Lord and who isn't. Change happens at different speeds in people, and we cannot investigate another person's heart. We may observe one weakness in another but not be aware of their strengths. Therefore, the maturity of others is not for us to judge, that is between them and God. We are warned throughout Scripture about judging one another (Matthew 7:1–2; Luke 6:37; Romans 14:3–4, 10; James 4:11–12).

The only time we are to judge others is when it comes to the leadership we are following. Even that is not so much a judgment of their maturity. It is primarily a judgment of their teachings so that we don't follow false teachers (Matthew7:15–20; 1 John 4:1). Therefore, we are not to be fruit inspectors of one another. Leave the fruit inspecting to the Lord. For we don't know if the fruit is righteous or if it is being faked. Also, fruit matures in different seasons, and some fruit is hidden. So let's leave the fruit inspection of our brothers and sisters in Christ to Him.

However, we can judge ourselves; we know better than anyone else if the change is happening in our lives. For it is nearly impossible to spend significant amounts of time with another and not have some change rub off on us. Pastor Tony Evans of Dallas said the following in his wonderful book, *Our God is Awesome:*

> Therefore, you cannot say you know God unless it's rubbed off in your history; unless it has

> affected how you treat your husband or your wife, how you raise your kids, how you spend your money, and how you relate to people. Unless the knowledge of God has changed you, you don't know Him.[4]

It is like what happens to old married couples. They know each other so well they sound like each other, they think alike, and they finish each other's sandwiches (ask your kids if you didn't get that one). Those of us who have been married for a few years can relate. We understand each other, both good and bad. We know what each other's buttons are. Our likes and dislikes often become the same. We know what the other person is thinking. My wife will often ask me, "Do you know where that thing is?" Strangely enough, I know which "thing" she is talking about.

We need to spend enough time and know God well enough that His character rubs off on us, and we become more and more like His Son. This is the secret to becoming like Christ—spending so much time with Him that we become like Him. We love the things He loves, hate the things He hates, and love others as He loves. We can't become like another person by just reading about them; we must be with them. Jesus Christ is our measure of maturity, not other humans. This is what Paul was telling the Ephesians:

> "For the equipping of the saints for the work of ministry, for the edifying of the body of Christ, till we all come to the unity of the faith and of the knowledge of the Son of God, to a perfect man, *to the measure of the stature of the fullness of Christ*. (Ephesians 4:12–13, emphasis added)

Jesus had the greatest discipleship program of all time. It consisted of just two words, *follow me*. He asked those twelve men to stop whatever they were doing and follow Him. They spent all their time with Him. It took around a week to walk from Galilee to Jerusalem.

Just imagine spending all day walking with the Lord. He taught them far more than is recorded in the Gospels. Christ rubbed off so much on these men that they were all willing to die for Him.

Knowing God Is Being Naked before Him

This one gets the attention of the college kids when I teach it especially the freshman homeschoolers. They are all thinking, *You can't say naked in Bible college*! Of course, I am not talking about physical nakedness; it is symbolic of openness in a human relationship. I believe this is the point God was making in the garden. Total transparency (nakedness) is an indicator of a deep relationship. When Adam and Eve sinned, their first consequence was shame at their nakedness. I believe it represented their loss of intimacy with God. It represented an indignity for their sin and that they could no longer stand pure before their God, so they hid.

Then God clothed them, representing the future sacrifice of His Son's blood to cover us in His righteousness which gives us the opportunity to stand before God without embarrassment. However, ever since Adam and Eve's sin, there has been this conflict battling within us. On the one hand, we were created with a desire for a relationship with God, and He has provided the restoration for that broken relationship. But our inherited sin nature is still ashamed, still fearful of intimacy, and we pull back from that relationship.

We don't like God too close especially if God is a deity we can't control. We have a primal fear of walking with God in the garden, naked, without clothing. We desperately want intimacy but when it comes, we pull back, fearful of a God who is too personal, too pure. We're much more comfortable with God at a distance.[5]

After all, intimacy can be threatening. Getting close to Jesus means we can no longer hide our inadequacies. His light illuminates everything that is wrong and ugly about our lives. Unconsciously, therefore, we may flee God's presence rather than pursue it. Intimacy with God may require leaving our comfort zones. Some people feel uneasy in the presence of God. They dismiss the act of worship as too emotional, preferring the intellectual pursuit of Bible study or doctrine. Or they simply have trouble being still because that's their personality. But regardless of our temperament, regardless of our emotional preference, we are called to intimacy with God.[6]

The problem isn't so much that we don't know how to have a relationship or that we don't believe God desires it. Sadly one of the major issues keeping us from a relationship with God is a fear of the relationship—a fear of intimacy. We will know that we are in fellowship with God when we can overcome our pride and be transparent with Him. The strange thing is that we can't hide anything from God anyway; He already sees our nakedness. It is a matter of pride that we must overcome. "God resists the proud but gives grace to the humble" (James 4:6).

I find it interesting that one of Satan's most powerful counterfeits is nakedness. Pornography is the bane of America. Almost every man I deal with in counseling is struggling with pornography. Women too; but while fewer are caught up in actual pornography, their hearts are drawn away from their husband by the romance novel, the soap opera, the chick flick. If any media portrays a romantic man who draws a woman from her husband, it is just as bad as pornography. Satan has made these things far more accessible than they used to be and far more socially acceptable. The ironic thing is Satan has taken away the shame of physical nakedness, but of course, this is not so we can be closer to God.

Knowing God Is Loving Obedience

As we discussed in chapter 2, obedience does not produce intimacy; obedience is the byproduct of intimacy. In other words, love does not produce obedience, but obedience does produce love. Jesus told us all that if we love Him, we will keep His commandments. The love part comes first. That is why the greatest commandment is to *love the Lord our God.* Therefore, obedience to God's Word is an indicator that we know Him.

"Now by this we know that we know Him, if we keep His commandments. He who says, 'I know Him,' and does not keep His commandments, is a liar, and the truth is not in him" (1 John 2:3–4).

John is saying here that those who know Jesus intimately keep His commandments. John is not talking here about knowing God for salvation, for salvation is not based on keeping God's commandments but on believing in Him. However, keeping God's commandments is important to have a good relationship with Him. The first word, *know*, is in the Greek present tense and, therefore, is just having general knowledge, something we know. But the second word, *know*, is in the Greek perfect tense and has the idea of knowing someone intimately. Like a husband knows his wife or a mother knows her son, it is a deeper knowledge than just generally to know.

Here is another example of God using the natural to explain the supernatural. When I was a child, keeping my parents' commandments had nothing to do with whether I was their child. Although there were times I am sure they wondered whose kid I was! For keeping their commandments did not determine if I was their child or not. But my behavior did affect our fellowship. When I did wrong, I was separated from them by being sent to my room. However, my behavior did not affect their love for me, for it was by their love that they disciplined me. My parents were just like God in that they did not chasten a child that was not theirs (Hebrews 12:5–8).

Again when it comes to obedience, we are also not to be fruit inspectors of one another. While loving obedience can be a good indicator of knowing God, it is not a perfect indicator. Obedience is very subjective from a human point of view; it can be faked, and disobedience is often hidden. In some false religions, their followers may look more righteous than some Christians. Others may have all the big sins taken care of, so they look obedient. However, they are still disobedient in the little sins like gossiping, complaining, anger, discontentment, fear, and worry. We all know from experience that we do not possess sinless perfection, and we occasionally stumble. So where is the breaking line? Ninety-five percent obedience? What if I am 94.8 percent? Does that mean I am not a child of God? We are often disobedient children, but that doesn't mean we thought we were His but weren't or somehow stopped being God's child.

Knowing God Is Our Purpose in Life

Most unsaved people think their purpose in life is happiness. Their decisions in life are being made with that purpose in mind. They will even put up with something unpleasant if it will ultimately lead to their happiness like working all week long at a dead-end job so that they can enjoy the weekend. Christians tend to fall into two camps of thought. One camp also thinks happiness is their purpose, but they seek that happiness in God rather than worldly things. The other camp is those that think their purpose is to glorify God. Neither goal is wrong. However, I have found that we cannot achieve either without first getting to know our God. That is why I believe knowing God is a better expression of our purpose.

The sad thing is, both camps often look down their noses at each other. They both have some truth in their beliefs. However, the other side's criticism of each can be true too. The happiness side thinks God wants us to enjoy Him, His creation, and one another. They think the glorify-God side is legalistic, only concerned with keeping the rules, and mostly grumpy. The glorify-God side thinks they please God by obeying His rules and that the happiness side loves the world too much and doesn't take sin seriously. There is some truth and exaggeration in both views.

The happiness camp points to the fact that the Greek word translated in the New Testament *blessed* could have been translated *happy*, and therefore, the Bible talks a lot about believers being happy. Their focus is primarily on the love of God. They point to verses such as these:

"Blessed *is* every one who fears the Lord, Who walks in His ways. When you eat the labor of your hands, you *shall be* happy, and *it shall be* well with you" (Psalms 128:1–2).

"Happy *are* the people who are in such a state; Happy *are* the people whose God *is* the Lord! (Psalms 144:15).

"Happy *is he* who *has* the God of Jacob for his help, whose hope *is* in the LORD his God" (Psalms 146:5).

The glorify-God camp thinks Christians should be more serious about their Christian walk and take their sin seriously. They see sin as the cause of all the discomfort in the world. They do believe that they can experience joy in the Lord but sometimes think happiness sounds too much like the world which they are to be separated. They focus on the holiness of God. They point to the tradition of the Westminster Catechism and point to verses such as these:

"A Psalm of David. Give unto the Lord, O you mighty ones, Give unto the Lord glory and strength. Give unto the Lord the glory due to His name; Worship the Lord in the beauty of holiness" (Psalms 29:1–2).

"Therefore, whether you eat or drink, or whatever you do, do all to the glory of God" (1 Corinthians 10:31).

What is the chief end of man? The chief end of man is to glorify God and fully enjoy him forever.[7]

However, the Westminster Catechism seems to include both. If we are to enjoy God fully, I think that would include being happy. I bring this all up to point out that if we are not careful, we can get out of balance in our walk with the Lord. Like I mentioned in the previous chapter, if we focus on just one or two of the attributes of God rather than all of them, we can take things to an extreme. To remain happy in Jesus Christ and glorify Him, we must remain focused on Him.

Glorifying God

Probably the most common belief for the Christian's purpose of life is to glorify God, at least in the circles I grew up in. They almost always point to 1 Corinthians 10:31, "Do all to the glory of God" as their proof text. However, there are a few problems with this belief. In the context of 1 Corinthians 10:31, Paul is actually talking about eating and drinking and to glorify God, we should not eat or drink anything that would offend a brother in Christ. The context is not really a summary of the entire Christian life and its purpose. Of course, we should give glory to God in all that we do, but I am not sure Paul intends 1 Corinthians 10:31 as a purpose statement for life. It has, over the years, become the traditional interpretation.

Besides if you were going to choose a purpose statement from 1 Corinthians, it would more likely be 16:14, "Let all that you do be done with love." Why wasn't 16:14 chosen? It is written in the same manner as 10:31, "All that you do." There are more poignant verses in 1 Corinthians on *love* than *glory*. There is the love chapter, chapter 13, which ends with, "Now abide faith, hope, and love, these three; but the greatest of these is love." Also 16:14 is at the end of the letter where more often, at least the purpose statement for the letter is written. Along with verse 22, "If anyone does not love the Lord Jesus Christ, let him be accursed." Of course, we know that Jesus said the greatest commandments were to love the Lord our God and our neighbor. In these two, all the commandments are summarized. The greatest commandment and summary of all was not glorify God.

It would seem that love is a closer purpose statement than glorify. That is why my definition of knowing God includes an intimate love relationship with Him. Also if *glorifying God* was our purpose in life, wouldn't it transcend time? That is, wouldn't it be expressed in the Old Testament too? Well, it does appear in the Old Testament, so yes, glorifying God is an important part of the believer's life. But is it the purpose of life? By doing a simple word search on *glory/glorify*, we see that the first use of the word is in Genesis 45:13. Here Joseph is telling his brothers to go back and tell their father about his glory in Egypt. In Exodus, we have quite a few times the glory of the Lord is spoken of but not until Leviticus 10:3 do we have anything about the people glorifying God. Here the sons of Aaron had been killed because they brought a "profane fire before the Lord." God's warning to Moses and Aaron was, "I must be glorified."

However, that passage in Leviticus is not really a command to all the people but more of a statement of fact about Aaron's work in the temple. It is also significant that nowhere in the law were the Israelites commanded to glorify God. The first clear admonition to glorify is in a Psalm of David's in 1 Chronicles 16. David lived in about 1,000 BC and even if we go back to Moses and Aaron, that was around 1,500 BC That is at least 2,500 years after Adam and Eve were created, and there is no mention of glorifying God. The church hasn't even been around for 2,500 years. I would think that if glorifying God was the purpose of humanity that God would have said so earlier.

Now of course, the term *knowing God* does not show up in that time frame either. However, we know that Adam and Eve had a close relationship with God before the Fall. They walked in the cool of the afternoon with God. As we saw in chapter 1, the institute of marriage was established before the Fall, and we are married to God. Finally when Adam and Eve sinned, they broke that love relationship with God and needed a blood sacrifice to re-establish that relationship. Just like we needed Jesus's death to reestablish our relationship with God before we could glorify Him.

My arguments aren't dogmatic; they are just observations for everyone to consider. If anyone is still adamant that glorifying God is our purpose of life, that is fine, I still love you (smile). I can put it this way then so we can still have fellowship together. God's purpose for our lives is to glorify Him by understanding and knowing Him.

> *But let him who glories glory in this, that he understands and knows Me,* That I *am* the Lord, exercising lovingkindness, judgment, and righteousness in the earth. For in these I delight," says the Lord. (Jeremiah 9:24, emphasis added)

What difference does it make which is the purpose? Why spend this much time talking about it? I believe if we don't get the correct purpose for our life that God intended, life can get out of balance. Like one pastor put it, we are the branches and He is the vine. But sometimes, we can get so caught up in improving the arbor that the branches and fruit sit on that we forget to abide in the vine. Or in other words, we often get so caught up in what we are doing as Christians, we neglect Who we should be knowing. For we cannot truly glorify, serve, worship, or obey that which we do not know.

Just like human relationships, they can get out of balance if the right purpose is not understood. If I have friends for what they can do for me, then I probably am not going to have those friends for very long. But even more specifically, Barb and I did not have kids for the purpose of obeying us, serving us, worshiping us, or glorifying us. We had kids because we wished to increase our loving relationships. Loving relationships, husband and wife, parents and children, best friends, are not based on what that person can do for you—at least they shouldn't be. They are based on loving one another. However, and let me make this very clear, how we treat each other is still very important. How we treat each other does affect how loving the relationship is.

The Wheel

Then where does glorifying God fall into the believer's life for clearly God does desire it? I see the believers' lives as being like a wheel. The hub of the wheel is what keeps everything in balance and connects us to the power plant. That hub is Jesus Christ. The outer wheel, where the tread is, that is where we touch the rest of the world (where the rubber meets the road). It is what we individually do to connect with the world and encourage them to have a relationship with God. Since we are all different wheels, we all have different ministries to the world. The spokes are those things that connect the hub to the tread. Glorifying God and being happy in God are two of those spokes. But worshiping God, obeying God, and serving God are also examples of spokes. These spokes are like the secondary purposes of life. They are all important to the believer's life, and they are all commanded by God. So important that without them, Christ does not touch the world through us. However, in our uniqueness of God creating us all a little different, we all have a little different preference to these spokes.

These differences in secondary goals are not right or wrong but just different. They are our God-created passions in ministry. They are an example of Him creating us as different vessels for different uses. Some are more in tune with the love of God, and they help bring into balance those who are more in tune with the holiness of God. For those who are passionate about serving others, it is good to remember that they also need to spend time worshiping God. For those who are passionate about studying God's Word in great depth, it is good for them to remember that there are people out there needing their example of Christ's love. In the previous ministry I was part of, we had numerous pastors, and each of us had a slightly different passion. I was passionate about individual ministries like counseling, mentoring, and discipleship. Our senior pastor was passionate about preaching and evangelism. Another loved music, another loved children, and one even loved teenagers.

Again in the human-relationship example, my wife and I help bring balance to each other. Not only the differing points of view that come from being male and female, but our personality strengths tend to help the other's weaknesses. Similarly the body of Christ each doing its part provides for the whole.

> But, speaking the truth in love, may grow up in all things into Him who is the head— Christ— from whom the whole body, joined and knit together by what every joint supplies, according to the effective working by which every part does its share, causes growth of the body for the edifying of itself in love. (Ephesians 4:15–16)

The picture of the wheel is both for the individual and the body of Christ. We all are centered and balanced around the hub, which is Jesus Christ, using our God-given passions and talents of worshiping, obeying, serving, and glorifying God to reach out and touch the world. So our testimony of connection to Christ might draw others into a relationship with Him.

We must start at the hub, for we cannot glorify, love, serve, or be happy in that which we do not first know. When talking about glorifying God, many point to Moses and how his face shone with the glory of God. Moses was a visible manifestation of God's essence. However, before Moses could glorify God, he had to be in the presence of God. Therefore God imparts Christ's righteousness in us at the moment of salvation so that we are forever qualified to be in the presence of God. While I strongly believe that glorifying God, being happy in God, serving, obeying, worshiping, and loving God are all vital parts of the believer's life, I also strongly believe that they all start with knowing Him.

Notice, if we were to put the hub where the spokes are, at glorifying, obeying, enjoying God, etc., the wheel would be out of balance just like we see in some churches today. Some are overly legalistic. Some are only concerned with worship, and others can get so consumed with serving the public that they forget about God. With Jesus Christ as the hub, things don't get out of balance. In fact, He brings balance both in churches and individuals.

Knowing God

As we finish this chapter, the following is what others and the Scriptures say about knowing God. Just in case anyone thinks I made all this up on my own, it should go without saying that just because I quote someone doesn't mean I agree with all his or her teachings. Of course, I do agree with all the Bible quotes (smile).

The first quote is from J.I. Packer. Another one of the early things I did in seeking to learn more about God was to go to my library. Nothing was more direct to the topic than J.I. Packer's book, *Knowing God.* The sad thing is that I had already read the book, but I didn't remember much. This time, it was a huge blessing. Reading the quote below is when I started believing that knowing God is our purpose in life.

> What were we made for? To know God. What aim should we set ourselves in life? To know God. What is the "eternal life" that Jesus gives? Knowledge of God. "This is eternal life; that they may know you, the only true God, and Jesus Christ, whom you sent." (John 17:3)

What is the best thing in life, bringing more joy, delight, and contentment than anything else? Knowledge of God. "This is what the Lord says: 'Let not the wise man boast of his wisdom or the strong man boast of his strength or the rich man boast of his riches, but let him who boasts boast about this: that he understands and knows Me'" (Jeremiah 9:23–24). What, of all the states God ever sees man in, gives God most pleasure? Knowledge of Himself. "'I desired... the knowledge of God more than burnt offerings,' says God" (Hosea 6:6, KJV).

In these few sentences, we have said a very great deal. Our point is one to which every Christian heart will warm, though the person whose religion is merely formal will not be moved by it (and by this very fact, his unregenerate state may be known) What we have said provides at once a foundation, shape, and goal for our life plus a principle of priorities and a scale of values.

Once you become aware that the main business that you are here for is to know God, most of life's problems fall into place of their own accord.[8]

The quote below from Charles Spurgeon was in Packer's book, *Knowing God.* The neat thing about this quote is that Spurgeon wrote it when he was only nineteen years old. Many people believe Spurgeon was a great man of God because of all the great things he did for God. No, Spurgeon was a great man of God because he learned very early that the most important thing was God Himself, not what he did for God.

> The proper study of the Christian is the Godhead. The highest science, the loftiest speculation, the mightiest philosophy, which can engage the attention of a child of God, is the name, the nature, the person, the doings, and the existence of the great God, which he calls his Father. There is something exceedingly improving to the mind in a contemplation of the Divinity. It is a subject so vast, that all our thoughts are lost in its immensity; so deep, that our pride is drowned in its infinity. Other subjects we can comprehend and grapple with; in them we feel a kind of self-content, and go on our way with the thought, "Behold I am wise."

> But when we come to this master science, finding that our plumb line cannot sound its depth, and that our eagle eye cannot see its height, we turn away with the thought "I am but of yesterday and know nothing."[9]

Following are additional quotes about knowing God from others whom God used because the understood the importance of a personal relationship with our Savior.

> It appears, therefore that the Bible answer to the question, "What is the purpose of life?" It is to know, and to love, and to walk with God.[10]

> Knowing God does not come through a program, a study, or a method. Knowing God comes through relationship with a person. This is an intimate love relationship with God. Through this relationship, God reveals Himself, His purpose, and His ways; and He invites you to join Him where He is already at work.[11]

> For it is not mere words that nourish the soul, but God Himself, and unless and until the hearers find God on personal experience, they are not the better for having heard the truth. The Bible is not an end in itself, but a means to bring men to an intimate and satisfying knowledge of God, that they may enter into Him, that they may delight in His Presence, may taste and know the inner sweetness of the very God Himself in the core and center of their hearts.[12]

> He made us with the intention that He and we might walk together forever in a love relationship. But such a relationship can exist only when

the parties involved know something of each other. God, our Maker, knows all about us before we say anything, but we can know nothing about Him unless He tells us. Here, therefore, is a further reason why God speaks to us; not only to move us to do what He wants, but to enable us to know Him so that we may love Him.[13]

It is not according to the nature of the human soul, to love an object which is entirely unknown. The heart cannot be set upon an object of which there is no idea in the understanding. The reasons which induce the soul to love, must first be understood, before they can have a reasonable influence on the heart.[14]

No single book could contain the whole of God's character. It will take eternity to grasp it. Why then is it so mandatory for us to know God now? The reason is that man is made in God's image; therefore, no person can love God, serve God, be encouraged by God, or walk with God until he knows God. To the degree that we know Him will determine everything about us.[15]

The great purpose toward which all the dispensational dealings of God tend is revealed to us in 1 Corinthians 15:28; "That God may be all in all." In agreement with this is the teachings of our Lord in John 17:3: "And this is [the object of] eternal life: that they might know you, the only true God, and Jesus Christ, whom you have sent." This being so, should we not act wisely by keeping this object before us in our daily life and study of God's holy Word?[16]

There is no greater goal in life than to truly know God. Experiencing Him and knowing Him intimately is a treasure far greater than any human achievement. God takes great pleasure in those who seek to know Him.[17]

Christians ought not to content themselves with such degrees of knowledge of divinity as they already obtained. It should not satisfy them, as they know as much as is absolutely necessary to salvation but should seek to make progress. This endeavor to make progress in such knowledge ought not to be attended to as a thing by the bye, but all Christians should make a business of it. They should look upon it as a part of their daily business, and no small part of it neither. It should be attended to as a considerable part of the work of their high calling.[18]

The excellency of the knowledge of God offers hope for the future, an example for the present, a longing to learn more, and a peace that will help us through everyday life. Is it worth it? Paul says in *Philippians 3:8* that *"I count all things but loss for the excellency of the knowledge of Christ Jesus my Lord."* You may collect many things, but none of them are worth the knowledge of God. In fact, all the things that you could collect during your life cannot compare to *"the excellency of the knowledge of Christ Jesus."* The only way that you will take the time to get to know God is by giving the gaining of this knowledge its proper place in your life. Paul continues by saying *"for whom I have suffered the loss of all things, and do count them but dung, that I may win Christ."* Paul was willing to lose all things. In his mind, all things of

> this world were worth a pile of manure compared to Christ. Yes! It is worth it![19]
>
> If I just do right, then I will be right. The Bible makes clear that it is not what you "do" that counts with God; it is what you "be" that is important. It is character over conduct. As we get to know God, His character rubs off on us, and our conduct becomes purely an extension of what we know. We have been told for so long to "stand up for Jesus." However, we must first learn to "sit down with Jesus." Our standing is merely a temporary exercise if we have not learned to sit at His feet.[20]

You can trust a person only to the extent you know him or her. And you can trust God only to the extent you know Him. We need to be well-acquainted with the person of our salvation. A person may know the doctrine of salvation fully yet never really know Jesus well enough to trust Him. J.I. Packer stresses that there is a distinct difference between knowing about God and knowing God. And there is no shortcut to the process of knowing a person. That is true not only between human beings but also between us and God. Many of our struggles in the Christian life stem from the fact that we know about Christ but have not gotten to know Him intimately.

Interestingly when Paul was nearing the end of his life as a veteran missionary, church planter, teacher, theologian, writer of Scripture, and prisoner for Christ, he said his supreme desire was to know Christ (Philippians 3:10). When we ask someone, "When did you come to know Christ?" we are referring to the day when that individual responded to the Gospel. However, for Paul, knowing Christ was also an ongoing, lifelong process. Being born again happens in a split second of time but coming to know Christ is a lifetime of learning of Him, walking with Him, and being made like Him. "But we all, with unveiled face, beholding as in a mirror the glory of the Lord, are being transformed into the same image from glory to glory, just as by the Spirit of the Lord" (2 Corinthians 3:18). All of us should share that ambition—to know our Savior more intimately and personally.[21]

The Knowledge of God

Even more important, of course, is what the Bible has to say about the knowledge of God. Throughout the Scriptures, God confirmed that the reason He created us was to have an intimate relationship with Him. At first, we were children of the Father then during maturity, we are the friend of the Holy Spirit and finally, for all eternity, we shall be Jesus's bride, an example of the three most intimate human relationships.

> The fear of the Lord *is* the beginning of wisdom, And the knowledge of the Holy One *is* understanding. (Proverbs 9:10)

> But the people who know their God shall be strong, and carry out *great exploits.* (Daniel 11:32)

> For this reason we also, since the day we heard it, do not cease to pray for you, and to ask that you may be filled with the knowledge of His will in all wisdom and spiritual understanding; that you may walk worthy of the Lord, fully pleasing *Him,* being fruitful in every good work and increasing in the knowledge of God. (Colossians 1:9–10)

> And we know that the Son of God has come and has given us an understanding, that we may know Him who is true; and we are in Him who is true, in His Son Jesus Christ. This is the true God and eternal life. (1 John 5:20)

Grace and peace be multiplied to you in the knowledge of God and of Jesus our Lord, as His divine power has given to us all things that *pertain* to life and godliness, through the knowledge of Him who called us by glory and virtue, by which have been given to us exceedingly great and precious promises, that through these you may be partakers of the divine nature, having escaped the corruption *that is* in the world through lust. (2 Peter 1:2–4)

And Pharaoh said, "Who *is* the Lord, that I should obey His voice to let Israel go? I do not know the Lord, nor will I let Israel go." (Exodus 5:2)

[Moses's prayer] Now therefore, I pray, if I have found grace in Your sight, show me now Your way, that I may know You and that I may find grace in Your sight. And consider that this nation *is* Your people. (Exodus 33:13)

For I desire mercy and not sacrifice, And the knowledge of God more than burnt offerings. (Hosea 6:6)

And those who know Your name will put their trust in You; For You, Lord, have not forsaken those who seek You. (Psalms 9:10)

As for you, my son Solomon, know the God of your father, and serve Him with a loyal heart and with a willing mind; for the Lord searches all hearts and understands all the intent of the thoughts. If you seek Him, He will be found by you; but if you forsake Him, He will cast you off forever. (1 Chronicles 28:9)

For I bear them witness that they have a zeal for God, but not according to knowledge. For they being ignorant of God's righteousness, and seeking to establish their own righteousness, have not submitted to the righteousness of God. Romans 10:2–3)

Oh, the depth of the riches both of the wisdom and knowledge of God! How unsearchable *are* His judgments and His ways past finding out! *"For who has known the mind of the LORD? Or who has become His counselor?"* (Romans 11:33–34)

Oh, continue Your lovingkindness to those who know You, And Your righteousness to the upright in heart. (Psalms 36:10)

"To the Chief Musician. A Contemplation of the sons of Korah. As the deer pants for the water brooks, so pants my soul for You, O God. (Psalms 42:1)

And this is eternal life, that they may know You, the only true God, and Jesus Christ whom You have sent. (John 17:3)

---

1. Richard Blackaby, M.Div., general editor, The Blackaby Study Bible: Personal Encounters with God Through His Word (Nashville: Nelson Bibles, 2006), 1074.
2. J.I. Packer, Knowing God (Downers Grove, Illinois: Intervarsity Press, 1973), 83.
3. Ibid., 88.
4. Evans, 22ff.

5. Miller, 118.
6. Joanna Weaver, Having a Mary Heart in a Martha World: Finding Intimacy with God in the Busyness of Life (Colorado Springs: Waterbrook Press, 2000), 60.
7. Westminster Catechism, https://reformed.org/documents/wsc/indExodu-shtml?_top=https://reformed.org/documents/WSC.html
8. Packer, 33ff.
9. Charles Spurgeon, as quoted by Packer, 17ff.
10. Roy and Revel Hession, We Would See Jesus (Fort Washington, PA: Christian Literature Crusade, 2000), 14.
11. Blackaby and King, 2.
12. A.W. Tozer, The Pursuit of God (Camp Hill, PA: Christian Publications, Inc., 1993) 9.
13. Packer, 110.
14. Jonathan Edwards, Jonathan Edwards on Knowing Christ (Carlisle, Pennsylvania: The Banner of Truth, 1997), 14.
15. Dan DeHaan, The God You Can Know (Chicago: Moody Press, 1982), 46.
16. J. Hudson Taylor, Union & Communion: A Devotional Study of How the Song of Solomon Reveals a Believer's Union with Jesus Christ (Minneapolis: Bethany House Publishers, 2000), 9.
17. Blackaby, 894.
18. Edwards, 16.
19. Sam Brock, My Biography of God: Discovering the Excellency of the Knowledge of God (Newberry Springs, CA: Iron Sharpeneth Iron Publications, 2008), 16.
20. Dan DeHaan, 17.
21. Earl D. Radmacher, Salvation (Nashville, Word Publishing, 2000), 15ff.

CHAPTER 5

God's Biography

His divine power has given to us all things that
pertain to life and godliness, through the knowledge
of Him who called us by glory and virtue.
—2 Peter 1:3

How well do you know God? In human relationships, we have different levels of knowledge. Do you know Dwight D. Eisenhower? Dwight was the supreme commander of the Allied Expeditionary Forces in Europe during World War II. He retired a five-star general and was our thirty-fourth president. Some of you have probably never heard of him while others may have heard of him but know just a little bit. After all, he is a few presidents back. A few of you may still remember his presidency; he was the first president to be affected by the two-term rule.

Even though I was only six years old when he died, I know quite a bit about Eisenhower. I have studied about him for most of my life. I have read nearly every book that was written about him. That is because he was my grandfather's hero. My grandfather was a mechanic in the engineer corps during World War II. He was in the second wave at Omaha Beach. It was while my grandfather oversaw the motor pool at Omaha Beach that he met Dwight Eisenhower. The mechanics worked through the night to keep the trucks moving inland during the day. General Eisenhower would come out and talk to the guys in the motor pool because he had a hard time sleeping. He would talk to my grandfather and the guys as they worked. My grandfather received a Bronze Star for his well-organized motor pool; General Eisenhower was the one who pinned it on Grandpa.

The general called my grandfather chief, but Eisenhower probably called hundreds of soldiers chief, not being able to remember everyone's name. So I doubt that after the war President Eisenhower would have remembered my grandfather. Besides this Kansas farm boy had befriended far more important people than my grandfather. During the war, General Eisenhower would work with the king of England, Winston Churchill, and President Truman.

Ironically on June 4, 1944, D-day, the day that brought all these men together, a few thousand miles away was a young man who knew Dwight Eisenhower better than all of them. That young man was John Eisenhower, and he was graduating from West Point. Unfortunately his dad couldn't be there; he was invading the French coastline. However, there was someone with John that day that new Ike better than anyone else—even better than his own mother. That person was Mamie Eisenhower, his wife. She lived with him for more than fifty years. Even though nearly the whole world knew Dwight D. Eisenhower, Mamie knew Ike better than anyone.

The Narrow Way

I told all this to illustrate how human relationships have differing levels of knowledge. In this illustration, I came up with seven levels: (1) never heard of, (2) heard of, (3) studied about, (4) met, (5) friend, (6) son, (7) bride. These levels picture the depths of relationship people can have with God. The never-heard-of and perhaps the heard-of would be unsaved. Starting with the studied-about would be the saved (although there could be those who have studied about God who are still not believers). Unfortunately most Christians have studied about God, but few have met Him. Many Christians, while saved, are not experiencing the abundant life that is available to all believers. To become a *friend* of God, to know the guidance only a *child* can, and to have the intimacy of a *bride*, we must know Him deeper. At what level of knowledge do you know God?

> Enter by the narrow gate; for wide *is* the gate and broad *is* the way that leads to destruction, and there are many who go in by it. Because narrow *is* the gate and difficult *is* the way which leads to life, and there are few who find it. (Matthew7:13–14)

I believe many have misinterpreted this passage. Usually it is taught as a comparison between the saved and the unsaved which has some truth to it as compared to all the world, there will be few who find Jesus Christ as their Savior. However, I believe Jesus is talking to the saved in this passage and saying few will find the abundant life in Him. In the parallel passage Luke 13:24, it says, "Strive to enter the narrow gate…" The Greek word is *agonizomai* (yes, it sounds like agonize). It was the word used of an athlete putting forth strenuous effort to compete in the games. So we know salvation is not by our hard work but by faith alone. However, running a good race is how Paul describes the Christian life, what we call sanctification. But justification is a one-time event, not a *difficult way* or path. Walking with the Lord down the way of life is a picture of sanctification.

Jesus is talking to His disciples in Matthew 5. He is explaining how their righteousness must exceed that of the Pharisees. In Matthew 5–7, Jesus is teaching His disciples how to live; he is not telling the lost how to be saved. In fact at this time, Jesus has not yet sent the Gospel to the Gentiles. In Matthew 10 and 15, Jesus says this:

> These twelve Jesus sent out and commanded them, saying: "Do not go into the way of the Gentiles, and do not enter a city of the Samaritans. But go rather to the lost sheep of the house of Israel. And as you go, preach, saying,

> 'The kingdom of heaven is at hand.' (Matthew 10:5–7)

> But He answered and said, "I was not sent except to the lost sheep of the house of Israel." Then she came and worshiped Him, saying, "Lord, help me!" But He answered and said, "It is not good to take the children's bread and throw *it* to the little dogs." And she said, "Yes, Lord, yet even the little dogs eat the crumbs which fall from their masters' table." Then Jesus answered and said to her, "O woman, great *is* your faith! Let it be to you as you desire." And her daughter was healed from that very hour. (Matthew 15:24–28)

I believe what Jesus is saying in Matthew 7 is that the way of the disciples is narrow and difficult, and few Christians find it. There will be Christians, while saved and going to heaven, who are content with the little knowledge of God that they have. Paul calls them carnal Christians (1 Corinthians 3:1; see also Hebrews 5:12–14). They are babes still needing milk and not able to eat meat. Some are afraid of the difficult path. However, it is not difficult to get to know God; the difficult part is dying to self. The agonizing part is humbling ourselves and giving up our desires so that we can seek after God. Just like I talked about in the previous chapter about time with God, we struggle just giving up 10 percent of our precious time to spend time alone with the Lord.

Who Is God?

Who is God and what is He like? Knowing this is critical: if you misdefine God, you've misdefined everything else because everything emanates from God. You can literally make sense of nothing if you have not first made sense of God.[1]

In chapter 3, I advised staying away from the devotion programs that were written for every believer. Now I am going to go against my advice and provide a devotion program written for everyone (smile.) However, I also said that we should try a lot of the different ways to do our devotions and to keep the parts we enjoy. So in this chapter, I want to recommend a project to know God better. It is a program that I came up with (mostly) by myself. I enjoy it greatly; but while it may not be as enjoyable for some, please give it a try. There is room in this program for a lot of variety. Hopefully it will be joyful for all. But the main reason I spend the time to present it is that unlike most other devotion programs, it gets right to the heart of God's change formula, knowledge of Him rather than a list of things to do.

This study is a concentration on what the Bible says about the character of God. Some call them the attributes of God, but I prefer to call them His perfections. Because we humans have been created in the image of God, we possess quite a few of His attributes: love, joy, peace, mercy, etc. However, God is the perfect expression of those qualities. The qualities are not part of God like they are part of us humans, these qualities *are* God. As John said, "Beloved, let us love one another, for love is of God; and everyone who loves is born of God and knows God. He who does not love does not know God, *for God is love*" (1 John 4:7–8, emphasis added).

I am going to show how to create a biography of God. When it is finished, it will provide all the Bible verses that talk about the different perfections of God. Remember when I wrote about the Holy Spirit impressing on my mind to teach about His goodness and mercy from Psalm 118 so that people would be thankful? After the Spirit impressed upon me to teach God is good and merciful, I started working on how to explain God is merciful. So I thought to myself, *What do I know already that the Bible says about God's mercy*? I thought I was doing pretty good when I came up with about 10 different verses. But to be safe, I decided I should at least check and see if there were a few more. After finding 292 verses on God's mercy, I was embarrassed to think that I somehow had believed I already knew about the mercy of God.

As I studied the other perfections of God, I began to realize that the Bible was mostly about Him. Another duh moment! I had been guilty of teaching that God's Word was like an owner's manual for life. I used to teach that like a car owner's manual—whenever something was broken, I went to the manual to find out how to fix it. Therefore, I had always presented God's Word as this giant fix-it manual and that when we had personal problems, we just had to find the right verses. I have a bunch of study helps that listed all the problems of life and where to go in the Bible.

I even had little pathways marked out in my Bible. If anyone came to me struggling with anger, then I would take them to the first verse. And next to the first verse, I would have written another verse to go to and so on. But as we have already discussed, this led to change by their hard work. So as I discovered more and more about the perfections of God, I realized the Bible isn't an owner's manual. Although the Bible does contain practical advice on living righteously, that is not its main purpose. I found that the Bible was more like a love letter from God, a letter to me explaining who He is so that I can know Him better. Like when I was learning about Barb while we were dating, the more I learned, the more I loved.

Have you ever gotten one of those notes that says, "I like you, do you like me? Check yes or no!" I got one in the fifth grade. It was from this little blond-haired girl. Charlie Brown had his little red-head girl, mine was blonde. Well, before that day, I hadn't paid much attention to her. Yes, she was cute, but I hadn't cared too much until she wrote me that note. Instantly I was interested, so much so that we sat next to each other on the bus for about a year. Anyway, I read that note probably a hundred times. It does something to the heart when you find out someone likes you. One of our deepest needs is a longing to be loved.

A pastor friend told me the story of his oldest son and his fiancée. My pastor friend asked his son, "Why do you like her?"

To which he replied, "Because she liked me first."

We were created with a desire to be loved and while humans do a so-so job at that, our God has perfect love for us.

I love my old Ford pickup; it is almost as old as I am. And I have a few owner's manuals on my bookshelf. No matter how much I love that truck, I don't take down one of those manuals and read it just for fun. But if we were to receive a letter from someone who loved us, we would probably read it over and over again. God has given us His love letter as the means to express His love for us that we might fall in love with Him, for we can't love what we don't know.

We have all probably heard a pastor say something like, "In this chapter, the writer uses the word *blank* twenty-three times, therefore, it is an important word for us to focus on." In the ancient Hebrew and Greek, repetition was a way to show significance: Holy, holy, holy is the Lord God Almighty or rejoice in the Lord, again I say rejoice. Well, the word used the most in the Bible is *God*, with all the Trinity's names, titles, and pronouns. Therefore, the most important thing we can learn from the Scriptures is not how we should behave, but who God is.

Before moving into the details of the biography-of-God notebook, there is something we must always do first. When seeking to understand God, we first want to pray and ask Him to reveal Himself. As James said, "You have not because you ask not" (4:2). We need to tell God we want to know Him better and ask Him to show us how. Now there's a prayer God is anxious to answer—He has been waiting a long time for us to pray it. We know that God answers all prayers, and sometimes that answer is no. Like when I asked for that brand-new Ford Raptor. But asking for a deeper relationship with Him is like my son asking if it is okay for him to clean his room. Definitely yes! But seriously, *we don't have because we don't ask.* The most important way to start our relationship with God is to ask Him. If His purpose for our lives is for us to have a loving relationship with Him, then it makes sense that His top priority is to provide that relationship.

> Anything significant that happens in your life will be a result of God's activity in your life. He is infinitely more interested in your life than you or I could possibly be. Let the Spirit

> of God bring you into an intimate relationship with the God of the Universe "who is able to do exceedingly abundantly above all that we ask or think, according to the power that works in us." (Ephesians 3:20)[2]

My Biography of God

In Old-Testament times, God required the king of Israel to make his own copy of the law which was the first five books of our modern Bibles. Of course, back then, no one had a copy of the Scriptures. The only copy was in the temple. So it was a very special thing for the king to have his own copy.

> Also it shall be, when he sits on the throne of his kingdom, that he shall write for himself a copy of this law in a book, from *the one* before the priests, the Levites. And it shall be with him, and he shall read it all the days of his life, that he may learn to fear the Lord his God and be careful to observe all the words of this law and these statutes, that his heart may not be lifted above his brethren, that he may not turn aside from the commandment *to* the right hand or *to* the left, and that he may prolong *his* days in his kingdom, he and his children in the midst of Israel. (Deuteronomy 17:18–20)

Notice that the king was to read it all his days. Wouldn't "all his days" imply every day? I like the part about how reading the Scriptures is so the king's heart would not be lifted above his brethren, a good point for us to remember as we learn more about our God. He warns us that knowledge can puff up. In fact, this can be a good measure of whether you are only growing in knowledge or growing in knowing God. Getting closer to God does not lead to pride, it leads to humility as we realize how great He is and how small we are. Beware of a Christian leader that has a lot of pride—that is a person who is not likely walking close to God no matter how much they know about God.

These days, we don't need to make our own copy of the Bible. We are spoiled these days; we have Bibles everywhere. I probably have twenty to thirty of them in my home. And on my smartphone, I can read nearly every version available. However, and this is a little off the subject for a moment, no extra charge, making a copy of the Bible or maybe a few books can be a profitable way to enjoy God's Word. I have done a little of this; I copied four or five different books of the Bible. I just got a notebook and copied them word for word. It sure gives you an appreciation for the old scribes making copies of books before the printing press was invented. But seriously, an advantage to doing this is that you slow down and see each word. It can be a real blessing, another devotion possibility to try.

Back to our biography of God. Simply explained, it is a collection of all the verses in the Bible for the different perfections of God like mercy, love, wrath, omniscience, etc. It will help answer questions like what does the Bible say about the mercy of God? Does God's mercy extend to both the believer and unbeliever? Are there any conditions for receiving God's mercy? While we don't need our own copy of the Bible, nowhere do we have a book of all the perfections of God. Sure there are some topical Bibles and books on the attributes of God. But they usually only list a handful of the key verses on each perfection. Nowhere, as far as I know, is there a book that has all the verses on each of the perfections. And even if someday one gets published, there still is a special blessing when we do it ourselves. Bible-reference books can be very helpful; I use them all the time. But there is a blessing to discovering God's truth through our hard work that cannot be duplicated. Remember this project isn't about just having a cool reference book. It is about us growing closer to God.

I am now going to describe the step-by-step process I used to create my biography of God. However, as I said before, there is plenty of room for variety. I recommend trying these steps first and then later adapting them to personal interests. Make the adaptations so it is something enjoyable, not just something to do.

Get a Notebook

First get some type of notebook, a spiral notebook, a three-ring binder, or a journal, anything with blank paper in it. Don't get anything too fancy yet. Do this project for maybe a month or so and see where it leads. After getting a feel for how to organize the notebook then spend a little more and purchase something that fits your style better.

Doing the notebook on a computer is another option. That is what I did after trying it out for a while. I found that there were a lot of verses that had two or three perfections of God and rather than write them out three times, I could cut and paste them. Also I ended up wanting the verses in biblical order. Using a computer makes this quite simple. But some may be a little more of a free spirit than me. They may want to collect them as they find them. And there is a benefit in writing the same verse two or three times—it helps to remember them better. Another benefit of having a paper notebook over doing it on the computer is that it can be worked on anywhere like sitting under a tree.

Read Your Bible

Read through the Bible as usual, but the focus is going to change. Instead of looking for what we are supposed to do (the list of rules), look for the character of God (however, if the Holy Spirit pricks your spirit about something you should do, don't ignore it). As we read each verse, we ask, "What does this verse tell me about God?" Of course, not every verse will have something. If there is nothing, move on to the next verse. No matter what book of the Bible we are reading, there will be something about God, but I recommend starting with Psalms. The Psalms are packed full of the perfections of God. For example, what does this verse say about God?

"Oh, give thanks to the LORD, for *He is* good! For His mercy *endures* forever" (Psalms 118:1).

Create Topic Pages

He is good, and His mercy endures forever. Now we want to create a page for each of these perfections. At the top of a sheet, put a title for each. The title could be numerous things: "God is Good" or "The Goodness of God." Be creative. I titled my topics by including the word *My*, *My God is Good*, and *My God is Merciful*. I include my to remind me that I have a personal relationship with God. At first, topics will be added quite often. Later we will talk about different categories and topics.

We also may want to combine keywords into one topic page like my God is longsuffering, slow to anger, and patient. There can be some verses that are talking about a perfection, but it doesn't use the keyword you are using. We will want to include these verses too. Now don't get hung up on which verses go where; the notebook won't be turned in for a grade. The notebook is for our edification and likely, no one else will ever see it. So don't get caught up worrying about doing it right or wrong, there isn't a wrong way to do it. If a verse is unclear, leave it out. Don't lose the joy of God by worrying if the notebook is being done correctly.

Copy the Verses

Then under each topic heading, copy the verse; in this case, Psalm 118:1. Of course, we could only write the address, but I highly recommend that the whole verse be written out. Sometimes I may even include a verse or two around it for context. Then copy that verse on any other topic sheet that applies. Writing out the verse helps us slow down and think about it. This project is not just something to hurry up and get done. In fact, with some of the other items we will talk about later, it could be a lifetime project.

Collecting Verses

There are multiple ways to continue to collect verses. We can collect them during our daily reading, in a Bible study or a church service. We can pick them up as we go throughout our week. If we are in a class or service and don't have our notebooks, we can underline the topics and copy them into our notebooks later. To make sure I don't duplicate verses, I put a small line under the verse numbers I have already added to my notebook. Then I don't have to go back and search through all the verses to see if I have already used it. Some of the topics will have hundreds of verses, so it is good to know which ones have already been added.

Another way to collect our verses is one topic at a time. I have done this at times when I wanted to preach or teach on that topic. For example, collecting all the verses on "My God Loves Me" (there are over a hundred). However, doing it this way requires a little extra help because we don't want to read through the entire Bible only looking for the verses on God's love. To do these topical studies, we need an exhaustive concordance or a word search. Most Bibles have a concordance in the back that lists keywords. But these concordances only list a few of the verses. An exhaustive concordance is a book that lists every word in the Bible and every verse it occurs in. They can be purchased online.

However, even easier with Bible software, we can do the same thing with a word search. After entering the word, the software will find for you every time the word occurs. These software programs range from just a few dollars to hundreds of dollars depending on what you want them to do. But the good news is that for simple word searches, there is free Bible software online. Just search "Bible word search" and try a few. However, after we have entered the keyword, we will have to weed through them and pull out the ones that apply to our topic. If we type in *love*, we will not only find verses about God's love but also things like loving our neighbor. Finally, as I mentioned having multiple descriptors sometimes for topics, we want to search synonyms for your keyword like loving kindness or charity.

Apply

Hopefully, this will be a challenging but enjoyable exercise but remember its ultimate purpose is not to keep busy. Its purpose is to help us grow in our knowledge and relationship with God. Therefore, occasionally we need to go back and read what we have collected. We should meditate on what the Scriptures are telling us about God, asking, "What does this knowledge of God challenge me to believe about Him?" and "How will that belief manifest itself in my everyday life?"

It can be a real blessing to the soul to read, for example, all the verses on God's love in one setting. Back in the late 1800s, early 1900s, when Christian-tent meetings were popular, one of the things they would do would be to have what was called a reading instead of a sermon. Someone would get up and read a series of verses on a single topic. And they would read it without commentary, just the words of God speaking to His children. For a lot of the people, it was their favorite service. Nowadays expository preaching has become popular, that is where the pastor preaches a whole chapter or section of Scripture, teaching the different issues as they come up. There is nothing wrong with that, but topical teaching is very helpful too.

Additional Information

As I promised, this is where you can make this project a lifetime blessing. First it may take quite a while to get through the Bible collecting all of God's perfections. My biography of God is probably only halfway done, and I have around 700 typed pages. However, I have added a few topics that are not quite the perfections of God. I have a section on "My God Commands Me to…" These are things like above in Psalm 118:1 where God commands me to give thanks. What He desires of me also tells me a lot about Him.

While primarily we want to fill our notebook with what the Bible says about God, we can use our topic headings as a place to store secondary information too. It could include things like a good-sermon outline, a poem, a song or even our private musings on the topic. It could also include a prayer request such as "Lord, help me to realize Your love for me." As I read books on the different perfections of God, I added quotes and interesting thoughts to my notebook. My notebook makes a good central place to store all the information on specific topics. This is especially beneficial if I might want to teach or preach on these topics someday.

For those who are studious and love to write, they can write a summary of each perfection like topical reports for school. As we finished school, most of us were no longer interested in writing papers. But part of the reason teachers assign papers is that writing fine-tunes our thoughts and beliefs on the subject. I took a graduate class on thesis writing that was so helpful; I wish I had taken it my freshman year. Our professor gave us a simple outline of how to develop a topical paper from a Biblical perspective. I share it here with you with a few modifications.

A. Start with a name, title, or perfection:
   Choose an interesting perfection to study.
   Choose a common topic. For now, avoid topics that only occur a few times.
B. Collect all the verses dealing with that topic:
   The biography of God may already have this done.
   Use study guides such a Bible software, concordances, and topical Bibles. Also collect applicable synonyms and other keywords.
C. Identify key verses:
   First verse, last verse, most familiar passage, best description of the topic, repeating phrases.
D. Define keywords:
   Use a common dictionary to understand the meaning.
   An older dictionary like Webster's 1828 can add additional insight.
   Define all keys words, not just the topic.
E. Divide into common themes:
   Categorize verses into common themes and ideas.
F. Collect other key thoughts and quotes:

What have others said about the topic?
Include notes from books and articles.
Include notes from sermons and lessons.
When quoting others include their source and page number (if applicable), you may want to return to it later.

G. Organize into a simple outline
H. How would someone teach or preach this topic?
I. Write paper or journal thoughts
J. Answer the question: what does this tell me about God?
K. How does it challenge me to change?
L. What must I choose to believe?

Advantages of Preparing a Biography of God

There are numerous spiritual blessings in doing this biography of God. Below I have summarized a few. There is no special grace for doing the biography. However, the benefits below should be considered for any devotion program chosen. One way or another, we need to increase in our knowledge of God, and it is important to be able to retain that knowledge.

Topic: With this study, we are collecting the very knowledge of God that begins the change process. This is not to say that we cannot study other topics from the Bible such as the people and their stories. Although in the other studies, we too can see the character of God; for now, we are concentrating on who God is.

Retention: Copying the information into a notebook or journal not only helps us remember those facts but allows us to return to that information later. This is very important especially as we get older (smile). I know we all think that when we are in the middle of something, *Oh, I'll remember that.* Then of course, two days later, we are wondering what it was that we had learned. Therefore, the more important the information, the more important it is to be able to recall it, especially in this day and age, when we are inundated with so much information.

Ministry: Having collected all this specific information about God provides an invaluable resource for preparing sermons, lessons, and Bible studies. If I ever become a senior pastor that needs to preach each week, I have, from my biography of God, over two hundred topics I could preach on. And with a lot of them being so extensive, that's enough sermons for about five years. Then I could start over again because like I just mentioned in Retention, most everyone will have forgotten the first lessons by then.

Enrichment: Like I mentioned before, being able to read all in one place every verse in the Bible that talks about God's love is extremely encouraging. If I have two hundred topics, that means I have two hundred days of individual readings on the character of God. The second book I am working on connects specific perfections of God with specific problems in life. If you are struggling with anger then read on the sovereignty of God, the love of God, and the will of God.

Before moving on to specific perfections and titles of God, I need to give due credit to a couple of people. While God Himself impressed upon me to begin collecting all that He said about Himself, I was also greatly influenced by two books: Sam Brock's *My Biography of God: Discovering the Excellency of the Knowledge of Go*[3] and Mardi Collier's *What Do I Know About My God.*[4] From Sam's book, I got the idea of a biography of God and collecting His attributes. From Mardi's book, I got the idea of labeling the topics with "My God." And one of the things I appreciate about Mardi's book is that in the second half of the book, she shares how specific qualities of God from her notebook affected specific problems in her life. For example, she shares how knowing God hates pride helped her overcome some self-pity in her family life. There is purchase information along with a broader description of these books and other good resources in chapter 10.

As we finish up this chapter, I wish to speak briefly on the perfections and titles of God to give you a better idea of what to look for in your Bible. Also in chapter 10, I have listed some of these perfections and titles, along with a few verses, to give a jump start on the notebook.

The Names of God

We start where God starts—with His name. How do most human relationships start? "Hi, my name is…" Now our names don't communicate as much as names did in ancient times. Back then, names were chosen for their meaning but not so much today. *Todd* supposedly means fox in old English. About the only significance that has is in my favorite movie, Disney's *The Fox and the Hound,* the fox's name is Todd.

On the other hand, my mother once ordered these name plaques from a Christian bookstore which said my name meant seeker of wisdom. I like that one, but I am not sure where or how they determined it. Although our names may not mean anything today, there are a few names we don't use anymore because of their unwanted meaning like Adolf, Judas, Benedict, Jezebel, etc. For us, our titles communicate more than our names like pastor, husband, father, Ford-truck owner, etc. But God's name and titles are packed full of meaning, and it is through them that God communicates to us.

God revealed His interests throughout the Old and New Testament. He revealed Himself not only through His glory and His attributes but also through the names of God. Those names describe the way God deals with us as well as tell of the things that excite Him. "God is the incomprehensible One, infinitely exalted above all that is temporal; but in His names, He descends to all that is finite and becomes like unto man." The names of God are not names men have chosen about Him. They are names given to us by God about Himself. They give His personal revelation of His divine Being.[5]

But if we would know what God says about Himself, it is necessary to study the revelation found in the great names and titles He has given us of Himself. God alone can reveal His character and will to man. The Unknown and the Unknowable, as far as fleshly wisdom is concerned, can only make Himself fully known.[6]

Herbert Lockyer's book *All the Devine Names and Titles in the Bible*[7] is a must for understanding the names and titles of God; it too is listed in chapter 10. As the book's title says, it lists all the names and titles of the Trinity along with a few devotional thoughts; it is a real blessing. Most of the following information is from Lockyer's research.

God the Father

Elohim: Is the first name of God, "In the beginning God (Elohim)" (Genesis 1:1). It describes God in the unity of His divine personality and power, a preview of the Trinity. Elohim is used over 3,000 times in the Bible.

El: means the Strong One. The most primitive Semitic name for God, it is also used for false gods, translated with a lower-case g in our English Bibles. Therefore, God the Father is frequently combined with nouns or adjectives to express the divine name concerning attributes of His being.

Elah: The Adorable One
El Elyon: God Most High
El Roi: The Lord that Sees
El Olam: God of Eternity
El Shaddai: The Almighty, All-Sufficient God

While God's names are translated in a masculine sense, we know that God is neither male nor female—He is Spirit. Both males and females are created in His image. There are a few instances where God is seen in the female sense.

Shaddai comes from the root *Shad* which means a breast and is so rendered in its first occurrence, "By the God of our father who will help you, And by the Almighty [El Shaddai] who will bless you with blessings of heaven above, blessings of the deep that lies beneath, blessings of the breasts and of the womb" (Genesis 49:25). Shad supplies us with a delicate yet precious metaphor, seeing it presents God as the One who nourishes, supplies, and satisfies. The word *Shaddai* goes further and suggest perfect supply and perfect comfort.[8]

"As one whom his mother comforts, so I will comfort you; and you shall be comforted in Jerusalem" (Isaiah 66:13).

"O Jerusalem, Jerusalem, the one who kills the prophets and stones those who are sent to her! How often I wanted to gather your children together, as a hen gathers her chicks under *her* wings, but you were not willing!" (Matthew 23:37).

Jehovah: Is the Eternal, Ever-Loving One. The Holy Name of God, it was also known as the name of four letters because from the Hebrew, it is spelled YHVH. In the original Hebrew, the vowels were not provided, so no one knows for sure how YHVH is pronounced. The most probable pronunciation is Yahweh.

Jehovah-Elohim: The Majestic, Omnipotent God
Jehovah-Hoseenu: The Lord, our Maker
Jehovah-Jireh: The Lord will provide
Jehovah-Rophi: The Lord, the Physician

Abba, Father: Is the distinguishing title of the New Testament. In the Old Testament, Israel had mostly known God as Jehovah but in the New Testament, the relationship changes to Abba, Father. Jesus came to earth to remind the Jewish people that there was an intimate relationship available with their God. While early believers like Enoch walked personally with the Lord, over the generations, the Jews had gotten away from this personal contact with God. When Jesus prayed, "Our Father which art in Heaven…" it would have been a big surprise for the disciples to hear God referred to as "Our Father."

God the Son

Most of the variety of names and titles are for God the Son. This would make sense as Jesus is central to the Gospel and when you have seen Him, you have seen God the Father. And as I have mentioned before, the titles of Jesus take on their normal meaning. *Word* for example is the basic element for communication. Jesus is the primary person for communicating who God is.

> "If you had known Me, you would have known My Father also; and from now on you know Him and have seen Him." Philip said to Him, "Lord, show us the Father, and it is sufficient for us." Jesus said to him, "Have I been with

> you so long, and yet you have not known Me, Philip? He who has seen Me has seen the Father; so how can you say, 'Show us the Father'? Do you not believe that I am in the Father, and the Father in Me? The words that I speak to you I do not speak on My own *authority;* but the Father who dwells in Me does the works. (John 14:7–10)

Some of the names and titles for the Son to collect are: The only Begotten Son, My Beloved Son, My Lord and My God, My Savior, God with Us, Jehovah, I Am, Creator, Word, Beginning, Alpha and Omega, Life, Messenger, Prophet, Servant, Carpenter, Worm, Accursed, Lamb of God, the Way, Good Shepherd, Branch, Bread, Hope.

God the Spirit

Often the most neglected of the Trinity is the Holy Spirit. The third person of the Trinity proceeding from the Father and the Son, of the same substance and equal in power and glory and is, together with the Father and the Son to be believed in, obeyed and worshiped throughout the ages.

Some of the misunderstandings on exalting the Holy Spirit comes from the translation of John 16:13 in the King James Version, "Howbeit when He, the Spirit of truth, is come, He will guide you into all truth: for He shall not speak of Himself…" Some have taken this to mean the Holy Spirit is taking on the trait of self-effacement and therefore, only exalts Jesus. This has led to thinking that the Holy Spirit shouldn't be exalted or worshipped. However, this is not what the Scripture is saying.

The translators of the NKJV translated it this way. "However, when He, the Spirit of truth, has come, He will guide you into all truth; for He will not speak on His own authority…" Meaning the Holy Spirit will not speak with a new authority. The Holy Spirit is not a new God; Jesus is affirming that God the Father, God the Son, and God the Spirit are all One.

Some of the names and titles for the Holy Spirit to collect are: The Spirit, the Spirit of God, the Spirit of Wisdom, the Spirit of Understanding, the Spirit of Knowledge and the Fear of the Lord, the Voice of the Almighty, the Gift of God, the Power of the Highest, His Witness, Comforter, Eternal Spirit, Wind, Water, Oil, Fire, Seed, Seal.

God considered His name so important that in the Ten Commandments right after commanding us not to have any other gods, He commanded that His name not be used in vain. I believe we have misinterpreted what God was saying when He commanded us not to use His name in vain. We most often think of using it with a curse word or saying, "Oh my god!" I think God had in mind something more than that. In *Webster's 1828 Dictionary*, it defines vain as "worthless; having no substance, value or importance."[9]

And I believe the Israelites missed it too when they refused to say the name of God. I believe God wanted the opposite. God wanted them and wants us to think of His name as so important that we use it to cry out to Him. God has such a desire to have a relationship with us, He wants us to use His name and use it often. As Jesus said, we can cry out *Abba, Father* to our God. Therefore, using the Lord's name in vain is to count it worthless or having no substance. I think we come close to using the Lord's name in vain when we fail to understand what His name is, how important it is, and fail to use it. Wouldn't it be silly if I never say the name of my wife?

Calling on the name or character of the Lord does not come naturally to people. It originates from a desire for God's holiness and love. It follows the recognition and acknowledgment of our own inability and God's all-sufficiency.[10]

> Following are some examples from Scripture on the importance of God's name. Give to the Lord the glory *due* His name; Bring an offering, and come before Him. Oh, worship the Lord in the beauty of holiness! (1 Chronicles 16:29)

But let all those rejoice who put their trust in You; Let them ever shout for joy, because You defend them; Let those also who love Your name Be joyful in You. (Psalms 5:11).

O Lord, our Lord, how excellent *is* Your name in all the earth, who have set Your glory above the heavens! (Psalms 8:1)

Some *trust* in chariots, and some in horses; But we will remember the name of the Lord our God. (Psalms 20:7)

Sing to God, sing praises to His name; Extol Him who rides on the clouds, By His name Yah, and rejoice before Him. (Psalms 68:4)

His name shall endure forever; His name shall continue as long as the sun. And *men* shall be blessed in Him; All nations shall call Him blessed. (Psalms 72:17)

He shall cover you with His feathers, and under His wings you shall take refuge; His truth *shall be your* shield and buckler. (Psalms 91:4)

Our help *is* in the name of the Lord, who made heaven and earth. (Psalms 124:8)

For unto us a Child is born, unto us a Son is given; And the government will be upon His shoulder. And His name will be called Wonderful, Counselor, Mighty God, Everlasting Father, Prince of Peace. (Isaiah 9:6)

> In this manner, therefore, pray: Our Father in heaven, Hallowed be Your name. (Matthew 6:9)

The Perfections of God

The attributes, or perfections as I prefer, are those character qualities that we share with God because we were created in His image. His perfections are qualities like love, joy, kindness, mercy, etc. However, it is important to remember that unlike our human examples of love, God is the perfect picture of love.

> Don't confuse God's love with the love of people. The love of people often increases with performance and decreases with mistakes. Not so with God's love. God's love never ceases. Never. Though we spurn Him. Ignore Him. Reject Him. Despise Him. Disobey Him. He will not change. Our evil cannot diminish His love. Our goodness cannot increase it. Our faith does not earn it any more than our stupidity jeopardizes it. God doesn't love us less if we fail or more if we succeed. God's love never ceases.[11]

> God's attributes are not merely a list of facts and features. They are truths that inform belief and inspire faith. God reveals truth about Himself in His Word, not for the sake of knowledge, but for the sake of relationship with us. He tells us about Himself so we will put our faith in Him, so we will treasure and worship Him and not waste ourselves on man-made idols. He wants our souls to soar in worship and communion with Him—not rot in our pursuit of sin or waste away in worry and fear.[12]

"The fear of the Lord *is* the beginning of wisdom, And the knowledge of the Holy One *is* understanding" (Proverbs 9:10).

Perfection Categories

Who My God Is

This category overlaps with the names of God. My God is my Father, Friend, Shepherd but includes other aspects of who He is—my God is able, almighty, awesome, eternal, good.

What My God Does

This category not only includes the works of God from a historical perspective, but it covers what our God does perfectly for us each day: He answers prayer, avenges, blesses, cares, protects. Also it includes what He will not do: He will not fail me, forget me, or leave me. It also includes the many things my God gives: He gives eternal life, joy, peace, safety.

What My God Wants

What my God wants of me communicates a lot about who He is and what is important to Him. My God wants me to believe, be content, be happy, and have humility. What my God does not want also communicates who He is. My God does not want me to be ashamed, be fearful, be proud, or to worry.

> Christians ought not to content themselves with such degrees of knowledge of divinity as they already obtained. It should not satisfy them, as they know as much as is absolutely necessary for salvation, but should seek to make progress. This endeavor to make progress in such knowledge ought not to be attended to as a thing by the bye, but all Christians should make a business

> of it. They should look upon it as a part of their daily business, and no small part of it neither. It should be attended to as a considerable part of the work of their high calling.[13]

Some of my students will ask, "How do I know when I know enough about God?" I know they are wondering how long they have to do this study.

To which I answer, "When you know as much about God as He knows about you, then you know enough."

Below are some of the warnings found in Scripture about not growing in our knowledge of God. By the way, all the different lists of Scripture throughout this book were easy for me to create because they were already in my biography of God.

> For forty years I was grieved with *that* generation, and said, "It *is* a people who go astray in their hearts, And they do not know My ways." (Psalms 95:10)

> Hear the word of the Lord, You children of Israel, For the Lord *brings* a charge against the inhabitants of the land: "There is no truth or mercy or knowledge of God in the land." (Hosea 4:1).

> For the wrath of God is revealed from heaven against all ungodliness and unrighteousness of men, who suppress the truth in unrighteousness, because what may be known of God is manifest in them, for God has shown *it* to them. For since the creation of the world His invisible *attributes* are clearly seen, being understood by the things that are made, *even* His eternal power and Godhead, so that they are without excuse. (Romans 1:18–20)

For I bear them witness that they have a zeal for God, but not according to knowledge. For they being ignorant of God's righteousness, and seeking to establish their own righteousness, have not submitted to the righteousness of God. (Romans 10:2–3)

Awake to righteousness, and do not sin; for some do not have the knowledge of God. I speak *this* to your shame. (1 Corinthians 15:34)

But then, indeed, when you did not know God, you served those which by nature are not gods. But now after you have known God, or rather are known by God, how *is it that* you turn again to the weak and beggarly elements, to which you desire again to be in bondage? (Galatians 4:8–9)

To the pure all things are pure, but to those who are defiled and unbelieving nothing is pure; but even their mind and conscience are defiled. They profess to know God, but in works they deny Him, being abominable, disobedient, and disqualified for every good work. (Titus 1:15–16)

You therefore, beloved, since you know *this* beforehand, beware lest you also fall from your own steadfastness, being led away with the error of the wicked; but grow in the grace and knowledge of our Lord and Savior Jesus Christ. To Him *be* the glory both now and forever. Amen. (2 Peter 3:17–18)

> Whoever abides in Him does not sin. Whoever sins has neither seen Him nor known Him. (1 John 3:6)

Anyone who continues to live in Him will not sin. But anyone who keeps on sinning does not know Him or understand who He is. (1 John 3:6, NLT)

---

1. Evans, 18.
2. Blackaby and King, 6.
3. Brock.
4. Mardi Collier, What Do I Know About My God? (Greenville, SC: Journeyforth, 2006).
5. Dan DeHaan, 88.
6. Herbert Lockyer, All the Divine Names and Titles in the Bible (Grand Rapids: Zondervan Publishing House, 1975), 1.
7. Ibid.
8. Ibid., 14.
9. Noah Webster, American Dictionary of the English Language, 1828 (San Francisco: Foundation for American Christian Education, 2002), "vain."
10. Blackaby, 7.
11. Max Lucado, Just Like Jesus: Devotional, A Heart Like His (Nashville: Thomas Nelson, 2003), 1.
12. Joshua Harris, Doug Down Deep: Unearthing What I Believe and Why It Matters (Colorado Springs: Multnomah Books, 2010), 44.
13. Edwards, 16.

CHAPTER 6

God's Way of Faith

But God, who is rich in mercy, because of His great love with which He loved us, even when we were dead in trespasses, made us alive together with Christ (by grace you have been saved), and raised us up together, and made us sit together in the heavenly places in Christ Jesus, that in the ages to come He might show the exceeding riches of His grace in His kindness toward us in Christ Jesus. For by grace you have been saved through faith, and that not of yourselves; it is the gift of God, not of works, lest anyone should boast. For we are His workmanship, created in Christ Jesus for good works, which God prepared beforehand that we should walk in them.

—Ephesians 2:4–10

The knowledge of God is vitally important for our maturity. For that reason, understanding God's Word is also vital, for the Bible is the primary means by which we get to know God. Thus, the most import question for our understanding of the Bible is our salvation. "For the message of the cross is foolishness to those who are perishing, but to us who are being saved it is the power of God" (1 Corinthians 1:18). Therefore, what is the answer to this question?

Which statement is true?

a) I am saved
b) I am being saved

c) I will be saved
d) All of the above

The answer to the above question is (d) All of the above. We briefly talked about this in chapter 3. These three tenses of salvation, or as I call them, the *trichotomy of faith*, are important for clearly understanding the Bible. I borrowed (with permission) the question above from my good friend Pastor James Hollandsworth.

A few years into my journey of learning God's growth formula, I was introduced to Pastor James at a Bible conference. There he preached on the kingdom of Jesus Christ which included this idea of the three tenses of salvation. God used the teachings of Pastor James to open my understanding even more of His Word. So much so that it became one of the top-three greatest spiritual events in my life, the other two being my salvation and the theology of knowing God. Of course, James's teachings were not some new revelation; they were right there in God's Word all along. But it was his presentation of these truths that enlightened me to so much about the Scriptures that I had missed before. Passages that had been tough to understand for years became very clear (references to James Hollandsworth's resources can be found in chapter 10).

I strongly believe that God intended His Word to be easily understood by all of us. God desires to have a personal relationship with every person in the world, but that relationship can only happen if we choose to believe in Him. Then that relationship grows with continued belief in Him. But belief in what? The knowledge of Him which grows that relationship comes from the Bible. Then it would make sense that He would communicate in a way that every person who desired it could understand. Wouldn't it be silly if my son wanted to have a relationship with a young lady but he had to depend on someone else to tell him about her?

Feed Yourself

Throughout the history of Christianity, there have been those who tried to convince the people that only they, the clergy, and spiritual leaders could properly interpret Scripture. Jesus dealt with this in His day with the Pharisees and scribes. They thought they had a monopoly on God's truth and the common folk needed to come to them to understand it. Then in the early church, it continued to be easy for church leaders to do this because copies of the Scriptures were not available to everyone. Unfortunately this limited access led to a lot of wrong theology. It is no coincidence that reformation came to Christianity soon after the invention of the printing press and the Bible became available to more people. When the common man could read the Scriptures for himself, he discovered the truth about God. Today with the Bible being available to nearly everyone, the clergy claiming superiority is not so much of a problem, though it continues to linger in some circles. The real problem is that since the common man broke free of that control, he gave it right back. People have become lazy in their personal Bible knowledge and have become content to let the clergy, once again, tell them what the Bible says and means. We stopped feeding ourselves.

When we go to church and listen to the sermon, that is like eating out. It is always nice to have someone else prepare the meal, but we know that eating out all the time is not physically healthy. Being fed *only* by our church is not spiritually healthy. That doesn't mean we shouldn't go to church; it means we need to learn to feed ourselves. When we stand before the judgment seat of Christ (Romans 14:10; 1 Corinthians 3:13; 2 Corinthians 5:10), Jesus will ask, "What did you do with the life I gave you, and as My bride, how did you prepare for My return?" We better have a good answer. We won't be able to give excuses and blame it on others. He won't accept "I didn't have the time to get to know You. My job, family, and hobbies kept me from learning about You." Nor will He accept an excuse like "No one ever said we had to get to know You." Jesus will reply, "I gave you all the time resources you needed to do everything I asked." We will all give an account of how we used His gifts of time and talent.

Furthermore, the excuse of "I couldn't understand the Bible" will also not be valid. God has provided His Word in an understandable way that no man or woman will have an excuse for not knowing His expectations for them. For Jesus has promised that if we seek

Him, we will find Him (Revelation 3:20). In this chapter, I will present some important concepts for understanding God's Word better.

Trichotomy of Faith

The first concept is the trichotomy of faith; *trichotomy* is just a fancy word meaning three parts. It is a way of describing a whole by dividing it into three components like dividing up an egg into the white, yolk, and shell. Each is singularly an egg and as a whole, they are an egg. As we have already talked about, our faith has three parts or tenses: past, present, and future. The Bible describes all three, and it is very important to understand which is being talked about as we read different passages of Scripture. For example, if someone is reading a passage about faith that includes good works and assumes the writer is talking about the faith of salvation, then he may mistakenly think salvation is by good works.

When I was in Bible college, we used Charles Ryrie's *Basic Theology* as our textbook. He said this about the three tenses of salvation:

> The inclusive sweep of salvation is underscored by observing the three tenses of salvation (1) The moment one believed he was saved from the condemnation of sin (Ephesians 2:8; Titus 3:5). (2) That believer is also being saved from the dominion of sin and is being sanctified and preserved (Hebrews 7:25). (3) And he will be saved from the very presence of sin in heaven forever (Romans 5:9–10)[1]

Context Determines Meaning

In the Old Testament, *salvation* and its other synonyms are primarily used in the context of being saved from temporal punishment. I have seen some commentators estimate that somewhere around 96–98 percent of the time in the Old Testament, the word *salvation* is used in this way. It is *not* being used as saved from eternal damnation. The estimate in the New Testament is around 80 percent. An example of this is Peter walking on water.

"But when he saw that the wind *was* boisterous, he was afraid; and beginning to sink he cried out, saying, 'Lord, *save me*!'" (Matthew 14:30, emphasis added).

Peter wasn't asking the Lord to save his spirit from hell but to save his body from drowning. The context determines the meaning of the word which is an important fact for all of us to remember. A word does not have a meaning without context: it only has possibilities of meaning.[2] For example, what does the word *trunk* mean? It could mean the trunk of a tree, the trunk of a car, the trunk of an elephant, a large box used for hauling clothes, or even swimming trunks. In the Bible, a lion can be just a lion; it can refer to the devil, or it can refer to Jesus Christ. We wouldn't want to mistakenly think that Jesus "walks about like a roaring lion, seeking whom he may devour" (1 Peter 5:8). That verse is talking about Satan. This principle is very important for understanding the Bible. For if we think *salvation/saved* always refers to our initial salvation, a lot of false theology can develop such as believing salvation is by good works or that bad behavior can cause someone to lose their salvation or isn't saved but thought he was.

Gift, Walk, Reward

The trichotomy of faith breaks out this way. For us who already believe, our salvation was in the past; this was the *gift by faith*. The salvation we need today and every day is our present salvation and is the *walk in faith*. The ultimate salvation we will receive in the future when we either pass away or Christ returns will be the *reward* of faith when we are in His presence. The *gift by faith* is when we were freed from the penalty of sin. The *walk in faith* is saving us from the power of sin which will not be completed until we step from this realm into the next. The *reward of faith* in the future will be when we will be saved from the presence of sin. We can see these three tenses in the verses below and the quote from Hudson Taylor.

> Therefore, having been *justified* by faith [past], we have peace with God through our Lord Jesus Christ, through whom also we have *access* by faith [present] into this grace in which we stand, and rejoice in *hope* of the glory of God [future]. (Romans 5:1–2, emphasis added)

The Lord Jesus received is holiness beginning, the Lord Jesus cherished is holiness advancing, the Lord Jesus counted upon as never absent would be holiness complete.[3]

As you see from the above verses, there are numerous ways these three tenses could be described. The most common is justification, sanctification, and glorification. That would mean that the *gift by faith* is justification, the *walk in faith* is sanctification, and the *reward of faith* is glorification. But I like *gift*, *walk*, and *reward* better. For one, they are not such big words and two, they are easier to remember. Plus it is my book, and I get to decide (smile). Seriously I do like the word pictures that *gift*, *walk*, and *reward* represent, and I believe that is why God used them. If Paul had used *rewards* (as he often does elsewhere) instead of *riches,* we would have had all three in this one passage of Ephesians.

> But God, who is rich in mercy, because of His great love with which He loved us, even when we were dead in trespasses, made us alive together with Christ (by grace you have been saved), and raised *us* up together, and made *us* sit together in the heavenly *places* in Christ Jesus, that in the ages to come He might show the exceeding *riches [reward]* of His grace in *His* kindness toward us in Christ Jesus. For by grace you have been saved through faith, and that not of yourselves; *it is* the *gift* of God, not of works, lest anyone should boast. For we are His workmanship, created in Christ Jesus for good works, which God pre-

> pared beforehand that we should *walk* in them.
> (Ephesians 2:4–10, emphasis added)

Before moving on, it is important for us to know that the term *gift by faith* should not be confused with the belief that only if God gives someone faith can they be saved, meaning not everyone can be saved, only the ones to whom God gives the *gift by faith.* While all good gifts do come from the Lord, God has also given us free will to choose Him or not. Like we discussed when talking about love, forced love is not really love. If God forced His salvation on us, then it would not truly be by love, "For God so loved the world" (John 3:16). Real love requires a choice. Also if God chooses some to be saved, that means he chooses the others to be lost, and therefore, He would be a liar when He said He desires all men to be saved. "For this is good and acceptable in the sight of God our Savior, who desires all men to be saved and to come to the knowledge of the truth" (1 Timothy 2:3–4).

What I am referring to in using gift by faith is our salvation that God gives us freely if we choose to believe in Him. Below are some of the verses that *gift by faith* comes Romans.

"Therefore, as through one man's offense *judgment* came to all men, resulting in condemnation, even so through one Man's righteous act *the free gift came* to all men, resulting in justification of life" (Romans 5:18, emphasis added).

"For the wages of sin *is* death, but the *gift* of God *is* eternal life in Christ Jesus our Lord" (Romans 6:23, emphasis added).

The *walk in faith* comes from verses like these:

"He who says he abides in Him ought himself also to *walk* just as He walked" (1 John 2:6, emphasis added).

"I say then: *Walk* in the Spirit, and you shall not fulfill the lust of the flesh" (Galatians 5:16, emphasis added).

"That the righteous requirement of the law might be fulfilled in us who do not *walk* according to the flesh but according to the Spirit (Romans 8:4, emphasis added).

The *reward of faith* comes from verses like these:

"For the Son of Man will come in the glory of His Father with His angels, and then He will *reward* each according to his works" (Matthew 16:27, emphasis added).

"But love your enemies, do good, and lend, hoping for nothing in return; and your *reward* will be great, and you will be sons of the Most High. For He is kind to the unthankful and evil" (Luke 6:35, emphasis added).

"And whatever you do, do it heartily, as to the Lord and not to men, knowing that from the Lord you will receive the *reward* of the inheritance; for you serve the Lord Christ" (Colossians 3:23–24, emphasis added).

Here are some other aspects of the Bible as seen in the trichotomy of faith:

Steps of Faith:

The *gift* is a single step of faith, a point in time decision.

The *walk* is multiple steps of faith over the process of life.

The *reward* is the final step of faith when the faithful rule and reign with Christ.

Relationship with God:

The *gift* is the start of the relationship.

The *walk* is the growing of the relationship.

The *reward* is fully enjoying the relationship.

God the Father:

With the *gift*, we are the children of God.

With the *walk*, we become the firstborn of God.

With the *reward*, we will be coheirs of God with Jesus.

Jesus, the Son of God:

As our *gift*, He is Savior (Messiah).

As our *walk*, He is Lord (Master).

As our *reward*, He is our King (Groom).

Righteousness:

The *gift* is the imputed righteousness of Jesus Christ.
The *walk* is yielding to the righteousness of Christ within us.
The *reward* is the fully-realized righteousness of Christ.

Putting Off and Putting On

With the *gift,* God puts off our unrighteousness and puts on us Christ's.

With the *walk,* we put off following the old nature and put on following Christ.

With the *reward,* God puts off our corrupt bodies and puts us a glorified body.

Another important connection is our own trichotomy. In 1 Thessalonians, we humans are described in three parts: body, soul, and spirit. "Now may the God of peace Himself sanctify you completely; and may your whole spirit, soul, and body be preserved blameless at the coming of our Lord Jesus Christ" (1 Thessalonians 5:23). The gift by faith is what saved our spirit. The walk in faith is what is saving our soul. The reward of faith is when our bodies will be saved. When we accepted Jesus Christ as our Savior, our spirit was saved. Someday in the future, our body will be saved when we get a new heavenly body. However, our souls are not yet saved; it is being saved. Our soul is who we are now—our thinking, our feeling, and what we do. The salvation of the soul is just another way of saying the sanctification process or the walk in faith. James M. Boice says the following in his *Foundations of the Christian Faith*:

> Spirit, soul and body are simply good terms to use to talk about what it really means to be a human being. The *body*, then, is the part of the person we see… The *soul* is the part of man that we call "personality." …what makes the individual a unique individual. Because we have souls we are able to have fellowship, love and communication with one another. But we do not have

> fellowship, love and communication only with others of our species. We also have love and communication with God, for which we need a *spirit*. The spirit is, therefore, that part of human nature that communes with God and partakes in some measure of God's own essence.[4]
>
> When Adam sinned, the spirit died instantly, with the results that all men and women since are born with what we call dead spirits. The soul began to die. In that area the contagion may be said to be spreading, with the result that we are increasingly captivated by sin. The remaining part of human nature, the body, dies last.[5]

The Salvation of the Soul

The word *soul* is often used interchangeably with the word *spirit* to refer to the spiritual side of man. As we are going to see, the Bible makes a distinction between the two words. Also the term *salvation of the soul* is not a term heard too much these days. Nonetheless, it has been around for some time and is very much biblical. I won't talk about it too much, for I have listed some good books on the subject in chapter 10. But I will briefly show where it comes from in the Scriptures for anyone struggling with the concept. "Receiving the end of your faith—the salvation of your souls" (1 Peter 1:9). At first glance, we might think Peter is talking about the initial salvation of the spirit. Except that later in his letter, he says the following about our souls.

> Since you have purified your *souls* in obeying the truth through the Spirit in sincere love of the brethren, love one another fervently with a pure heart, *having been born again*, not of corruptible seed but incorruptible, through the word of God which lives and abides forever. (1 Peter 1:22–23, emphasis added)

> Beloved, I beg *you* as sojourners and pilgrims, abstain from fleshly lusts which war against the *soul*, having your conduct honorable among the Gentiles, that when they speak against you as evildoers, they may, by *your good works* which they observe, glorify God in the day of visitation. (1 Peter 2:11–12, emphasis added)

> Therefore let those who suffer according to the will of God commit their *souls to Him* in *doing good*, as to a faithful Creator. (1 Peter 4:19, emphasis added)

These verses show Peter was not talking about salvation that comes with the gift by faith but salvation that comes by the walk in faith—our continuing sanctification. Another example is that James, in his letter to his fellow believers says, "Let him know that he who turns a sinner from the error of his way will save a *soul* from death and cover a multitude of sins" (James 5:20, emphasis added). Again this verse looks like it is talking about the salvation of the spirit and turning an unsaved person to Jesus Christ. However, in the previous verse, James says, "*Brethren,* if anyone among you wanders from the truth, and someone turns him back" (James 5:19, emphasis added). James is talking to a community of believers, his brethren, throughout the letter. *Brethren* is used fifteen times in the book of James, and nowhere in the New Testament is *brethren* used to describe the unbeliever. James is telling these Christians that if anyone among them falls away from the walk in faith, then they should draw him back.

In Hebrews, the author says, "But we are not of those who draw back to perdition, but of those who believe to the saving of the *soul* "(Hebrews 10:39, emphasis added). Just like James, the author of Hebrews has been warning believers not to draw back in their walk in faith but to continue to the saving of their souls. We know that these are believers because ninety-nine times, the author includes himself in his warnings just as he did in the above verse. The author of Hebrews later says:

> But do not forget to *do good* and to share, for with such sacrifices God is well pleased. Obey those who rule over you, and be submissive, for they watch out for your *souls* as those who must give account. Let them do so with joy and not with grief, for that would be unprofitable for you. (Hebrews 13:16–17, emphasis added)

As a pastor, I never looked out for a believer's spirit, for it was already saved. But I did look out for their souls by teaching them and counseling them to walk with God. M.R. DeHaan said this in his commentary on Hebrews:

> It [Hebrews] is not written to half-saved professors who are threatened with being lost after all. Instead it is written to believers who *are saved* and *cannot be lost* again, but they can lose their *reward.* The warning is to believers coming short of God's best, and becoming subject to the chastening of the Lord, and loss of reward at the Judgment Seat of Christ. These Hebrews knew they had in heaven a better and more enduring substance and were admonished by the Holy Spirit to hold fast their confidence.[6]
>
> Salvation is far more than being delivered from hell and going to heaven when we die. These are incidentals and by-products—bonuses of salvation. His real purpose is to make perfect saints out of worthless sinners. There are then two possibilities of Christian experience. One is to have salvation, *period;* and the other is to have salvation, *plus.* One is to be just saved by grace; the other is to know a life of power, victory, joy, service and fruitfulness and a reward at the end of the way. And it all depends on what we do

> with God's gift of salvation. We can develop it or neglect it.[7]

One more thing on the salvation of the soul and the walk in faith. Understanding these different tenses helps us better understand the Scriptures. Look at what a difference in understanding it makes knowing about the soul in Jesus's teachings.

> Then Jesus said to His disciples, "If anyone desires to come after Me, let him deny himself, and take up his cross, and follow Me. For whoever desires to save his life [soul] will lose it, but whoever loses his life [soul] for My sake will find it. For what profit is it to a man if he gains the whole world, and loses his own soul [life]? Or what will a man give in exchange for his soul [life]? For the Son of Man will come in the glory of His Father with His angels, and then He will reward each according to his works. (Matthew 16:24–27)

The word translated twice as *life* in verse 25 is the same Greek word *psyche* translated *soul* in verse 26. It is, therefore, talking about our everyday life. Yet these verses are, more often, used to talk about the unsaved and to warn them that if they don't give up the things of this world and accept Jesus as their Savior, they will lose everything. Consequently we tend to read these passages and move on because we think they are for the unsaved. But notice in verse 24, Jesus is talking to His already-saved disciples. The warning was specifically for them; they were the ones who would be tempted to either return to their old lives or go on for Jesus. For in the previous verses, Jesus was warning them that He must go to Jerusalem and die. He knew that they would have to count the cost of being His disciple. The same decision faces us today. If we give up the things of this world, we too can experience the abundant life that comes from following Jesus. Without understanding this about the walk in faith and the salvation of the soul, we might have missed this challenge to our souls. Watchman Nee puts it this way:

> How is the spirit saved? "That which is born of the Spirit is spirit" (John 3:6). We are told in the context of John 3 that he who believes has eternal life. To the believing one, his spirit is saved. Accordingly, the salvation of the spirit means having eternal life. But how is the soul saved? The passage [Matthew 16:24–27] we have been considering tells us that if we lose our soul for the Lord's sake, our soul shall be saved. And hence the salvation of the spirit is to have eternal life while the salvation of the soul is to possess the kingdom.
>
> The spirit is saved through Christ bearing the cross for me; the soul is saved by my bearing a cross myself.
>
> The spirit is saved because Christ lays down His life for me; the soul is saved because I deny myself and follow the Lord.
>
> The spirit is saved on the basis of faith: once having believed, the matter is forever settled, never again to be shaken. The soul is saved on the basis of following: it is a life-long matter, a course to be finished.
>
> By faith the spirit is saved, because "he that believeth on the Son hath eternal life" (John 3:36). Through works of the soul is saved, because "then shall [the Lord] render unto every man according to his deeds." (Matthew 16:27)[8]

Determining Gift, Walk, or Reward

How then do we know which one, gift, walk, or reward, is being used in the Scriptures? As we mentioned before, context determines the meanings of words. For this reason, we must first look at the context of the passage we are reading. If the passage is talking about faith alone like John 3:16 and 5:24, the passage is talking about the gift by faith. If the passage includes good works and obedience by faith even though it may include the words *saved* or *salvation*, the passage is most likely talking about the walk in faith. Of course if the passage is talking about future things, rewards, or crowns, the passage is talking about the reward of faith.

The gift by faith, the salvation of our spirit, is by grace alone, through faith alone, in Jesus Christ alone. The key word being *alone.* Salvation has nothing to do with good works. Good works and good behavior do not gain us the salvation of our spirit; there is nothing we can do to earn that salvation. We simply accept by faith—the free gift God gives. Neither can work or behavior take away salvation of the spirit. God does not take back His gift. Even little kids realize it is not right to take back a gift. Nor does our good works or right behavior determine if our spirit is saved. As we talked about before, while we should be growing in good works and right behavior, they can be poor indicators of whether the spirit is saved or not. That would be like giving someone a gift and saying, "Now prove to everyone I gave you a gift and that you deserve it." Curiously the grammar check on my computer wants to remove *free* from the above sentence where I typed *free gift.* Even the computer realizes that *free* is redundant when talking about a gift for there are no payments required for a gift.

From the time of birth, there is a continuing process of growth. This is the walk in faith or the salvation of the soul; its byproduct is obedience. The walk in faith not only includes good works and behavior change but also the chastisement of disobedient children. Along with the many passages of what the walk in faith looks like, there are also many verses warning the believer to remain faithful in that walk. Therefore, in the New Testament, all the instructions on how the Christian should live and the warnings for not doing so are part of the walk in faith.

For the reward of faith, the salvation of the body, there are two parts. It is a future reward of being in the presence of God. But there is also a present reward of experiencing the abundant life in Christ—the love, joy, and contentment that comes by following Him. The future reward is also twofold; it is a reward for all believers and rewards for those who were faithful in their walk. We see this in the passages below and many others. The reward for all believers is an eternity in the presence of God. However, the reward of ruling and reigning with Christ will only be for the faithful. There will be levels of rewards in Jesus's parables of the talents and cities (Matthew 25:14–30; Luke 19:1–27). We also see this in the fact that Jesus promised the twelve disciples that they would sit on twelve thrones and judge the twelve tribes of Israel. Jesus didn't promise thrones to all His followers, only the twelve. As we see below, not everyone's work will withstand the test of God's fire.

> Now if anyone builds on this foundation *with* gold, silver, precious stones, wood, hay, straw, each one's work will become clear; for the Day will declare it, because it will be revealed by fire; and the fire will test each one's work, of what sort it is. If anyone's work which he has built on *it* endures, he will receive a reward. If anyone's work is burned, he will suffer loss; but he himself will be saved, yet so as through fire. (1 Corinthians 3:12–15)

As we see, the important indicator of which one of the three tenses the Scripture are speaking of is their context. To summarize it, when the context is talking about faith alone then likely, the passage is talking about the gift by faith which is the salvation of our spirit. When the context is talking about good works, righteous behavior, and/or warnings to remain faithful then likely, the passage is talking about the walk in faith which is the salvation of our soul. When the context is talking about the future, future rewards, and future judgment then likely, the passage is talking about the reward of faith which is the salvation of our body.

Another indicator of which tense is being used is the proportions of Scripture. As we saw earlier when talking about the use of the word *salvation*, most of the Bible is talking about the walk in faith. Of course, the Scriptures also talk about how to be saved and the future with God, but most of the Bible is about how we should live now, which makes sense, as the Bible was written chiefly to us who believe, and the thing we need most is how to live a faithful life. Thus, our first leanings should be to the walk in faith when interpreting the verses under consideration unless otherwise indicated.

Along with the proportion of Scripture, the audience that the writer is addressing is a strong indicator. Like I just said, most of Scripture is written to us believers, not to the lost. Sure the author may include all three of the tenses in his writings. But if he is writing to saved brethren, then he is probably writing to them about the walk in faith. The Apostle John follows this pattern of gift, walk, and reward in his writings. The Gospel of John is the most evangelistic book in the Bible, dealing mostly with the gift by faith for the lost. It has this stated purpose, "These are written that you may believe that Jesus is the Christ, the Son of God, and that believing you may have life in His name" (John 20:31). Revelation is the book that speaks the most about future events—the reward of faith. However, 1, 2, and 3 John, along with most of the other books of the New Testament, were written primarily to believers about their walk in faith. Look at some of these introductions:

> To all who are in Rome, beloved of God, called *to be* saints: Grace to you and peace from God our Father and the Lord Jesus Christ. (Romans 1:7)

> To the church of God which is at Corinth, to those who are sanctified in Christ Jesus, called *to be* saints, with all who in every place call on the name of Jesus Christ our Lord, both theirs and ours. (1 Corinthians 1:2)

> Paul, an apostle of Jesus Christ by the will of God, To the saints who are in Ephesus, and faithful in Christ Jesus. (Ephesians 1:1)

> To the saints and faithful brethren in Christ *who are* in Colosse: Grace to you and peace from God our Father and the Lord Jesus Christ. (Colossians 1:2)

> Simon Peter, a bondservant and apostle of Jesus Christ, to those who have obtained like precious faith with us by the righteousness of our God and Savior Jesus Christ. (2 Peter 1:1)

> Jude, a bondservant of Jesus Christ, and brother of James, to those who are called, sanctified by God the Father, and preserved in Jesus Christ. (Jude 1:1)

> The Revelation of Jesus Christ, which God gave Him to show His servants--things which must shortly take place. And He sent and signified *it* by His angel to His servant John. (Revelation 1:1)

The last indicator is keywords. Not to contradict the principle of context determines meaning for that will always be true. Nevertheless, there are some keywords for the three tenses that are true most of the time. When we see these words, it is highly likely that the context is of that tense.

The Gift by Faith:

Justification, belief, believe, believers, born again, children of God, everlasting life, grace.

The Walk in Faith:

Sanctification, good works, disciples, firstborn, perfect, followers, walking in the Spirit, walking in the light, sin, confession, repentance, eternal life, love, obedience, flesh, law, righteousness, holiness, brethren, peace, contentment, joy, blessed, one another.

The Reward of Faith:

Glorification, rewards, crowns, overcomers, the bride of Christ, friends of the Groom, the judgment seat of Christ, inherit the kingdom, marriage supper of the Lamb, coheirs, reign and rule with Christ.

Of course, none of these indicators are absolutes and true 100 percent of the time. For example, justification in the book of James is used in a walk-in-faith sense. "You see then that a man is justified by works, and not by faith only" (James 2:24). We know from many other passages that initial salvation is not by works but by faith alone. Thus, James is not talking about the justification of God for salvation but our justification before men which is showing them that we walk by faith. Those who believe salvation is by works point to this verse as proof. But we can say, "No, James is not talking about the gift by faith, he is talking about the walk in faith because of the context of his statement." See, we are already conquering some of the tough passage of Scripture.

Gift, Walk, and Reward in Scripture

Now let us look at some of the keywords in the Scriptures that use all three tenses and see how knowing this helps with the interpretation. An important one for understanding the Scriptures is *eternal life* or *everlasting life.* Eternal life in the context of the gift by faith is when we receive the gift of eternal life to be with our heavenly Father forever. Eternal life in the context of the reward of faith is when we will fully realize that eternal life and be in His presence. But eternal life in the context of the walk in faith is a *quality* of life more than a period of time as seen in the gift and reward. Jesus said, "I have come that they may have life, and that they may have it more abundantly" (John 10:10). When the Bible talks about eternal life, it is not only talking about that eternity with God but also about the quality or abundant life we can have right now in Christ.

"And this is eternal life, that they may know You, the only true God, and Jesus Christ whom You have sent" (John 17:3).

This verse is part of Jesus's prayer for His disciples in John, chapter 17. When Jesus prays about eternal life, He is not praying for His disciples to have the salvation of their spirits. His disciples do not need that salvation; they already have it. What they need is to continue to grow in their relationship with their God so that they can experience the abundant life. As we have stated many times, the salvation of the spirit is by believing in God and His Son. Knowing God and His Son is the walk in faith and how we have the abundant life that Jesus promised.

Here is another example of eternal life being part of the walk in faith.

> But in accordance with your hardness and your impenitent heart you are treasuring up for yourself wrath in the day of wrath and revelation of the righteous judgment of God, who *"will render to each one according to his deeds" eternal life* to those who by patient continuance in doing good seek for glory, honor, and immortality; but to those who are self-seeking and do not obey the truth, but obey unrighteousness--indignation and wrath, tribulation and anguish, on every soul of man who does evil, of the Jew first and also of the Greek; but glory, honor, and peace to everyone who works what is good, to the Jew first and also to the Greek. (Romans 2:5–10, emphasis added)

On the one hand, it sounds like Paul is writing about the unsaved when he talks about indignation and wrath. But on the other hand, he is also talking about glory, honor, and peace. Then in the middle, we have eternal life for those who are *doing good.* A lot of ink has been used trying to explain these verses. One group looks at them and says this is the lost vs. the saved, hence salvation is by works. But there are many other verses that disprove salvation by good works. Another group says both groups are saved, and this proves that salvation can be lost. Except that there are many other verses teaching the believer cannot lose their salvation. Then another group says those who do good are the ones who are saved; the others thought they were saved, but their bad behavior proved they weren't. But as we discussed before, just because a child is disobedient doesn't mean they are not a child of God.

Which interpretation is correct? Well, using what we have learned about the three tenses, what can we determine about this passage? Most likely, Paul is talking about the walk in faith and not the gift by faith. For one, the passage doesn't say anything about belief or faith. Second the passage talks about good works, and the audience are the *saints* in Rome (Romans 1:7). These are both walk in faith indicators. Also vs. 9 talks about *anguish, on every soul;* we know that the soul is the being-saved part of man, not the already-saved part. The correct interpretation is more likely a warning from Paul to the believers in Rome to continue in their walk with Christ. Paul is telling them that they are in danger of the wrath of God because of their hardness and impenitent hearts. When the spirit is saved, we don't get a new heart, for it is part of the soul. Thus, a changed heart is part of the salvation of the soul. We Christians are susceptible to the hardening of our hearts. When King David sinned with Bathsheba, it was because his heart was hardened. In his repentance, he asks God to give him a new "heart" (Psalms 51:10). David also says, "The sacrifices of God are a broken spirit, a broken and contrite heart—these, O God, You will not despise" (Psalms 51:17).

One of the struggles many Christians have today is with verses like these when they say anything about judgment, punishment, or negative consequences. Many assume the Bible must be talking about the unsaved, for it surely can't be talking about the saved. I think this comes from pride like what the Jewish leadership had in Jesus's time. The leadership knew they were God's chosen people but rather than using that to bring the world to God, they looked down their noses at the Samaritans and Gentiles. I think many in Christianity today think that because their little sins are not as great as the world's big sins, that any condemnation found in the Scriptures must be directed to the lost. While it is true, there are warnings to the wicked, there are also many warnings to the disobedient believer. The book of Hebrews is full of warnings to believers to not pull away from their faith.

Consequently when many Christians today see verses like the above that talk about wrath, self-seeking and do not obey, they immediately assume they are talking about the lost and move on. When they do that, they miss the teaching the Holy Spirit has for them. This is a dangerous habit for us Christians. In the Old Testament, there are numerous examples of the Jewish people being disobedient, self-seeking, and walking away from God who then experienced the wrath of God. Both 1 Corinthians and Hebrews use the Jewish people's escape from Egypt and their failure to enter the Promised Land as examples for us not to be disobedient lest we too experience the wrath of God's judgment. There were many times in the wilderness that God punished and even killed those of His people who disobeyed.

But the most tragic of all are those who reach a place where God ceases to deal with them and leaves them alone until the judgment seat of Christ. For it is impossible to renew them again unto repentance. Like Israel, they are out of Egypt, under the blood, but die in the wilderness before ever reaching the Canaan of victory, assurance, fruitfulness and blessing.[9]

> Moreover, brethren, I do not want you to be unaware that all our fathers were under the cloud, all passed through the sea, all were baptized into Moses in the cloud and in the sea, all ate the same spiritual food, and all drank the same spiritual drink. For they drank of that spiritual Rock that followed them, and that Rock was Christ. But with most of them God was not well pleased, for *their bodies* were scattered in the wilderness. Now these things became our examples, to the intent that we should not lust after evil things as they also lusted. And do not become idolaters as *were* some of them. As it is written, "*The people*

> *sat down to eat and drink, and rose up to play."* Nor let us commit sexual immorality, as some of them did, and in one day twenty-three thousand fell; nor let us tempt Christ, as some of them also tempted, and were destroyed by serpents; nor complain, as some of them also complained, and were destroyed by the destroyer. Now all these things happened to them as examples, and they were written for our admonition, upon whom the ends of the ages have come. Therefore let him who thinks he stands take heed lest he fall. (1 Corinthians 10:1–12)

> Therefore, as the Holy Spirit says: "Today, if you will hear His voice, Do not harden your hearts as in the rebellion, In the day of trial in the wilderness, here your fathers tested Me, tried Me, and saw My works forty years. Therefore I was angry with that generation, and said, 'They always go astray in their heart, And they have not known My ways.' So I swore in My wrath, 'They shall not enter My rest.' Beware, brethren, lest there be in any of you an evil heart of unbelief in departing from the living God; but exhort one another daily, while it is called "Today," lest any of you be hardened through the deceitfulness of sin. (Hebrews 3:7–13)

Some attempt to explain away this chastisement of God by saying Israel is different from the church and that those in the wilderness that died weren't saved, and we can't look to them as examples for us today. Yes, I know and believe that God's dealings with Israel and the church are two different things. But the Holy Spirit points out in both books that these things that happened to Israel were given to us as our examples (1 Corinthians 10:11; Hebrews

3:12). As far as some Israelites being saved and some not, notice that in the 1 Corinthians passage, Paul uses the word *all* five times, all the Israelites drank of the water which was Christ. All were saved, but God was not pleased with all. When we start to realize that, the majority of the New Testament is talking to us believers about our walk in faith, warnings included, we begin to realize that God's expectation of our growth in a personal relationship with Him is a serious matter and not to be taken lightly. Too often, we treat this relationship with God as an optional thing, something we do if we have any spare time.

> Do not be deceived, God is not mocked; for whatever a man sows, that he will also reap. For he who sows to his flesh will of the flesh reap corruption, but he who sows to the Spirit will of the Spirit reap everlasting life. And let us not grow weary while doing good, for in due season we shall reap if we do not lose heart. Therefore, as we have opportunity, let us do good to all, especially to those who are of the household of faith. (Galatians 6:7–10)

Yes, we will reap what we sow. If we sow small amounts of time getting to know our God, we will reap a shallow relationship. But if we sow a significant amount of time with our God, we will reap a deep and loving relationship with Him. Sowing and reaping are what we do day in and day out; it is part of the walk in faith. So the everlasting life talked about in verse 8 is the abundant life in Christ Jesus. If verse 8 were talking about the salvation of our spirit, then that salvation would be the result of our sowing, not by faith alone.

I hope you are seeing and understanding these different tenses and how they are helpful in understanding God's Word. God does not wish for you to be ignorant of Him or His ways. His one desire for you is to know and love Him. He has left you a love letter to accomplish that goal. You cannot understand and know God if you do not understand and know His Word. Feed yourself!

---

1. Charles Ryrie, Basic Theology: A Popular Systematic Guide to Understanding Biblical Truth (Chicago: Moody Publishers, 1999), 319.
2. J.P. Louw, Semantics of New Testament Greek (Philadelphia: Fortress Press, 1982), 40.
3. Hudson Taylor, http://www.crossroad.to/heaven/Excerpts/books/faith_under_fire/hudson-taylor/exchanged-life.htm
4. James Montgomery Boice, Foundations of the Christian Faith: A Comprehensive and Readable Theology (Downers Grove: InterVarsity Press, 1986), 152ff.
5. Ibid., 204.
6. M.R. DeHaan, 20.
7. Ibid., 34.
8. Watchman Nee, The Salvation of the Soul (Richmond: Christian Fellowship Publishers, 2009), 11ff.
9. M.R. DeHaan, 134.

CHAPTER 7

God's Children

Assuredly, I say to you, unless you are converted and become as little children, you will by no means enter the kingdom of heaven.
—Matthew 18:3

Kids! Gotta love them, right? Well, of course, we always love them, but there are some times we don't necessarily like them (smile.) If *change* is the most loved and hated word in our language, then *children* is a close second. No, we don't hate them. However, we are often saddened by their choices in life. Our children are going to put two things on their mother's tombstone, "I love you" and "Make good choices." The two statements they hear from their mom probably every day. Especially "Make good choices" as they got old enough to drive. I imagine God is the same way with us. He loves us greatly, yet He is not always happy with the choices we make.

A few years ago, Barb and I were visiting a good pastor friend and his wife in Bullhead City, Arizona. Our two oldest boys were somewhere around five and seven years old. While we were there, our friends left to go to the store, and we stayed at their home to watch the kids. So Barb and I were relaxing in the living room while the boys played outside. Back then, you could let your kids play outside without worrying about them. Anyway as we were sitting there, I heard the garage door go up and shortly after, go back down. I figured our friends must be home. However, no one came into the house, and I heard the door go up and down again. Being a typical dad, after about the fourth or fifth time, I figured I better go and see what was going on.

I stepped out into the garage just in time to see our youngest, who will remain nameless (smile), push the garage door button and run over to the garage door. As the door got about eye level to him, he grabbed on and proceeded to ride the door all the way to the top. When the door stopped, he let go and dropped back down to the floor. It was only then that he noticed me along with his older brother who was standing there, watching, probably waiting for his turn. Of course, I yelled, "What are you doing!"

To which the little one answered, "Nutin." I gave them one of my dad lectures in my stern dad voice. Yet I was thinking to myself, *That was brilliant, I wish we had electric garage door openers when I was young*. After they promised not to do it anymore, I went back into the house. As I returned to the living room, Barb asked what was going on, and I told her. Then I got that infamous parent line, "That's your kid!"

I wonder if Mary ever said to Joseph, "That's your kid." We know Jesus was sinless, so He must have been a pretty good kid. But did Jesus ever act like a child? Did He ever bring His dead hamster back to life? Or did He ever make a cat turn around and roar like a lion when a dog was chasing it? I hope that's not disrespectful, I don't mean it to be, but I love wondering about Jesus and His childhood. I wonder if the angels ever said to God, "That's Your kid." Does God ever turn to Jesus while they are watching us and say, "That's Your kid?"

Reverse Maturity

I bring this all up because being a *child* of God has a special application to our Christian maturity. It is important for us to understand how that works. Once again, God uses the natural to help explain the supernatural. I am sure God looks at us as a loving parent, always wishing for our best, for our success, and our enjoyment of life. He is also disappointed when we don't follow His ways. He knows if we would mature, we would truly enjoy Him. Except in this case of the natural explaining the supernatural, things work in reverse order from the natural. With natural maturity, we parents try to help our children grow from a dependent child to an independent adult. We want them to grow up, leave the house, maybe have a family of their own and someday, have enough money to take care of us in our old age. God's model of maturity is the opposite; He wants to take an independent adult (symbolically no matter what age we were saved) and help us mature to *dependent children*.

How much does a fifty-year-old depend upon his parents? Not much, he probably thinks he doesn't need them at all. He is now old enough to handle anything and usually doesn't want any interference from his parents. How much does a twenty-five-year-old depend upon his parents? Maybe a little more especially since young people are getting married older these days. How about a fifteen-year-old? While he or she probably doesn't think they need their parents at all, they still do, more than the twenty-five-year-old. What about a five-year-old, five-month-old, or a five-day-old. An infant is fully dependent upon his or her parents for everything; they can do nothing for themselves. Strangely this is exactly where God wants to take us. He wants us to do nothing in our strength, but to depend fully upon Him, doing only His will. Jesus left us an example of this in the Gospel of John. In many different ways, Jesus says to His Father, "Not My will but Your will be done."

> Then Jesus answered and said to them, "Most assuredly, I say to you, the Son can do nothing of Himself, but what He sees the Father do; for whatever He does, the Son also does in like manner. (John 5:19)

> I can of Myself do nothing. As I hear, I judge; and My judgment is righteous, because I do not seek My own will but the will of the Father who sent Me. (John 5:30)

For I have come down from heaven, not to do My own will, but the will of Him who sent Me. (John 6:38)

Jesus answered them and said, "My doctrine is not Mine, but His who sent Me. If anyone wants to do His will, he shall know concerning the doctrine, whether it is from God or *whether* I speak on My own *authority.* He who speaks from himself seeks his own glory; but He who seeks the glory of the One who sent Him is true, and no unrighteousness is in Him. (John 7:16–18)

Then Jesus cried out, as He taught in the temple, saying, "You both know Me, and you know where I am from; and I have not come of Myself, but He who sent Me is true, whom you do not know. (John 7:28)

Then Jesus said to them, "When you lift up the Son of Man, then you will know that I am *He,* and *that* I do nothing of Myself; but as My Father taught Me, I speak these things. (John 8:28)

And I do not seek My *own* glory; there is One who seeks and judges. (John 8:50)

Do you not believe that I am in the Father, and the Father in Me? The words that I speak to you I do not speak on My own *authority;* but the Father who dwells in Me does the works. (John 14:10)

He who does not love Me does not keep My words; and the word which you hear is not Mine but the Father's who sent Me. (John 14:24)

Become as Little Children

It is good for us to remember that Jesus lived His life as an example for us. The new life He gave us no longer belongs to us; He wants to live His life through us. Christ-like maturity looks like us being dependent upon God. Not our will but His, not our words but His, not our actions but His, and not our feelings but His. These are the character qualities of a completely dependent child. This is what Jesus was trying to teach His disciples.

> At that time the disciples came to Jesus, saying, "Who then is greatest in the kingdom of heaven?" Then Jesus called a little child to Him, set him in the midst of them, and said, "Assuredly, I say to you, unless you are converted and become as little children, you will by no means enter the kingdom of heaven. Therefore whoever humbles himself as this little child is the greatest in the kingdom of heaven. Whoever receives one little child like this in My name receives Me. (Matthew 18:1–5)

> Then little children were brought to Him that He might put *His* hands on them and pray, but the disciples rebuked them. But Jesus said, "Let the little children come to Me, and do not forbid them; for of such is the kingdom of heaven." And He laid *His* hands on them and departed from there. (Matthew 19:13–15)

We might think that it was the disciples who were acting childish, wanting to know who was going to be greatest in the kingdom. Not so—that is actually how adults act. When we think about what we want our children to mature into, it usually includes things like being honest, kind, responsible, independent, loving, caring, and trustworthy. As a counselor for many years, I have found that the words that more often describe adults are *angry, bitter, gossips, liars, cheaters, backstabbers*, and *greedy*. I sometimes think being an adult is overrated. The disciples were acting like adults; they were so concerned with their position in the kingdom that they were missing what Jesus was trying to teach them. Just like what He taught Martha when He visited her and her sister Mary. Mary was sitting at the feet of Jesus, listening to Him teach. Martha was running around obsessed with making dinner. "Martha, Martha, you are worried and troubled about many things. But one thing is needed, and Mary has chosen that good part, which will not be taken away from her" (Luke 10:41–42). We too are often running around so obsessed with life that we miss the teachings of Jesus.

Before we move on to the positive qualities of childlikeness, we want to briefly deal with what seems like a contradiction to this teaching. That is 1 Corinthians 13:11, "When I was a child, I spoke as a child, I understood as a child, I thought as a child; but when I became a man, I put away childish things." First it should be obvious that the Holy Spirit is not going to guide Paul to contradict the teachings of Jesus. Second the keywords are, *spoke, understood,* and *thought*. The context of this verse is that it is in the middle of Paul talking about how our knowledge is partial now. When "that which is perfect has come" (verse 10), we will know in full. Paul is saying that our knowledge of God is childlike and limited, he is not talking about putting away the positive behavior that children have. Which was the same thing Jesus was teaching His disciples, that maturing in our knowledge of Him is actually to stop acting like a typical adult. C.S. Lewis put it this way, "When I became a man, I put away childish things, including the fear of childishness and the desire to be very grown up."[1]

Children ride in strollers—they sit back and enjoy the ride, often falling asleep without care. Adults drive cars—they decide where they are going and how fast they will get there. Adults often struggle to fall asleep. And Roy Hession said this:

> All we need to know of the Father has been revealed by the Lord Jesus with such simplicity

> that a child can understand... perhaps with such simplicity that unless we become as little children we will not understand, for so often it is our intellect that gets in the way.[2]

There used to be a bumper sticker going around that said, "God is My Copilot." Then one came out saying, "If God is Your Copilot? Trade Places!" Probably all of us as a child thought sometimes, *I can't wait until I grow up and nobody can tell me what to do.* Yes, it is often our pride that gets in the way of understanding the simplicity which is in Christ. Unfortunately our pride grows right along with our natural growth. The older we get, sometimes, the prouder we get of our knowledge. When Paul said, "We know that we all have knowledge. Knowledge puffs up, but love edifies" (1 Corinthians 8:1). Paul was addressing ordinary people without much, if any, formal education. He was not talking about the knowledge that comes from education although that knowledge can also puff up. As we mature with or without formal education, we can be in danger of pride. We must remember to remain childlike, and here are a few examples of what it looks like to be childish. Interestingly the character qualities are truer usually the younger the child is; even young children begin to quickly move away from these as they get older.

Children Are Not Afraid to Be Naked

Every parent has had a kid get loose and run around without their cloThessalonians I love it when moms are chasing them through the store and the kids are just having a grand old time. I was driving home one afternoon and after turning into our neighborhood, I found a little guy standing naked on the sidewalk. He was probably about three years old, and no one else was around. I pulled over, concerned about him being all alone. As I started walking toward him, he ran into a nearby house. I thought to myself, *I hope that's where he lives.* I knocked on the door to make sure, and I told the young lady who answered what I had just seen. She sighed and told me that her husband was swimming in the backyard with the kids. After thanking me, I got the impression that her husband was about to be in a lot of trouble.

As I mentioned in chapter 2, I believe the nakedness of Adam and Eve in the garden is symbolic of complete transparency before God. When they sinned, they became ashamed of their nakedness because the relationship with God was broken. Consequently we adults have been ashamed of our physical nakedness since then. I believe our shame is a reminder that God still desires that transparent relationship with us, but our sin prevents it.

We adults are to be like children and not ashamed of our spiritual nakedness and accept the open relationship God desires. God is not ashamed of our nakedness; nothing is hidden from Him anyway. Like a mom walking in on her child changing and answers her child's horror with, "It's nothing I haven't seen before." God already knows our deepest sins; the issue is, will we get over our pride and accept that kind of transparent relationship?

Children Have a Simple Faith

Kids will believe anything. Like most dads, I used to mess with my kids with those not-so-truthful reasons for stuff. My favorite was the trees moving back and forth is what causes the wind to blow. Or when I would swerve the car a little and yell, "Snake!" and get them all screaming. I still remember when my oldest did the same thing to his friend from Taiwan, the poor kid about had a heart attack. Okay, maybe not a good thing to lie to your children. Nevertheless, I use it to illustrate that as we mature naturally, we tend to get skeptical, cynical, and jaded to what others tell us.

We live in a time, like no other, when we have almost unlimited information available, sometimes as close as our phone. With the Internet, we can find out about everything. Unfortunately we also find out people lie—and lie a lot; fake news, scams, and exaggerations. We have rightly learned to weigh all that information and to accept or reject that advice we receive. Consequently we tend to treat God's Word in the same way as if it's just helpful advice that we can take or leave. The Bible says God hates divorce; we think, "Well, maybe, does God really not want anyone to get divorced?" I have heard so many times in counseling that even though God doesn't want us to divorce, He still wants us to be happy, so we are going to leave each other. We treat God's commandments as if they are optional.

As we saw in the four Ts, trust is vitally important to a relationship. If we are not going to trust/believe in God's ways, how can we expect to have an intimate relationship with Him? Yes, it is dangerous for children to believe any old thing the world tells them, that is part of natural maturing. However, when it comes to God, we adults need to become like children and unconditionally believe all that God says. God loves us more than we can comprehend, He will not lie, and we can have faith that *all things work together for our good.*

Children Are Quick to Forgive and Forget

As parents, we are lucky our children so easily forgive—at least, they do when they are young. New parents make a lot of mistakes raising their children. One of the biggest is, perhaps unwittingly, taking advantage of that easy forgiveness. When we are young parents, we are usually beginning to build our careers and, therefore, are always busy. This busyness sometimes causes us to neglect our children and because they so easily forgive our missed time with them, we keep on doing it. Then when we are settled into our careers, we wonder why our teenagers don't want to spend any time with us.

This willingness to forgive and forget seems to be proportional to age. The younger we are, the easier it is to forgive. The older we get, the more likely we are to harbor grudges, bitterness, and unforgiveness. Jesus told us that if we didn't forgive one another, He would not forgive us (Matthew 6:15). Also Paul told us as much as we can, we should live at peace with everyone (Romans 12:18). We are to keep short accounts with our fellow humans and quickly forgive not only because God wishes all men to live at peace with one another but also because God is a jealous God. God is so jealous of our relationship that He doesn't want us distracted from Him by disputes with others.

When we are angry and unforgiving to others, we are usually concentrating on the wrong they did to us. God does not want us to take our eyes off Him; He wants our full attention. He doesn't get that when we hold grudges and stew on our bitterness. Therefore, we are to be like young children—not being offended so easily and quick to forgive. Again as a counselor, I found that people will often cling to their bitterness like a family heirloom. They don't want to forgive; they seem to get a certain amount of joy or energy having something to stew over. It's like they are afraid of settling the matter because then, they won't have anything to gossip about.

Children Love Unconditionally

There is nothing more heartwarming than to come home and have your kids run up to you with lots of hugs and kisses. Probably nowhere else do we get as close to the unconditional love of God as the love of a young child. Sure the love of a husband and wife is close. However, children have that unconditional trust and forgiveness, the lack of which can taint the husband-and-wife relationship. Of course, that is not how God intended it. He intended us to love everyone unconditionally. Unfortunately in counseling, I have run across couples that love their children more than each other.

Sin has corrupted our view of love; it has become conditional. We will love others if they do the things we want. Thus, the high rate of divorce; as soon as we stop getting what we want, we go looking for it elsewhere. Unknowingly we often treat God the same way. If life feels good, we are quick to praise Him. Nonetheless, if life becomes uncomfortable, we are just as quick to blame Him.

As adults, we need to return to loving unconditionally like children. This is the condemnation Jesus had for the church at Ephesus, "You have left your first love" (Revelation 2:4). After being Christians for a few years, we can become complacent with God. I heard someone once say that he thought that the opposite of love was not hate but indifference. Which seems to be very true, we don't go from loving God to hating Him but being indifferent to Him. That is until life goes bad, then we wonder why God isn't around to take care of us. Also our unconditional love for others is the distinguishing factor of following Christ. The world will know we are Jesus's disciples by our love for one another (John 13:35). We are called to love the unlovable, for anyone can love someone who loves them back (Matthew 5:43–48).

Children Have No Confidence in Self

The distinguishing factor of natural maturity is independence. We want our children to grow up and be able to take care of themselves. I remember the first time our oldest made cereal for himself, and I no longer had to fix him breakfast, yay! And wow! All the free time I have now that they can all drive. Part of that training of independence is getting the child to have confidence in himself to try new things and to take some risks while still under our protection. For example, when our kids started liking the opposite sex, we didn't let them go on dates all alone. When they were young, temptations toward impurity were too strong. We did, nonetheless, allow them to group date (get together with a bunch of friends) because we wanted them to build confidence in socializing with the opposite sex, for we didn't want them to live with us forever (smile).

Again God's desire is the opposite. He does not want us to have confidence in self. Apart from Jesus, we can do nothing. Even Jesus realized that apart from the Father, He could do nothing.

> Then Jesus answered and said to them, "Most assuredly, I say to you, the Son can do nothing of Himself, but what He sees the Father do; for whatever He does, the Son also does in like manner. (John 5:19)

> I can of Myself do nothing. As I hear, I judge; and My judgment is righteous, because I do not seek My own will but the will of the Father who sent Me. (John 5:30)

> I am the vine, you *are* the branches. He who abides in Me, and I in him, bears much fruit; for without Me you can do nothing. (John 15:5)

> Not that we are sufficient of ourselves to think of anything as *being* from ourselves, but our sufficiency *is* from God. (2 Corinthians 3:5)

> We can, however, *do all things through Christ who strengthens us*, the key being *in Christ.* God wants all our confidence to be in Him, not in our strength, knowledge, or wisdom. We are not commanded to bear fruit, we are commanded to abide in Christ, and He will bear fruit through us. (John 15:4)

Children Will Ask for Anything and Everything

We all have experienced this or at least done it ourselves as a kid. "Can I have this, can I have this, can I have this?" Of course, this is rude behavior in children who are not afraid to ask for what they want. But for adults, it illustrates our independence. Especially for us men, we hate to ask for help from anyone. Our pride can cause us even to have a reluctance to ask God for help, and we miss out on His provision. We think we are all grown up now; we don't need to bother God with these little needs, we can take care of it ourselves. We generally only ask God for the big stuff. When Jesus taught His disciples to pray, part of that prayer was, "Give us this day our daily bread" (Matthew 6:11). The needs of life don't get any more basic than our daily bread. God desires that we ask for everything, even for the little stuff. Of course, that doesn't mean we get every cheap little toy we ask for; but like a good father, He will not withhold any good gift.

A friend of ours told us about the time she lost the keys to her car. It was time to take her boys to school, and she was frantically searching the house for them. After looking for a while, her youngest spoke up and said, "Why don't we pray and ask Jesus to show us where they are?" She said she was cut to the heart; her six-year-old son had more faith in their God then she did. So they prayed for the keys and sure enough, in a couple of minutes, they found them. What a wonderful illustration of what we are talking about. Although God does not want us to be rude, asking for every little toy that catches our fancy. He does want us to set aside our pride and be like a child, not afraid to ask Him for all our basic needs. (We have not because we ask not) (James 4:2–3).

> Ask, and it will be given to you; seek, and you will find; knock, and it will be opened to you. For everyone who asks receives, and he who seeks finds, and to him who knocks it will be opened. Or what man is there among you who, if his son asks for bread, will give him a stone? Or if he asks for a fish, will he give him a serpent? If you then, being evil, know how to give good gifts to your children, how much more will your Father who is in heaven give good things to those who ask Him! (Matthew 7:7–11)

Children Don't Have to Be Perfect

When I am talking about *perfect* in this context, I am not referring to the biblical definition of perfection as we have talked about before which means growing into maturity. What I mean by perfect here is the traditional definition of being without fault or defect. Again as adults, our pride gets in the way, and we think that we cannot appear to be wrong in any way. We all know that person that thinks they are always right; they will fight to the bitter end rather than admit they were wrong. These are the people that when anyone gets close to proving them wrong, they strike back with personal attacks and name-calling. Just watch the nightly news. However, a sign of spiritual maturity is when we don't always have to prove that we are right. Now that doesn't mean we can't stand up and defend what we know to be true. What I am talking about is having the wisdom to know when we are "casting our pearls before swine" (Matthew 7:6). That is, knowing that arguing with this person would be a waste of the time God has given us.

Children don't always have to be right; they are teachable, willing to accept their weakness. That is before they become teenagers (smile). Young children are willing to grow in their knowledge of God. Sadly many Christians get what they think is all their theology lined up and are unwilling to admit there might be something new they can learn. They become content in what they know about God and in their pride, don't think there is any more to learn. These are also the Christians who think their behavior is perfect, and they judge everyone else's sins. They make me think of the Pharisees' attitude toward the disciples, "Who are these men, they are unlearned and mere fishermen." Therefore, don't be like those spiritual leaders, be as humble children that know they aren't perfect. For the humble will find God.

> In that hour Jesus rejoiced in the Spirit and said, "I thank You, Father, Lord of heaven and earth, that You have hidden these things from *the* wise and prudent and revealed them to babes. Even so, Father, for so it seemed good in Your sight. (Luke 10:21)

Children Don't Like Rules

None of us like rules except when we are making them for others. Logically we cannot get rid of the rules nor am I suggesting it. We need rules for order and safety. Children though usually think relationships are more important than rules. In school, what is it that kids do the most to get themselves in trouble? Talking in class. They have an instinct that connecting with their friends is more important than following the rules. They don't want to go to bed; they want to stay up with Mom and Dad. Or the worst one of all—they don't want to sleep in their bed, they want to be in ours. Again not suggesting we get rid of the rules. What I am getting at is back to the change formula, obedience does not produce love, but love does produce obedience. Another way of putting it is, rules without relationship lead to rebellion. We adults can get so caught up in the rules sometimes that we miss relationships.

Jesus broke the rules quite often, that is the false rules/traditions, that the Pharisees had burdened the people with.

> And when the Pharisees saw *it,* they said to Him, "Look, your disciples are doing what is not lawful to do on the Sabbath!" But He said to them, "Have you not read what David did when he was hungry, he and those who were with him: how he entered the house of God and ate the showbread which was not lawful for him to eat, nor for those who were with him, but only for the priests? Or have you not read in the law that on the Sabbath the priests in the temple profane the Sabbath, and are blameless? Yet I say to you that in this place there is *One* greater than the temple. But if you had known what *this* means, *'I desire mercy and not sacrifice,'* you would not have condemned the guiltless. For the Son of Man is Lord even of the Sabbath." (Matthew 12:2–8)

When a lawyer asked Jesus what the greatest rule was, He answered, love God with all your heart, mind, and soul, and love your neighbor. He also said that these two rules sum up all of them (Matthew 22:36–40). I hope you understand what I am saying. We adults need to spend less time worrying about the rules and more time loving our God and neighbors. If we did that, would we need any other rules?

Children Have Awe of Creation

These last two are perhaps my favorite. I am a big fan of God's creation. Especially His creation of trees. I already have dibs on being

God's forest ranger on the new earth. Yes, I am a *tree hugger;* I give them a little hug right before I cut them down. Now don't get me wrong, I do believe we need to be good stewards of what God has provided for us and not squander those resources. I also don't worship trees; I worship their Creator who gave them to us to use. I love seeing God in His creation of wood. I do some woodworking as a hobby to relax and unwind. I started off making toys for the kids; but now, as I am currently waiting for grandkids, I have branched out to other things. Right now, I like to make wooden pens; they don't take long, and I can give them away as gifts. The neat thing about making pens is I don't need a lot of wood; so I have been experimenting with all types of exotic woods. These woods normally would be too expensive to use in large amounts, but I can afford them in small pieces. I am amazed at all the different colors, smells, and the different hardness of woods. Not every type of wood floats; some types sink in water.

I could go on for another whole book just on trees and the glorious things God has done with them. What I am getting at though in this section is that sometimes, we adults lose some of our awe of God's creation. Even for us who like to be out in nature, we seldom connect its beauty with God's greatness. The Scriptures are clear that God also gave us His creation to teach us about Him. Sure it is not as specific as His revelation in His Word, yet we should not neglect the awesomeness of this world. Children have that awe—the first time they feel the grass under their feet, the first time they see snow, or when they first notice their shadow, they are giddy with excitement. For my kids, who were born in Arizona, it was the first time they saw actual water flowing in a river.

I am in awe of the simple seed. Everything alive today would die in a few days without water, yet a tiny seed can be stored without water or light for hundreds, even thousands of years. Though when we add a little light and water, it springs to life. Supposedly scientists have been able to germinate seeds as old as four thousand years. How does God keep that little spark of life in a seed for so long without it having any of the things that sustain life? Sometimes we busy adults need to slow down and watch the trees grow.

Children Love a Good Story

We talked before about not being the author of our stories and enjoying the story God is writing for our lives. Now we are going to look a little deeper into loving God's story. My children loved storybooks; I will never forget *One Fish, Two Fish, Red Fish, Blue Fish.* Back in the day, I nearly had that whole book memorized. I used to try to read it faster each time, but that only meant the kids wanted another story. Even we adults love a good story; although we don't read as much as we use to, we love the stories in the movies and on TV. I believe this love for stories is part of our being created in the image of God. God is the Master Storyteller; He is writing the story of all our lives. Paul Miller, in his wonderful book *A Praying Life,* talks about the story God is telling, he says, "To see the marvel of the stories that our Father is telling, we need to become like little children."[3]

When I first read the above statement is when I started thinking about spiritual maturity being like a child. Most of what I have written in this chapter was inspired by this thought. While we adults love a good story, we are skeptical, knowing most stories are made up. We could say that we don't fully trust in the story, at least not like a child. Children believe the stories they hear and get all caught up in them. Now it is, of course, foolish for us to believe in manmade fairy tales. We can, nonetheless, fully believe in God's stories. That's the whole point, we adults need to let ourselves go and fully trust in the Storyteller and His story.

What is the story that God is telling? The greatest story ever told is the story of God's Son.

The Gospel, the Father's gift of His Son to die in our place, is so breathtaking that since Jesus's death, no one has been able to tell a better story. If you want to tell a really good story, you have to tell a Gospel story.[4]

After the good news of Jesus Christ, the next best gospel story would be our own, how Jesus saved us. There is probably nothing better than hearing the testimonies of how people got saved. All our stories are different in the details but with the same result. It is a blessing to hear how God's grace turns around lost lives. At the point of our salvation, we gave up and yielded to God's control to save our lives. Unfortunately not too long after our salvation, we have a bad habit of taking back control of our lives. It's like that natural maturity again, we revert to being independent and say, "Lord, thanks for saving me, nevertheless, I can take it from here." One of the keys to enjoying the story God is writing is to stop trying to control its outcome.

When you stop trying to control your life and instead allow your anxieties and problems to bring you to God in prayer, you shift from worry to watching. You watch God weave His patterns in the story of your life. Instead of trying to be out in front, designing your life, you realize you are inside God's drama. As you wait, you begin to see Him work, and your life begins to sparkle with wonder.[5]

If we stop fighting and embrace the gospel story God is weaving in our lives, we will discover joy. Part of our discomfort in the Christian life is the battle of who is in control of it. There are three types of suffering that every believer experience. One is the suffering and persecution we receive for being a Christian. We can't do much about that. Two is the suffering we receive because this is a sin-filled world and others sin against us. Not much we can do about that either. Three is the suffering we bring upon ourselves because of our pride, wanting to do things our way. That suffering we can avoid if we yield control to the Storyteller.

Both James and Peter said, "God resists the proud, but gives grace to the humble" (James 4:6; 1 Peter 5:5). When we think of pride, we often think of a person saying, "Hey, look at me," like someone doing a victory dance after scoring a touchdown. However, the way God uses *pride* in His Word is doing things *our way.* It matters not whether we are seeking attention or not. Therefore, being humble is saying, "Not my will, Lord, but Your will be done." Sometimes that is a tough way to go, like asking for forgiveness from someone you have wronged. The good news is God has promised the grace we will need to go His way. We need to be like little children and sit back on God's lap and listen to the story. Then ask Him to read it again.

Perhaps the greatest Christian children's story writer was C.S. Lewis, *The Narnian.* Following are some observations by Paul Miller on how much C.S. Lewis loved God's story.

> Lewis' mind was above all characterized by a willingness to be enchanted, and it was this openness to enchantment that held together the various strands of his life—his delight in laughter, his willingness to accept a world made by a good and loving God, and (in some ways above all) his willingness to submit to the charms of a wonderful story.[6]
>
> How did we lose the enchantment? When did we lose our willingness to be delighted?
>
> In most children, but in relatively few adults, at least in our time, we may see this willingness to be delighted to the point of self-abandonment. This free and full gift of oneself to a story is what produces the state of enrichment. But why do we lose the desire—or if not the desire, the ability—to give ourselves in this way? Adolescence introduces the fear of being deceived, the fear of being caught believing what others have ceased believing in. To be naïve, to be gullible—these are the great humiliations of adolescence. Lewis seems never to have been fully possessed by this fear.[7]

As adults, we have a fear of giving ourselves to God's story wholeheartedly. We have lost the joy of imagination. We have become old fuddy-duddies who can't enjoy the unpredictability of God's story. Our sin nature has created in us a fear of giving ourselves over completely. We have within us a natural self-protection mechanism that makes it nearly impossible to give 100 percent of ourselves to any cause. No matter how much a coach talks about giving 110 percent, we always hold back a little. We can't really give 110 percent anyway; we can't give more than we are. But we don't even give the 100 percent for if we give a full 100 percent and we still fail, then we are failures. For instance, if a student were to spend all the time he had available studying for a test yet still failed, it would crush his spirit. However, if that student goofs off a little bit and then fails, he can always excuse it away. "Well, I wouldn't have failed if I had just spent more time studying." It is a built-in self-preservation measure that keeps us from feelings of failure.

I see this self-preservation in failing marriages. Society has made us leery of loving each other completely. When a popular TV host tells her audience that they should have their secret savings account in case their husbands cheat on them, she is setting them up for failure. Unfortunately we treat God that way too. He wants a 100 percent buy-in to the story He is writing. Unfortunately we fear that what if God's ways don't work? What if I lose all those earthly things I love most? What if God is not really there? Some parents are now discouraging their children from going to the mission field. They don't want them to live a life of sacrifice and poverty. They also fear that their child may die on the mission field.

I know it can be hard to give yourself completely to the Lord. No one is saying it will be easy. These other aspects of being a child of God are difficult too. It goes against your instincts; you don't want to be a child again, you want to be an adult and in control. You don't want to forgive quickly; you kind of like that energy you get from stewing on your problems. You like following the rules; they are easier than having a real relationship with God. It will not be easy becoming a child. However, as you saw from God's Word, He will give you His grace if you turn over your will to His story.

Below is a slightly modified list from Miller on how to enjoy the enchantment of your Father's story.

1) Don't demand that the story go your way (in other words, surrender completely).
2) In all things, look for the Storyteller. Look for His hand and then pray in light of what you are seeing (in other words, develop an eye for God).

3) Stay in the story. Do not shut down when it doesn't go the wrong way I wanted (in other words, do not give up on God's story for you).[8]

---

1. C.S. Lewis, http://cslewiswisdom.blogspot.com/2011/07/in-defense-of-childishness.html
2. Hession, 33.
3. Miller, 210.
4. Ibid., 213.
5. Ibid., 74.
6. Ibid., 210.
7. Ibid., 210.
8. Ibid., 201.

CHAPTER 8

God's Full Joy

And these things we write to you that your joy may be full.
—1 John 1:4

If you were to die today, would you spend eternity with Jesus Christ? That question is often used in witnessing to the unsaved. But it is just as important of a question for the saved. Do you have assurance of your salvation? Why is this important? Wouldn't our lives be miserable if we spent every day worried about if we are going to heaven when we die? Our eternal joy is not only affected by the answer to the questions but our daily joy is too. Satan loves to discourage us by inserting doubt into our beliefs, and one doubt can start an avalanche! He cannot steal away our eternal security, but he can steal away our abundant life if we do not grow in our knowledge of God's truth. God, like a loving Father, wants us to be fully confident of our security in Him for eternity and our everyday joy.

> My sheep hear My voice, and I know them, and they follow Me. And I give them eternal life, and they shall never perish; neither shall anyone snatch them out of My hand. My Father, who has given *them* to Me, is greater than all; and no one is able to snatch *them* out of My Father's hand. (John 10:27–29)

Unfortunately there are some misunderstandings about salvation that Satan is using to cause Christians to doubt their assurance, and therefore, they lose out on God's full joy. The false theology takes on the form of believing that our good works and obedience to God's Word is part of the salvation of our spirit. That right behavior must be done to earn our salvation. Or that the lack of right behavior causes us to lose our salvation. Or most commonly, that right behavior is proof that we have salvation. But as we have seen previously, all these leave the Christian hoping their good outweighs their bad and with no assurance of salvation. Below is a culmination of conversations over many years with those who believe good works determines whether a person is saved. John is not a specific person but just a name to represent the whole. The conversation usually goes something like this:

TODD. So, John, you believe salvation is by faith alone.

JOHN. Yes, Todd, I believe salvation is by faith alone, but the faith that saves is never alone.

TODD. What does that mean?

JOHN. It means that the faith that saves us is seen in our faithfulness to God's Word, that we bear fruit, keep His commandments, and do good works. Someone who claims to be a Christian but doesn't bear fruit and doesn't deal with their sin may think they are saved, but they really aren't. First John 2:3 says, "Now by this we know that we know Him, if we keep His commandments. He who says, 'I know Him,' and does not keep His commandments, is a liar, and the truth is not in him."

TODD. But you do believe that people cannot earn salvation by their good works?

JOHN. Yes, and neither can someone lose their salvation by doing wrong.

TODD. Let me see if I have this right then. People can do nothing to earn their salvation and once they have it, they can do nothing to lose it. But if someone claims to be a Christian but doesn't do good works and keep God's commandments, they are not saved?

JOHN. That is correct.

TODD. Okay, I agree that people can do nothing to earn or lose their salvation. But I am not too sure about what a person does proves or disproves they are saved. It seems subjective. Which commandments must be kept, all of them or just the ones in the New Testament? What is bearing fruit? How does someone know they are bearing fruit? Where does the Bible define what fruit is? What are good works? Is there a definition? Where does the Bible say someone has to do all this to prove they are saved?

JOHN. Well, like I already mentioned, 1 John 2:3 says those things about Jesus's commandments. In fact, the entire book of 1 John is a test of salvation. It gives all the details of what a person must do to know that they are saved. First John 5:13 says, "These things I have written to you who believe in the name of the Son of God, that you may know that you have eternal life, and that you may continue to believe in the name of the Son of God." First John gives us a list of Christian attributes that must be evident for the person to be saved such as being sensitive to sin and confessing our sins, obeying God's Word, rejecting evil in the world, and loving others.

TODD. Okay, I would agree. Those are all good things that a believer should be doing. I am familiar with these tests of salvation from 1 John and throughout the New Testament. The problem I have is one person has eleven tests, another has nine, and another only has six. Although each list was very similar, they each had some the others didn't, and I could think of a few more they missed. So which list is correct: six, nine, eleven, or thirty-two? What if I use the wrong list? What if I miss some? What if I am only doing well for nine of the eleven? Does God grade on a curve? Does this mean if I am a true Christian, I will never sin again?

JOHN. No, it doesn't mean we will be sinless. We all know that Christians occasionally sin. But it means we will sin less and less and produce more fruit over time. True believers may fall away from doing right for a little while, but they will always come back.

TODD. You are saying that if there is an upward trend, kind of like a chart, there can be a dip here and there as long as the general trend is up.

JOHN. Yes.

TODD. That adds more questions to my mind. I am not trying to be argumentative but something as important as eternal life, I want to make sure I have it right. You said I wouldn't necessarily keep God's commandments all the time, but how often do I have to keep the commandments to be sure it is an upward trend? How many times can I hate someone before it starts going down? How many fruits do I have to produce? Is it one a day, one a week? How many a year is an upward trend?

JOHN. I am not sure I understand?

TODD. Well, if we created a continuum, a line with zero on one end and one hundred on the other, the zero would represent never doing good works or never keeping God's commandments. And the one hundred represents always doing good works and always keeping God's commandments.

JOHN. Okay.

TODD. I agree with you that on the zero end, if someone never did good works or never kept God's commandments that it may be reasonable to wonder if that person is saved. And on the other end, none of us will ever achieve sinless perfection. What I am asking is then where the line between saved and unsaved is? Is it just past 50, so the trend is upward? But what if someone is 49.999? Will they go to hell just because they missed it by less than 1 point? And if we move it to 49, then what about the person who is 48.999? It still seems very subjective to me.

JOHN. That will be up to God. We will have to trust in Him that it will all work out.

TODD. Are you saying then that we can't know for sure if we are saved or not? For now, I am even less certain that I am saved. What happens if I do pretty good for most of my life but at the end, I mess up? I know

King Solomon, in the Old Testament, was loved by God and wrote three books of the Bible. But God was angry with him at the end of his life because he started worshipping false gods. That's serious. Does that mean Solomon is not in heaven? Do you know if you're saved or not?

JOHN. Well, I guess not. I suppose you have to wait until you die to see if you did enough.

TODD. Isn't that the very definition of a false religion? That you hope your good outweighs your bad and you make it into paradise? I thought you said that is what 1 John was all about, *that you may know that you have eternal life.* Is John lying to us? I thought we could have assurance of our salvation? There is not going to be much joy in life if I am always worried about whether I am saved!

After that, the conversation usually goes one of two ways. Most often, they change the subject and don't want to talk anymore. But a few will want to know more, and we can go on to discuss it. Which is what we will be doing for the rest of the chapter. Why all the discussion? Because it sounds logical that if a person is born again and the Holy Spirit dwells within them that there should be some evidence of that, yet He does not want us to lose our joy by doubting our salvation.

Not only is losing our joy a danger of this theology; another consequence is that we can miss out on the teachings from God that do affect our joy. When Christians believe the test of salvation theology, they start to think that the warning passages in the New Testament are for the unsaved and not the saved. Because the consequences of disobedience sound so dire and the truly saved almost always are obedient, then the writer must be talking about the unsaved. Therefore, they miss out on some very important teaching from the Holy Spirit on how to live. The Holy Spirit is often warning the believer to remain faithful to God or suffer some serious consequences such as the chastisement of the Lord (Hebrews 12:5–11), a sin that leads to death (1 Corinthians 11:30), or being ashamed at the return of Jesus Christ (1 John 2:28).

Thus, I am spending a chapter talking about it, plus it gives me a chance to introduce 1 John. This little book by John is perhaps one of the most beneficial for helping believers walk with God and experience the joy of the abundant life in Christ. It is the book I use the most in counseling. Unfortunately the mistaken idea that its purpose is a test of salvation has greatly affected the blessings of the joy of fellowship. As I have mentioned before, John's writings are a wonderful example of the gift, walk, and reward of faith. First John falls into that category of the walk in faith and the salvation of the soul, not the spirit. John himself said he wrote it that our joy would be complete (1 John 1:4).

However, when Christians see 1 John as a test of salvation of the spirit, they then see all the rules that must be kept proving they are saved. Below is the list compiled myself from other such list to give you a sampling of what they look like. The very fact that there are multiple lists prove my point that they are a poor indicator of salvation. For which, manmade list, is correct, the one that has eleven characteristics or the one with only six? What if I am doing pretty good at nine of the eleven? Does God grade on a curve?

Biblical Tests of Genuine Salvation:

Those who are saved:

1) Sin

   Are sensitive to sin, do not habitually sin, avoid sin and anything that leads to sin, strive against the flesh, have a decreasing pattern of sin, reject this evil world, and have feelings of bitterness when they offend God

2) Obedience
Obey God's Word, live obediently, adhere to the apostolic teachings, live according to God's will, do the things that please God, avoid the things that God hates, and grow in holiness.
3) Love God
Enjoy fellowship with Christ and the Father, desire God earnestly, and consider God's grace a precious jewel.
4) Love Others
Love other Christian brothers and sister, have a positive influence on others, have a special love for all true disciples of Jesus, rejoice in other's salvation, and love the ministers of God's Word.
5) Bear Fruit
Are fruit bearing, do good works, and have the fruit of the Spirit
6) Jesus Christ
Trust in Christ, confess Jesus is the Messiah, and believe Jesus Christ is the only Savior.
7) Holy Spirit
Experience the ministry of the Holy Spirit and testify that the Holy Spirit is within you.
8) World
Can discern between spiritual truth and error, does not use the world's opinions or standards, have suffered rejection from the world, reject the evil of the world, and have new desires and perspectives
9) Prayer
Call upon God earnestly with tears and have experienced answered prayers
10) Christ's Return
Are eagerly awaiting Christ's return, desiring Jesus's second coming, persevering in all these things until Christ returns or you die.

When a Christian looks at a list like this, they start thinking, *I need to buckle down and start doing better.* Then when they can't keep all these expectations, they either keep trying harder or give up. Those who try harder most often end up in self-righteousness and fruit inspection of everyone else. Those that give up often become what I call Christian couch potatoes doing just the bare minimum and hoping their good outweighs their bad. Neither lead to assurance of our salvation, for both groups are left hoping they have done enough to satisfy God. Just like in Jesus's time on earth, the Pharisees thought they had to keep all the commandments to please God, and those who didn't were lost. Then there were the harlots and tax collectors that gave up on keeping the law and just hoped for the best. We know they weren't completely devoid of conscience, for more of them than the Pharisees were willing to believe in Jesus.

As we can see, that list is very compelling. It is how every Christian should live, for it is right from God's Word. Also I agree that the Holy Spirit can and does change the believer and if a person has no change at all, perhaps he does need to do a little soul-searching. However, I don't believe behavior, good or bad, is a reliable test of salvation of the spirit.

Good Behavior, a Poor Salvation Indicator

Therefore, behavior is a poor indicator of salvation of the spirit for multiple reasons. One, it is too subjective. As we saw above in the conversation with John, there was no way to measure if we have done enough to prove we are saved. It is a truth of even the natural realm that a test must be measurable. When we take a test, there is always a minimum that we must get right to pass. Tests always have a pass-and-fail point, a means to know if someone has done enough. We would have gone bonkers going through twelve grades of school not knowing if we had done enough to graduate especially if we thought we were doing well only to fail the last test.

Second, behavior is a poor indicator because we have free will, and the greatest commandment is to love the Lord our God will all our heart, soul, and mind. As we spoke about before, we cannot love

God if we don't have the option to hate God. If only true believers persevere to the end, then their free will to sin would have to be removed to guarantee that happens. Otherwise they might goof up just before their death.

The third reason that behavior is a poor indicator is found in the Old Testament. We know that there is a difference between God's covenant with Israel and His covenant with the church. However, the way of salvation has been the same throughout time. Where is the test of salvation for the Israelites? It was not the law, for the law did not make them an Israelite. The law was what kept them in fellowship with God, not what saved them. Paul tells us in Galatians 3:10–11 that the law was a curse. The law was to show the Jews that they could not keep fellowship with God through their hard work. They struggled with self-righteousness just as much as we do. The law did not make them Israelites; not keeping the law didn't cause them to stop being Israelites nor did keeping the law prove they were Israelites. However, because they were born an Israelite didn't mean they had salvation either, they had to individually believe in God as exemplified by placing the blood over the doorpost during the Passover (Exodus 12:11). Salvation was by faith alone for the Jews too.

Even if the law saved or was a test of salvation for the Israelites, what about everyone before the law? There were at least 2,000 years of humanity before God gave the law. Adam, Eve, Enoch, Noah, and Abraham had no list of rules. Their salvation was just as much about faith alone as ours is. Also just like us, it was their fellowship with God that was determined by their behavior. We see this in the Garden of Eden when Adam and Eve disobeyed God; they lost fellowship with Him. They did not stop being His children or realize they only thought they were His children but weren't. They still believed in God; if anyone did, they did, for they had literally walked with Him. Throughout the history of mankind, eternal salvation of the spirit has been by faith alone in God. Our good behavior has never caused us to receive that salvation. Our lack of good behavior has never caused anyone to lose that salvation. Nor has our good behavior or lack of it ever proven we have that salvation.

That doesn't mean I believe Christians can do whatever they want and not take God's commandments seriously. I do believe that good or bad behavior is an indicator of whether the salvation of the soul is occurring. It is in the walk in faith that we cooperate with the Holy Spirit in getting to know God better, continuing to believe in Him, and yielding to His change in us. Also our good works/behavior is what will be judged at the judgment seat of Christ, and it is that faithful behavior which will be rewarded while our lack of will be burned up like hay (1 Corinthians 3:12–15). Thus, good behavior is vitally important for living the abundant life in Christ. When we confuse the gift of faith with the walk in faith, we miss out on the joy of the faithful walk with our Lord. Below is how M.R. DeHaan, coeditor of *Our Daily Bread*, puts it:

> There is a vast difference between coming to Jesus for salvation, and coming *after* Jesus for service. Coming to Christ makes one a believer while coming after Christ makes one a disciple. All believers are not disciples. To become a believer one accepts the invitation of the Gospel; to be a disciple one obeys the challenge to a life of dedicated service and separation. Salvation comes through the sacrifice of Christ; discipleship comes only by sacrifice of self and surrender to His call for devoted service. Salvation is free, but discipleship involves paying the price of a separated walk. Salvation cannot be lost because it depends upon God's faithfulness, but discipleship can be lost because it depends upon our faithfulness.[1]

Eternal Life in 1 John

Now let us take a closer look at 1 John. Like I said before, many teach that 1 John is a test of salvation which I would agree with if they were talking about the salvation of the soul. But no, they are thinking of salvation from eternal condemnation—the salvation of the spirit. That belief comes from this passage, "These things I have written to you who believe in the name of the Son of God, that you may know that you have eternal life, and that you may *continue to* believe in the name of the Son of God" (1 John 5:13).

Of course, when people see *eternal life*, they immediately assume salvation from eternal damnation. But as we have already seen, eternal life does not always mean the salvation of the spirit. Here are a few of the problems with the test-of-salvation view. Why would John be writing to people he knows are saved, about them, knowing they are saved? "I have written to you who believe...that you may know you have eternal life." Both the terms *believe in the name of the Son of God* and *have eternal life* are descriptions of a saved person. It would be as if John was saying, "I am writing to you who are saved that you might know you are saved and that you might continue to be saved." That would be like writing a book to people who live in Arizona about how to know they live in Arizona. "If there is a huge hole in the ground (Grand Canyon), if there are cacti growing in your yard, and if it is hotter than the sun, you might live in Arizona." Not sure that book is selling much?

But it would be reasonable to write a book to people who live in Arizona on how to enjoy Arizona. "Since you live in Arizona, you should visit one of the seven natural wonders of the world. You should try growing cacti to show your northern friends and wait until December, the weather is fantastic." Look at what John says at the beginning of his letter, "These things we write to you that your joy may be full" (1:4). I believe John is just repeating what he heard Jesus say so many times to him and the other disciples, that He wanted their joy to be full (John 15:11; 16:24; 17:13). While there is initial joy at the point of our new birth, in the Gospel of John, Jesus was talking to His disciples about the joy of the abundant life in Him, the walk in faith.

Another issue is the word *know* in verse 13. This is a different Greek word than what we talked about in 1 John 2:3 which was *ginosko*—to be aware of, to understand. The Greek word in verse 13 is *eido*, to behold, to consider, to look at. *Eido* is translated *know* 281 times and translated *see* 314 times. It is translated *see* in verse 16, "If anyone *sees* his brother sinning." Both are proper translations, for *eido* has the meaning of both *see* and *know*. The issue is that it has a slightly different meaning than *ginosko.* First John 5:13 could rightly be translated, "that you might see that you have eternal life." Because John knew the meaning of both *ginosko* and *eido* but choose to use *eido* in verse 13, I believe John was pointing the readers back to the beginning of his letter. John wanted them/us to see eternal life and that eternal life is Jesus Himself (verse 2).

> That which was from the beginning, which we have heard, which we have *seen* with our eyes, which we have *looked* upon, and our hands have handled, concerning the Word of life— the life was manifested, and we have *seen*, and bear witness, and declare to you that *eternal life* which was with the Father and was manifested to us— that which we have *seen* and heard we declare to you, that you also may have fellowship with us; and truly our fellowship *is* with the Father and with His Son Jesus Christ. (1 John 1:1–3, emphasis added)

For that reason, John's desire for them to "continue to believe" makes more sense. Continuing to believe is how they would see and experience that abundant life which would fill them with joy. Continuing to believe is a walk-in-faith term. It is the present-tense idea of the soul being saved. First John is packed full of good works, obedience, and love. Throughout his letter, John is telling the readers how their joy will be full when they look upon Jesus. He is showing them how to have fellowship with God and one another. That fellowship comes from confessing sin, knowing Jesus, keeping His commandments, abiding in Christ, and loving the brethren. Also John says in 3:3, "And everyone who has this hope in Him purifies himself, just as He is pure." This verse parallels 1 Peter 1:22, which we looked at, that talked about purifying our souls. These are all aspects of the walk in faith. Therefore, 1 John 5:13 should be understood as Paul saying, "I have written these things to you who believe in the Son of God, that you may see the abundant life which is in Him and that you would continue to believe in the Son of God."

More evidence, remember when we talked about understanding the audience to help us determine if the author is talking about the gift, walk, or reward? If the audience is obviously saved, then the letter is most likely about the walk in faith. Look at some of these references to John's audience.

> I have not written to you because you do not know the truth, but because you know it, and that no lie is of the truth. (1 John 2:21)

> But the anointing which you have received from Him abides in you, and you do not need that anyone teach you. (1 John 2:27)

> I write to you, little children, because your sins are forgiven you for His name's sake. I write to you, fathers, because you have known Him *who is* from the beginning. I write to you, young men, because you have overcome the wicked one. I write to you, little children, because you have known the Father. I have written to you, fathers, because you have known Him *who is* from the beginning. I have written to you, young men, because you are strong, and the word of God abides in you, and you have overcome the wicked one. (1 John 2:12–14)

Along with those verses, ten times John refers to his readers as little children or children of God, another four times as brethren, and four more times as beloved. It seems obvious from verses 2:21 and 2:27 that the audience knew they were saved. They know the truth, and they have been anointed by God, and they don't need anyone to teach them. They have been forgiven of their sins, they overcome the wicked one, and they know the Father. It sure sounds like these people were saved, and they knew it. Why then do so many believe John is telling them how to know they are saved? It is because people have interpreted 1 John 5:13 in the context of more modern times.

It is understandable why others would assume John is telling them how to know if they were saved, for it has been a problem in the modern church for many centuries. After the Roman Emperor Constantine in AD 313 stopped the persecution of Christians, he established the first state church. Although it provided freedom to worship God, it also began the corruption of the purity of the church by allowing the unsaved to become members. In many countries, the church roll of members would become the state's census and a means of taxing the people. Thus, church membership would become mandatory for most everyone, believer and nonbeliever. Which would lead to many false believers and wrong theologies like salvation by works, infant baptism, and unconditional election. By the time of the Reformation, there were more people in churches that were not saved than there were saved. Although the Reformation brought about some change, the same problem continues in many churches today. Not so much from mandatory membership anymore but from wrong ideas of salvation. So it is understandable how some could see 1 John as a test of salvation of the spirit.

Yet at the time of John's writing of 1 John, I doubt that this was the issue. The church was still young; there were no outside pressures to join, no mandatory membership. In fact, the opposite was true; because of the persecution of the church, there would be more pressure not to join. Being a follower of Jesus Christ back then might cost them their livelihood, houses, families and even their lives, and so there probably weren't many fake Christians. In John's time, to be a follower of Jesus Christ took a real commitment. A similar thing is happening today in China with the persecution that is going on there. I doubt there is much of a problem in the Chinese church with people being unsaved yet willing to be identified as a Christian and thrown into prison or even killed. Thus, I don't believe not knowing if someone was saved or not was a big problem for John and his fellow believers.

Even yet, another clue that John is talking about the walk in faith is how he used *eternal life* elsewhere in this letter.

"Whoever hates his brother is a murderer, and you know that no murderer has eternal life abiding in him" (1 John 3:15).

As we have seen before, eternal life does not always mean the salvation of the spirit. Now I am pretty sure that John is not saying that no murderer will go to heaven. For that would mean none among Moses, David, nor Paul will be in heaven. It would mean that likely none of us are going to heaven, for who hasn't hated someone else in their heart.

"You have heard that it was said to those of old, '*You shall not murder*,' and whoever murders will be in danger of the judgment.' But I say to you that whoever is angry with his brother without a cause shall be in danger of the judgment" (Matthew 5:21–22).

But it does make sense that a murderer would not be experiencing the abundant life in Christ. Therefore, if we harbored hatred toward the brethren rather than love, we would be out of fellowship with God and one another. Also in 1 John 2:25, John uses eternal life, and here, it is used in the context of abiding in Jesus Christ. If we continue to abide in Christ, we will experience the joyful life. Abiding is an act of sanctification and part of the salvation of the soul.

Full Joy in Fellowship

When we are in fellowship with God and one another, we will experience the full joy of the Christian life. I am not sure why anyone would think this letter is about a test of salvation of the spirit. Having fellowship with my wife does not prove we are married—the marriage license does. Sometimes our fellowship is sporadic, and we don't treat each other nicely. Also sometimes the busyness of life or business trips keep us from each other. Neither of those determines whether we are married, but they do affect the joy of our relationship.

Therefore, some have said that 1 John is not a test of salvation but a test of fellowship which would be a lot closer. However, I am not too sure as there is not much joy in tests (smile). I prefer to see it more like a how-to book. It is a letter to the believers on how to experience the full joy of the eternal life which is Jesus Christ. As a loving father, which am I more likely to give my children, a test of whether they love me or the means to love me. I know as a human father I was constantly correcting my children and showing them how to remain in good fellowship with their mother and me. Also it would be just as poor a test of fellowship as it is a test of salvation, for it would be just as subjective. A believer in fellowship with God should act this way; but again, behavior can be faked. Unsaved people can still have good behavior, and good works are sporadic. I prefer to see 1 John as *providing* fellowship and joy, rather than *proving* fellowship.

The proof of both salvation and fellowship lies in our hearts for we know if we believe in God and we know how well we are following Him. But even more important, the ultimate proof lies with God Himself—be sure God is not mocked or fooled. He knows who truly believes in Him and who doesn't. There will not be a single person in heaven who fooled God and shouldn't be there. Nor will there be a single believer not in heaven who should have been there. Also when our faithfulness is tested by fire, there will not be a single test result that is inaccurate. While we may fake our Christianity among one another, God still knows the truth.

We will spend the rest of this chapter looking at how we might have full joy in eternal life (Jesus Christ). This list will sound a lot like the list above. But as I said before, the list is not necessarily wrong, for it comes right from the Scriptures. The difference being these instructions on how to have joy in our Christian lives. Thus, the list will be of much more use to us than as a list of character qualities we would never be able to meet to prove we are saved. But first, let me remind you that this list is not about us trying hard to accomplish the list in our own strength. The change formula still applies. John is showing us that the result of knowing God intimately is that we will keep His commandments, sin less often, love our brothers and sisters in Christ, and abide in Jesus. All of which will bring the joy of fellowship with God and one another.

Fellowship is one of God's greatest gifts; the believer delights to be in intimate relationship with fellow Christians. At the same time, he longs to enter into an increasingly intimate relationship with the Father and the Savior. We were created with the need for fellowship, and we are restless and insecure until this becomes our living experience.[2]

A relationship brings with it certain rights and privileges but not necessarily peace, joy, love, and happiness. These internal riches are the "Fruit of Fellowship," my suggested theme for 1 John. If you are a believer in Jesus Christ, you have been born into God's family. He is your heavenly Father. That is a permanent, eternal relationship. But to enjoy that relationship, you need His fellowship. The beautiful thing about fellowship with our heavenly Father is that it is available to anyone who believes in His Son.[3]

Walking in the Light: 1:5–7

Of course, walking in the light goes right along with the walk in faith. It is another way of saying the same thing. Nothing complicated here, walking is walking. It is the idea of taking a walk with someone. You go in the same direction, and it is a good time to have a conversation. Walking in the light corresponds to God's love for us and His desire to have an intimate relationship with us. My wife and I love to take walks together especially on vacation and if there are some trees. We did this before we were married and have continued throughout our marriage. I look forward to when I can walk with Jesus in the forests of the kingdom. That should take a few billion years; then we can walk back.

Jesus wants to have that walk with all of us. Not just in the kingdom but starting here on earth, just as He did from the very beginning with Adam and Eve when He walked with them in the garden, in the cool of the day (Genesis 3:8). He wants those times of fellowship so that we can talk unlike running together which means we are too winded to talk. Running with Jesus is what we are doing now in our busy lives; we are so winded we only get in a couple of words. Walking together therefore represents time and talk from the Ts of relationship building.

Walking in the light represents guidance, for it is hard to see in the dark. Jesus wants us to walk close enough to His light that the path is clear. As a kid, we used to take night hikes at summer camp. It was important to stay in the light of the flashlight for if we got out of the light, it was easy to stumble and fall. I know, I have the scars to prove it just like I have scars in my soul from walking outside of Jesus's light.

Therefore, to experience joy in our Christian lives, we must choose to believe that Jesus wants to walk with us, that He enjoys that fellowship, and wants to guide our lives so we will not stumble. We must choose to believe that His path is the only correct one and that it is out of love that He wishes us to walk this narrow way. When we believe, then we will walk in the light of Jesus Christ, and our desire to follow our path will diminish.

Confessing Sin: 1:8–2:2

We will spend a good amount of time here on confessing sin, for sin is at the root of all the issues which steal away our joy in Christ. Sin, after the salvation of our spirit, will not cause us to lose that salvation but that sin will cause us to lose our fellowship with God. There is good news though, for "He is faithful and just to forgive us our sins and to cleanse us from all unrighteousness" (1 John 1:9). The good news is that when we do sin, we can almost instantaneously restore the fellowship with God through confession.

This is a glorious example of God's grace! If we sin in second number one but confess it in second number two, in second number three, God will forgive us and restore all fellowship. Now here comes the grace part that if in second number four, we do the same sin again yet confess it in second number five, God will again forgive us in second number six. Glory!

That grace makes us wonder, though—wouldn't we take advantage of it? Wouldn't we sin more? Well, Paul dealt with this very question in his letter to the Romans.

"What shall we say then? Shall we continue in sin that grace may abound? Certainly not! How shall we who died to sin live any longer in it?" (Romans 6:1–2).

We will talk later about willful sin and its dangers but first, let us concentrate on the grace of God. Sure we would be tempted to sin more but not if we fully understand God. Jesus is so passionate about having free-flowing fellowship with us that He will set aside, what we might call, His right to retribution for our sins and forgive us immediately. He loves us so much and wishes our broken fellowship to immediately be restored that He is willing to give us this undeserved gift of grace. When we understand the depth of this love, we no longer wish to take advantage of it. If I could ever find another human to love me as much as Jesus did, I would not chance breaking that relationship by sinning against him.

The best definition of confession is "to agree with," that means we are to agree with God about our sin. Unfortunately we tend to think that means just to agree that what we did is a sin. Our thoughts go something like, *Yep, did that sin again, sorry, God, I will work harder at giving it up*. While we technically did confess it as a sin, John is talking about something deeper. Confessing your sin to God means to agree fully—actions, thoughts, and feeling—with God. Not to just agree it was a sin but to think the same as God about that sin, to feel the same, and do the same as God about that sin. To see the sin as God does. It means to understand the heart of God and be fully disgusted by our sin.

I have done a lot of counseling for couples dealing with pornography. It truly is the bane of our society today. One of the problems is that men do not fully understand how their casual approach to viewing pornography tears at their wife's heart and spirit. For a man, looking at pornography is just like any other activity—eating, sleeping, going to work; it has very little to do with emotional connections. A man can look at pornography and still feel he loves his wife. Of course, that is ridiculous. It is not real love, and there is no excuse for doing it. What he doesn't understand is how much of a betrayal it to his wife's heart. To her, it is a rejection of her very being; it is just as bad as if her husband had physically cheated on her. She very much feels he has cheated. If a man were to fully understand the damage he does to his wife, there would be many who would cease looking at pornography.

That is what John was getting at when he talked about us confessing our sins. It is so much more than just agreeing that it was a sin. It is knowing God so well that we are truly grieved that we have hurt Him with our sin. Therefore, we will experience joy in our walk with Jesus when we completely deal with sin. This comes from getting to know how much Jesus hates sin and recognizing that He sacrificed His own life for our forgiveness. The writer of Hebrews had this to say about continuing to take sin lightly:

> For if we sin willfully after we have received the knowledge of the truth, there no longer remains a sacrifice for sins, but a certain fearful expectation of judgment, and fiery indignation which will devour the adversaries. Anyone who has rejected Moses' law dies without mercy on the testimony of two or three witnesses. Of how much worse punishment, do you suppose, will he be thought worthy who has trampled the Son of God underfoot, counted the blood of the covenant by which he was sanctified a common thing, and insulted the Spirit of grace? For we know Him who said, *"Vengeance is Mine, I will repay,"* says the Lord. And again, *"The Lord will judge His people."* It is a fearful thing to fall into the hands of the living God. (Hebrews 10:26–31)

As verse 29 is saying, when we willfully sin and don't recognize/confess it as it is, it is like spitting on Jesus Christ as He hung on the cross, dying to forgive us of that sin. That is what it means to count His sacrifice a common thing. So while God is full of grace, long-suffering, and love, we are not to insult the Spirit of grace by dealing with sin lightly. "It is a fearful thing to fall into the hands of the living God" (verse 31). That warning is in the context of sinning willfully.

Isn't all sin willful, we might ask? Yes, there is a sense in which we choose to do all our sins. The difference is that there are sins of immaturity, and then there are willful sins. It was like when my children were young; they would all play in the front yard with the neighborhood kids. I would sit on the front porch and keep an eye on them. We lived in a quiet neighborhood with very little traffic. The kids still had a rule of not running out into the street without first checking for cars. Now occasionally in the heat of the battle, a ball would roll out onto the street, and one of my kids would forget to stop and look for cars. Then I would correct them and remind them of the rule. Although I might yell a little, my correction wasn't too harsh as I knew they were young and learning.

My kids' forgetting the rules is what I would call a sin of immaturity. However, if in the same scenario, one of my kids, while running after a ball, stopped at the street, turned around, looked at me, and stuck out his tongue before running into the street—now that would be a willful sin, a sin of rebellion, and that little one would feel the full wrath of Dad. This is what the writer of Hebrews is warning us believers about. If we stick out our tongue at the sacrifice His Son made for our sin, we too will feel the wrath of God.

This passage in Hebrews is a perfect example of what we have been talking about when it comes to those warning passages for believers. Because of the terms, *judgment*, *fiery indignation*, and *no longer remains a sacrifice*, many Christians believe these verses can't possibly be talking about believers. Well, let us use the principles we have learned so far about the gift, walk, and reward. The first thing we notice is in verse 26, the author includes himself in the warning "if *we* sin willfully after *we* have received the knowledge of the truth" (emphasis added). Hence, these passages cannot be addressed to someone who has lost their salvation nor someone who thinks they are saved but isn't.

Also in verse 29, the author says, "Counted the blood of the covenant by which he was sanctified a common thing." The unsaved are not sanctified and cannot call the blood they were saved by a common thing. Only saved people could do this. Then in verse 30, the author quotes Deuteronomy 32:35, saying, "The Lord will judge

His people." That should be clear that the Holy Spirit here is warning us to take our sin seriously. Those who believe good works prove whether a person is saved will be critical of those of us who don't. They will accuse us of teaching that Christians can do whatever they want and not deal seriously with their sin, but I point to these verses in Hebrews 10. That is not true. The Bible clearly warns us against taking a lackadaisical attitude toward our sins. The difference is that our sin affects our fellowship, not our salvation.

Then what does the Holy Spirit mean about these extreme consequences of no repentance and fiery indignation? We need to ask ourselves, is there any time when God didn't allow a sacrifice for repentance? We have a clue from chapters 3 and 4 of Hebrews. Here the author has been warning his audience not to be like Israel in the wilderness after their escape from Egypt.

> While it is said: *"Today, if you will hear His voice, do not harden your hearts as in the rebellion."* For who, having heard, rebelled? Indeed, *was it* not all who came out of Egypt, *led* by Moses? Now with whom was He angry forty years? *Was it* not with those who sinned, whose corpses fell in the wilderness? And to whom did He swear that they would not enter His rest, but to those who did not obey? So we see that they could not enter in because of unbelief." (Hebrews 3:15–19)

> Let us therefore be diligent to enter that rest, lest anyone fall according to the same example of disobedience. (Hebrews 4:11)

We know from 1 Corinthians 10 that we looked at before, that while all the Israelites drank of the Rock which was Christ (verse 4), God was not pleased with most of them (verse 5). God gave us this story as our example that we too might not fall away (verses 6, 11–12). The story is when the Israelites came to Kadesh Barnea and were faced with entering God's Promised Land. Entering the

Promised Land is not a picture of salvation but sanctification, entering the abundant life of sweet fellowship with God. For after eventually entering the land, there were still strongholds of sin that they would need to destroy; if it were a picture of entering heaven, it wouldn't still have sin. However, after the spies reported back that there were giants in the land, the Israelites responded this way:

> So all the congregation lifted up their voices and cried, and the people wept that night. And all the children of Israel complained against Moses and Aaron, and the whole congregation said to them, "If only we had died in the land of Egypt! Or if only we had died in this wilderness! Why has the Lord brought us to this land to fall by the sword, that our wives and children should become victims? Would it not be better for us to return to Egypt?" So they said to one another, "Let us select a leader and return to Egypt." (Numbers 14:1–4)

The people were afraid to trust in God and enter the Promised Land. They wanted to return to their old lives in Egypt; they wanted to return to the slavery of sin. The picture the Holy Spirit is painting for us in 1 Corinthians and Hebrews is that we are like these Israelites, and we too are faced with a decision. We can either trust the Lord and enter the abundant life of Jesus Christ or out of fear that it will be too hard and dangerous, we can choose to return to the slavery of sin and face the wrath of God. Here is God's response to the Israelites' decision:

> Then the Lord said to Moses: "How long will these people reject Me? And how long will they not believe Me, with all the signs which I have performed among them? I will strike them with the pestilence and disinherit them, and I

> will make of you a nation greater and mightier than they." (Numbers 14:11–12)

God had had enough of their disobedience, and He was ready to destroy them all. But Moses and Aaron pleaded with God not to, and God repents, though there will still be consequences for their lack of trust. The Israelites are sentenced to wander the wilderness for forty years before returning to the Promised Land. Also everyone over twenty years old will die in the wilderness and never see the Promised Land. When the people heard this, they were deeply saddened and repent, seeking God's forgiveness. They even tried to enter the promised land on their own.

> Then Moses told these words to all the children of Israel, and the people mourned greatly. And they rose early in the morning and went up to the top of the mountain, saying, "Here we are, and we will go up to the place which the Lord has promised, for we have sinned!" And Moses said, "Now why do you transgress the command of the Lord? For this will not succeed. Do not go up, lest you be defeated by your enemies, for the Lord *is* not among you. For the Amalekites and the Canaanites *are* there before you, and you shall fall by the sword; because you have turned away from the Lord, the Lord will not be with you." But they presumed to go up to the mountaintop; nevertheless, neither the ark of the covenant of the Lord nor Moses departed from the camp. Then the Amalekites and the Canaanites who dwelt in that mountain came down and attacked them, and drove them back as far as Hormah. (Numbers 14:39–45)

Then some forty plus years later after Joshua had led the survivors into the Promised land, he gives the children of God a similar warning. In Joshua 24, just before his death, he reminds the people of all the things the Lord has done for them. This is where Joshua says those words most of us have posted somewhere in their home, "As for me and my house we will serve the Lord" (Joshua 24:15). He then goes on to remind the people that there is no repentance for sins of rebellion.

> But Joshua said to the people, "You cannot serve the Lord, for He *is* a holy God. He *is* a jealous God; *He will not forgive your transgressions nor your sins*. If you forsake the Lord and serve foreign gods, then He will turn and do you harm and consume you, after He has done you good." And the people said to Joshua, "No, but we will serve the Lord!" (Joshua 24:19–21, emphasis added)

Yes, there was a time when there was no sacrifice for repentance. The Israelites had overrun the longsuffering of God and even though they were sorry, God did not change His mind about their consequences. There was no sacrifice the Israelites could make for the repentance of their judgment. This is the warning that Hebrews 10 is trying to pass on to us. While God is very patient and longsuffering with our sins of immaturity, He is not as merciful with our sins of rebellion.

What about the judgment and fiery indignation for us? I believe that these warnings refer to the test of fire at the judgment seat of Christ in 1 Corinthians 3 which is in the same letter of the example we have been looking at in 1 Corinthians 10. This is curiously parallel to Hebrews. While we don't know for sure who wrote Hebrews, with all the parallels to Paul's writings, if it wasn't Paul himself, it was someone greatly influenced by Paul.

> Now if anyone builds on this foundation *with* gold, silver, precious stones, wood, hay, straw, each one's work will become clear; for the Day will declare it, because it will be revealed by

> fire; and the fire will test each one's work, of what sort it is. If anyone's work which he has built on *it* endures, he will receive a reward. If anyone's work is burned, he will suffer loss; but he himself will be saved, yet so as through fire. (1 Corinthians 3:12–15)

Also I don't think that it was mere coincidence that right before 1 Corinthians 10, Paul himself worried that he would be disqualified in his Christian race of life. "But I discipline my body and bring it into subjection, lest, when I have preached to others, I myself should become disqualified" (1 Corinthians 9:27). This sounds a lot like Hebrews 10:26 when the author includes himself in the warning of willful sin. Paul knew that any Christian, including himself, could fall away from Christ and return to the slavery of sin. In 1 Timothy 1:15, Paul said he was the chief of sinners. This was near the end of his life, and he was talking in the present tense, not the past. This did not mean they would lose their salvation or that they never had it; it means that the disobedient child of God is in danger of the chastisement of God (Hebrews 12).

Now lest anyone is worried about whether they have such a serious sin in their lives. First if we are worried about such a sin, it is probably not in our lives, for those who are in open rebellion usually are not concerned about it. Like most of the Pharisees in Jesus's time who were so blinded by their pride, they could not see Jesus. Therefore, if our hearts are still tender unto the Lord and ache because of our sin, repentance is still available.

All this to say if we want our joy to be full in Jesus, we need to confess our sin truly and flee from it. This all corresponds with believing that Jesus is holy and cannot be in the presence of sin, and our sin takes us out of fellowship. It also reflects on the love of God in that He is not a tyrant only wanting us to keep the rules. No, for just like a human father, He knows that these rules keep us from hurting ourselves. Just like my son running onto the street, he wants to keep having fun. But I know if he doesn't obey me, he may be killed. Finally confession reflects on God's desire for fellowship when

His grace will so quickly forgive our sins of immaturity. These are the character qualities of God we must choose to believe if He is going to change our hearts towards confession.

Knowing Him: 2:3–5, 5:20

We have already talked about this a lot so just some reminders. This path to joy corresponds with Jesus's desire to have a relationship with us. We know it is meant to be an intimate relationship because we are called to be the bride of Christ for all eternity. When my wife fell in love with me, no one had to tell her she needed to deepen that relationship. It was the simple byproduct of love.

Not sinning: 3:4–10, 5:18

These have been some of the hardest passages to understand especially when people try to tie not sinning with salvation of the spirit. Those who believe 1 John is a test of salvation point to these verses as proof that if a person continues in sin, then he is not a Christian. As we saw previously, not sinning is very subjective and a poor indicator of salvation of the spirit. However, for the salvation of the soul, it is hugely important. How we deal with sin in our lives does affect our joy in the Lord.

Another reason sinning is a poor indicator of salvation of the spirit is that we tend to concentrate on the *big* sins. We think we are doing pretty good because we don't have those big sins that the unbelievers do like murder, adultery, drunkenness, drug abuse, divorce, homosexuality, etc. Yet we still struggle with sins such as anger, pride, discontentment, lust, complaining, gossip, worry, lying, bitterness, etc. For a good study on this, see Jerry Bridges' book *Acceptable Sins.* It is a common fault of humanity that when we start thinking we are doing pretty good, our pride rolls back in, and we start judging others in our self-righteousness. Therefore, while we might be doing pretty good on the big sins, we believers still struggle with sin.

There isn't such a thing as *big* sins. The Bible tells us that when we transgress against one of God's commandments, we are guilty of all (James 2:10). Yes, there can be bigger consequences for some sins over others. But all sin, large or small, keep us from fellowship with God. Then Jesus made it even tougher in His Sermon on the Mount where He explained the difference between the spirit of the law and the letter of the law.

> You have heard that it was said to those of old, *"You shall not murder,* and whoever murders will be in danger of the judgment." But I say to you that whoever is angry with his brother without a cause shall be in danger of the judgment. And whoever says to his brother, "Raca!" shall be in danger of the council. But whoever says, "You fool!" shall be in danger of hell fire. Therefore if you bring your gift to the altar, and there remember that your brother has something against you, leave your gift there before the altar, and go your way. First be reconciled to your brother, and then come and offer your gift. (Matthew 5:21–24)

> You have heard that it was said to those of old, *"You shall not commit adultery."* But I say to you that whoever looks at a woman to lust for her has already committed adultery with her in his heart. (Matthew 5:27–28)

Which one of us has not lusted after another in our heart or looked at another with hatred? By that standard, we are all adulterers and murderers. By that standard, we are likely guilty of breaking all Ten Commandments. The Bible is packed full of sinning believers; there is example after example of God's disobedient children. That is because God's story is about His grace and mercy toward His disobedient children and not about how perfect His kids can be in their strength. But like we have already talked about, that doesn't mean we are to take sin lightly. It's just that our everyday sins were never about salvation of the spirit, but they are a huge part of our salvation of the soul. Consequently they are a large part of our joy too.

Therefore, because we cannot get away from sinning believers, some have watered down the thought of a believer never sinning by saying what John means is the believer doesn't practice unrighteousness. For just like in sports or playing an instrument, what you practice, you get better at. So John is saying the true believer practices righteousness and no longer practices unrighteousness. Those who are doing better with sin over time are the ones that are saved. It is kind of like a sales chart—it may have a dip or two but if it is a continuous upward trend, they are good. The problem with this view is that how do we measure practicing? How many times can I do a sin before I am practicing unrighteousness? How much of practicing righteousness is enough? How much unrighteousness is too much? Again it sounds like hoping that our good outweighs our bad. Also while the chart may be going upward with not doing those big sins, it may be going downward with those little sins of complaining and self-righteousness.

What then is John talking about when he says we will no longer sin? The answer is in 1 John 3:6.

"Whoever abides in Him does not sin. Whoever sins has neither seen Him nor known Him" (1 John 3:6).

John is saying that when we abide in Jesus, we will not sin. However, when we are not abiding in Jesus, we will sin. John is not saying that believers will never sin again. He is saying that if we want full joy in Christ, we must remain abiding in Jesus. For when we are abiding in Him, we will not sin. Therefore, when we do sin, it is because we are no longer abiding in Him. The Greek word *meno* which is translated *abide* simply means to take up residence or to live somewhere. We are to live constantly in the presence of God. His life is to be our life. His character is to be our character. This again suggests the marriage relationship. When a couple gets married, they move in together. They then *abide* with one another for the rest of their lives. If I am not living with my wife, of course, our fellowship is going to be hindered.

Abiding in Jesus is optional for the believer. He must choose to abide in Christ.

"He who says he abides in Him *ought* himself also to walk just as He walked" (1 John 2:6, emphasis added).

"He who loves his brother abides in the light, and there is no cause for stumbling in him. *But* he who hates his brother is in darkness and walks in darkness, and does not know where he is going, because the darkness has blinded his eyes" (1 John 2:10–11, emphasis added).

"Therefore let that abide in you which you heard from the beginning. *If* what you heard from the beginning abides in you, you also will abide in the Son and in the Father" (1 John 2:24, emphasis added).

"No one has seen God at any time. *If* we love one another, God abides in us, and His love has been perfected in us" (1 John 4:12, emphasis added).

John is pointing back to his time with Jesus when he wrote one of the most important verses in the Bible. "And the Word became flesh and dwelt among us, and we beheld His glory, the glory as of the only begotten of the Father, full of grace and truth" (John 1:14). The world translated *dwelt (skenoo)* means to reside, to dwell, to tent or encamp, to tabernacle. John's Jewish audience would have immediately thought of God in the desert coming down and dwelling in the holy of holies of the temple. However, in those times, only the priest could enter the presences of God. There was a large curtain separating man from God but when Jesus died on the cross, that curtain was torn in two. Now we who believe can abide with Jesus.

Unfortunately we can choose whether to stay in the holy of holies and abide with Christ. When we sin, we are choosing to walk out of the holy presence of Jesus and follow our own path. When we sin, we are no longer abiding in Christ, we have left His dwelling place and returned to living in the world. But yes! When we abide with Jesus Christ, we do not sin.

Therefore, as we see that Jesus wants to abide with us and wants us to abide with Him and we believe that, then God will draw our hearts away from sin. For just like my relationship with my wife, if

I sin against her, our abiding will be a struggle. But when I abide with her in love, I tend not to sin against her. Of course, when I am not sinning against her, there is great joy in the relationship—happy wife, happy life. The word translated *dwell* back in John 1:14 also means to occupy as a mansion. Jesus has gone to prepare a place, a mansion (John 14:2) that we may abide with Him for all eternity.

Finally what about 1 John 3:10? "In this the children of God and the children of the devil are manifest; whoever does not practice righteousness is not of God, nor is he who does not love his brother." This sure sounds like John is talking about the saved and unsaved. Except we know that loving your brother and practicing righteousness are not the means of salvation. So John must be talking about something else. I believe John remembers back to what he heard Jesus say to Peter. "Get behind Me, Satan! You are an offense to Me, for you are not mindful of the things of God, but the things of men" (Matthew 16:23). While we don't know how much time has passed but just a few verses before this, Peter had proclaimed that Jesus was "the Christ, the Son of the living God" (verse 16). On this proclamation, the church would be built. So obviously in verse 23, Jesus is not saying Peter is Satan or that he wasn't saved.

What I believe Jesus and John are saying is, "Stop acting like Satan, you are thinking just like him." There are only two ways a human can act—like Jesus or like the devil. Therefore, when we are sinning, we are no longer acting like our Savior but acting like the devil. The same as what I would say to my kids when they were younger and misbehaving, "Stop acting like Scott Farcus down the street! You are a Tjepkema. Start acting like one."

We have come to the end of the chapter; I leave the rest to you to explore. Below is a general list of what is left. Also in chapter 10, I have listed for you some good commentaries on 1 John. Read through the passages for each and ask yourself, "What must I believe about God to experience joy from these instructions?" Remember, the joy doesn't come from trying hard to keep the commandment. The joy comes when you see Christ in these passages, understand who He is, and believe in it. Then God will make the change in your heart that makes keeping these commandments quite easy.

"And this is His commandment: that we should believe on the name of His Son Jesus Christ and love one another, as He gave us commandment" (1 John 3:23).

"For this is the love of God, that we keep His commandments. And His commandments are not burdensome" (1 John 5:3).

Additional

Keeping His Commandments: 2:3–4; 3:22–23; 4:21–5:3
Perfected Love: 2:4; 4:17–19
Abiding in Him: 2:6, 24–29; 3:17; 24; 4:13–16
Loving the Brethren: 2:7–11; 3:11–18; 4:7–12; 20–21; 5:16–17
Not Loving the World: 2:15–17; 5:4–5; 5:19
Avoiding False Teachers: 2:18–23; 4:1–6
Asking God: 5:14–15
Keeping from Idols: 5:21

---

1. M.R. DeHaan, 117.
2. J. Dwight Pentecost, The Joy of Fellowship: A Study of First John (Grand Rapids: Kregel Publications, 1977), 7.
3. David R. Anderson, Maximum Joy: First John—Relationship or Fellowship? (The Woodlands, Texas: Grace Theology Press, 2013), 22.

CHAPTER 9

God's Motivation for Us

The fear of the Lord is the beginning of wisdom,
And the knowledge of the Holy One is
understanding.
—Proverbs 9:10

What motivates you? What turns your crank? What pushes your buttons? What are you passionate about? They say that without passion in life, humans lose hope, so much so that it often leads to suicide. For some, what we are passionate about is the same as our purpose in life. But for most, what they are passionate about is usually what they like to spend their spare time doing. Tell me where you spend your extra money and time and I can probably tell what your passions are. Also I can tell what your passion is by what you talk about the most.

I have one friend who loves sports. When we go out to lunch, he pretty much always talks about sports. He loves them all and when he has spare time, he is either going to see a game or playing one himself. I have another friend who loves sports too, but he also loves board games. He especially likes those games that take a lot of strategy and planning. He has a huge collection of games, and he will stay up late, even into the next morning, playing them. Another friend loves history especially war history, and he knows a lot about old and new firearms. Another one of my friends also loves firearms, but he loves being out in nature too; his interest is survival skills. He probably knows a dozen ways to start a fire. All these guys love to talk about their hobbies, and that is why they are my friends because those are some of the things I love to do and talk about too although maybe not as much as they do.

My passion is trees. I love walking in the forest and looking at the trees. This fall, my wife and I celebrated our thirtieth wedding anniversary. We spent a week walking around the Redwoods in northern California. Also I have a woodworking shop in our garage. I could spend every day out there; I love the smells of the different woods. Olive wood smells like green olives, tulipwood smells like tulips but unfortunately, zebrawood smells like zebras. God is amazing! The other thing I love about trees and wood is seeing God's creativity in His creation, so many different densities, colors, and smells.

Trees play an important part in the Bible too. There is the Tree of Life which we will spend all eternity eating from (Revelation 2:7; 22:14). Wisdom is also called a tree of life (Proverbs 3:18). We are to be like a tree (Psalms 1:3; 92:12; Proverbs 11:30; Jeremiah 17:8). King David, when he was being chased around the desert by Saul, compared himself to a "green olive tree in the house of God" (Psalms 52:8). Trees will rejoice and praise God (Psalms 96:12; Isaiah 55:12). Of course, our Savior died on a tree (Galatians 3:13) that we might be reconciled to God and be able to spend eternity walking in the trees with Him.

One of the categories in my biography of God is "My God Loves Trees." It is a list of all the verses talking about trees. I have drawn a little symbol of a tree by all those verses in my Bible. The study of the trees of the Bible is very interesting; there are a few good books available on the subject. Did you know there is no such thing as gopher wood, the wood supposedly used to build Noah's Ark? Scientists have not been able to identify any such wood. True it was before the flood and possibly could no longer exist. But more likely the word translated *gopher* in Genesis 6:14 is a scribal error as there is only a one-letter difference between the Hebrew word for gopher (*goper*) and pitch (*koper*) which is used at the end of the verse. It is more likely, and would make more sense, that God told Noah to make the ark out of pitched (*koper)* wood because it would keep the ark waterproof. Besides who would name a tree gopher wood? Gophers don't have anything to do with trees.

Another fun fact is that there are many trees wrongly identified in our English versions of the Bible. None of the translators of the King James Version had ever been to Israel or the surrounding areas. Therefore, when they came to translate the different trees in the Scriptures, sometimes they were unfamiliar with the Hebrew or Greek word for a species. Thus, they used the tree names they knew about in England and Europe. I hope this doesn't destroy anyone's childhood, but Zacchaeus probably didn't climb up into a sycamore tree. Sycamore is a European tree and not native to the Middle East. Neither is the apple tree, at least in Bible times; the Bible was more likely describing an apricot tree.

But I digress, I could go on for an entire book about how God is glorified through his creation of trees (maybe my next book?). I could tell you about how lodgepole pine are trying to take over the world by creating their own forest fires to destroy their enemies. Or how the largest living organism in the world is an aspen tree in Utah. Or I could tell you about how one of the oldest trees on the earth, the redwoods, maybe even older than their tree rings indicate. For after they fall over, they often send up new shoots that are a continuation of the original tree.

Motivating God's Children

All that because our passions are often what motivates us to get out of bed each day. God uses motivators to encourage us to grow in maturity, become Christ-like, and have an intimate relationship with Him. Having a passion for something or someone is not wrong. God created us with that character quality, it reflects His image, for He is passionate about a relationship with us. He gave us our feelings of passion that they may be directed toward Him. He has created within all humanity a passion for knowing and understanding God, but not everyone yields to that passion. He is not concerned if we have other passions, for He wishes us to enjoy life; the problem is when He is not our first passion. When we yield to our selfish nature, we neglect that desire to know God; therefore, God uses multiple motivators to draw us to Him. For God is singular in purpose; He wants our love which then leads to glorifying, worshiping, obeying, and serving Him.

For those of you with children, how do you motivate them? We have four different children and five different personalities (smile). What we learned was what motivates one child doesn't necessarily motivate another. To be a good parent, we need to understand our children's differences to love and discipline them. Like a good parent, God uses multiple ways to motivate us, too. There are three major motivators found in Scripture, and they seem to follow right along with the trichotomy of faith we have been talking about. The three motivators the Scriptures refer to the most are the fear of God, the love of God, and the rewards of God. The fear of God is what most often motivates people to the gift by faith. The love of God most often motivates the walk in faith. Then the rewards of God are what usually motivates the reward of faith. While there are definite overlaps of the three and one doesn't leave after the other is experienced, they tend to fall out that way. That means that while we might move from the fear of God to the love of God, we should still fear God.

Fear of God

We start with the fear of God for that is where God starts. Proverbs says that the "fear of the Lord is the beginning of knowledge" (Proverbs 1:7). The first consequence of sin was fear and shame when Adam and Eve hid from the Lord. As parents, our initial motivation concerning instruction of our children is fear—a fear of punishment. Of course, we wish our children would be motivated to clean their room by their love for us. Just as God wishes His children would be motivated by love. But because of our immaturity, fear of punishment is more often needed. Most people come to Jesus for salvation because of the fear of eternal punishment for their sins. Some evangelists say, "You can't get people saved if you don't first get them lost." Well, I am not so sure about that; I believe Jesus is just as welcoming of someone who wants to love Him. God will use whatever it takes to draw the lost to Him, and fear is a powerful motivator.

I am afraid that some pastors water down the idea of the fear of God. They often say things like, "Fearing God doesn't mean we are to fear God is out to get us but that we should treat Him with awe and respect." I think these pastors fear a contradiction to their teaching of a loving God, for they seem to contradict one another. We will see that this is not true; fear and love can live together. Also if we look up *awe* in the dictionary, it usually says something like to have fear and awe. It ends up being kind of circular reasoning. To fear is to have awe; to awe is to have fear. I believe God intended both to be true. We are to have awe, respect, and reverence for our God while also fearing Him in its fullest meaning. I don't think fear and love contradict; I want my children to have a healthy fear of their old dad along with knowing I love them. I know a healthy fear of my dad kept me from doing some stupid stuff when I was younger. "No, I am not going to drive 110 mph down the freeway. My dad would kill me if he ever found out."

I have a section in my biography of God on the wrath of God. There are hundreds of verses on God's wrath, and they are not all in the Old Testament. It is hard to read these and not believe that God intends our fear of Him to be anything less than real fear.

> For after seven more days I will cause it to rain on the earth forty days and forty nights, and I will destroy from the face of the earth all living things that I have made. (Genesis 7:4)

> I *am* the Lord your God, who brought you out of the land of Egypt, that *you* should not be their slaves; I have broken the bands of your yoke and made you walk upright. But if you do not obey Me, and do not observe all these commandments, and if you despise My statutes, or if your soul abhors My judgments, so that you do not perform all My commandments, *but* break My

covenant, I also will do this to you: I will even appoint terror over you, wasting disease and fever which shall consume the eyes and cause sorrow of heart. And you shall sow your seed in vain, for your enemies shall eat it. I will set My face against you, and you shall be defeated by your enemies. Those who hate you shall reign over you, and you shall flee when no one pursues you. And after all this, if you do not obey Me, then I will punish you seven times more for your sins. I will break the pride of your power; I will make your heavens like iron and your earth like bronze. (Leviticus 26:13–19)

God *is* a just judge, And God is angry *with the wicked* every day. If he does not turn back, He will sharpen His sword; He bends His bow and makes it ready. He also prepares for Himself instruments of death; He makes His arrows into fiery shafts. (Psalms 7:11–13)

Your hand will find all Your enemies; Your right hand will find those who hate You. You shall make them as a fiery oven in the time of Your anger; The Lord shall swallow them up in His wrath, And the fire shall devour them. (Psalms 21:8–9)

Because you disdained all my counsel, and would have none of my rebuke, I also will laugh at your calamity; I will mock when your terror comes, When your terror comes like a storm, and your destruction comes like a whirlwind, when distress and anguish come upon you. (Proverbs 1:25–27)

The Son of Man will send out His angels, and they will gather out of His kingdom all things that offend, and those who practice lawlessness, and will cast them into the furnace of fire. There will be wailing and gnashing of teeth. Then the righteous will shine forth as the sun in the kingdom of their Father. He who has ears to hear, let him hear! (Matthew 13:41–43)

Or do you despise the riches of His goodness, forbearance, and longsuffering, not knowing that the goodness of God leads you to repentance? But in accordance with your hardness and your impenitent heart you are treasuring up for yourself wrath in the day of wrath and revelation of the righteous judgment of God, who *"will render to each one according to his deeds":* eternal life to those who by patient continuance in doing good seek for glory, honor, and immortality; but to those who are self-seeking and do not obey the truth, but obey unrighteousness--indignation and wrath, tribulation and anguish, on every soul of man who does evil, of the Jew first and also of the Greek. (Romans 2:4–9)

Knowing, therefore, the terror of the Lord, we persuade men; but we are well known to God, and I also trust are well known in your consciences. (2 Corinthians 5:11)

Therefore I was angry with that generation, and said, "They always go astray in their heart, and they have not known My ways." So I swore in My wrath, "They shall not enter My rest." Beware, brethren, lest there be in any of you an evil heart of unbelief in departing from

> the living God but exhort one another daily, while it is called *"Today,"* lest any of you be hardened through the deceitfulness of sin. (Hebrews 3:10–13)

> For we know Him who said, *"Vengeance is Mine, I will repay,"* says the Lord. And again, *"The Lord will judge His people."* It is a fearful thing to fall into the hands of the living God. (Hebrews 10:30–31)

The Lord, our God, is to be feared and is not to be taken lightly. While He is also loving and longsuffering, we should not take His grace for granted. It is a combination of fear with love like a child has for a parent. My favorite illustration of the fear of God is the relationship a sea captain has with the sea; it is both fear and love. Once he has spent some time sailing the seas, he no longer wants to be on land for very long. His heart yearns to be back out to sea with the salty breeze filling his lungs. Yet he also knows the danger and power of the ocean. He knows that if he does not respect that power, it can, in almost an instant, swell up and kill him. He knows that neither his skills nor the size of his ship is a match for the awesomeness of the mighty oceans.

Therefore, like the sea captain, if we respect the sea and don't sail into the storm, we need not fear tragedy. In the Bible, most of the context around fearing God involves being obedient and the dangers of not obeying Him. Thus, the warning of fearing God is to those falling away from their relationship with Him. It is to those who do not take God's commandments seriously and count the sacrifice of His Son a common thing (Hebrews 10:29).

One of the hardest activities we humans must do is keep life in balance. There are those who fear the Lord so much that they are obsessed with their obedience and everyone else's. They are so focused on obeying God that they lose out on the love and joy of God and steal His joy from others. Then there are those who think God is just a big softy and that they can do whatever they want. They can disobey God because He has promised to forgive them. They may think they are enjoying life now, but they may miss out on the joy of hearing "Well done, good and faithful servant" at the end of their lives.

When I was younger, growing up in the farmlands of Oregon, one thing we kids did was walk the fence rail, that is, trying to balance while walking on the top rail of a two-and-a-half-inch-wide fence. It was fun to challenge each other to see how far we could make it before falling off. An even greater challenge was when we walked the stretch of fence with blackberry bushes on one side and cows and manure on the other. That was when we really concentrated on staying balanced. Yet if we wanted to get somewhere fast, like to the swimming hole, we had to jump off the fence so that we could run. We couldn't get anywhere quickly if we stayed on top of the fence. Life is like that. It is much easier not to live in balance; balance takes too much time, thought, and concentration. It is much easier to take life to one extreme or the other. For example, one church will say no one can ever get a divorce while another church says anyone can get a divorce. Churches do this sometimes because it is easier than listening to all the facts and making a tough decision. After twenty-five-plus years of counseling, I know firsthand that there are no cut-and-dry cases when it comes to couples wanting to break up.

God wants us to live in balance, desperately depending on Him to keep us in that balance. God does this on purpose, for the only way to have true balance in the Christian life is to be walking close to God, in His light, so we can easily see the path. When I ran my own life, I would try to balance my relationship with God, my family, my friends, my job, my ministry, and my spare time. It never worked; it seemed as if someone was always mad that I wasn't spending enough time with them. Now as I have made my time with God a priority, I go to Him first each day to get my marching orders, and I let Him balance the relationships and duties in my life. This all comes from another aspect of fearing God, the fear of failure, for I am not qualified to run my life. I can't know beyond the present moment, but God knows my entire life. He is the only one qualified—He created me! Of course, He knows what I need and how to balance my life.

I don't want to be that guy who failed his marriage, whose kids are no longer talking to him, and who doesn't have much to show for twenty-five years of ministry. Most of all, I fear standing before my God and hearing, "You lazy and slothful servant, you did nothing with the life I gave you."

Love of God

We have already talked a lot about the love of God as our motivation to have a relationship with Him because love is the primary motivator in the walk in faith. I also believe love is the greatest of God's motivators. Like good parents, we all wish our kids would obey us out of love rather than fear. God too wishes we would take His loving teaching and direction, believe it, and follow it. He knows if we would, life would be so much more joyful even in the times of tribulation. God's desire for us to love Him is found throughout the Scriptures.

> You shall not make for yourself a carved image, or any likeness *of anything* that *is* in heaven above, or that *is* in the earth beneath, or that *is* in the water under the earth; you shall not bow down to them nor serve them. For I, the Lord your God, *am* a jealous God, visiting the iniquity of the fathers on the children to the third and fourth *generations* of those who hate Me, but showing mercy to thousands, to those who love Me and keep My commandments. (Exodus 20:4–6)

> Hear, O Israel: The Lord our God, the Lord *is* one! You shall love the Lord your God with all your heart, with all your soul, and with all your strength. (Deuteronomy 6:4–5)

> Then one of them, a lawyer, asked Him a question, testing Him, and saying, "Teacher,

which *is* the great commandment in the law?" Jesus said to him, "You shall love the Lord your God with all your heart, with all your soul, and with all your mind. This is the first and great commandment. And the second is like it: You shall love your neighbor as yourself. On these two commandments hang all the Law and the Prophets." (Matthew 22:35–40)

Beloved, let us love one another, for love is of God; and everyone who loves is born of God and knows God. He who does not love does not know God, for God is love. In this the love of God was manifested toward us, that God has sent His only begotten Son into the world, that we might live through Him. In this is love, not that we loved God, but that He loved us and sent His Son *to be* the propitiation for our sins. Beloved, if God so loved us, we also ought to love one another. (1 John 4:7–11)

Jesus summarized all the commandments into two: loving God and loving one another. Which really is one commandment for John says, "For he who does not love his brother whom he has seen, how can he love God whom he has not seen" (1 John 4:20). Jesus's two commandments are interdependent upon each other so that they form one commandment. We cannot love God without loving one another, and we can't love one another without loving God. We express our love for God primarily through our love for one another. For there is not that much I can physically do for God; I can't repair His car, give Him a ride to the doctor, or take Him to lunch. But I can show my love for Him by doing those things for others.

Then the righteous will answer Him, saying, "Lord, when did we see You hungry and feed *You,* or thirsty and give *You* drink? When did

> we see You a stranger and take *You* in, or naked and clothe *You?* Or when did we see You sick, or in prison, and come to You?" And the King will answer and say to them, "Assuredly, I say to you, inasmuch as you did *it* to one of the least of these My brethren, you did *it* to Me." (Matthew 25:37–40)

It has been said that if we want to experience *joy* in our lives, we need to love Jesus, Others, and You—in that order which is very much true, for we can't truly love others in a Christ-like manner without first loving Christ. We also don't properly understand the love for self unless we first love others. The secular world tends to do this in reverse, that would be YOJ. I call YOJ the god of self. The world believes we need to love self first (self-esteem), then we can love others; and if there is anything left, love what we recognize as a god. Most people believe that the problems of the world are caused by people not loving themselves enough. No! The problem is we love ourselves too much and don't love God and others enough.

By worshiping YOJ, the world is only finding temporal joy; it will not last nor will it satisfy. For lasting joy, we must love the Lord our God with all our heart, soul, and mind. However, I found in Scripture that there is a step of love that comes before loving God. It is that we must first understand the depth of God's love for us. Although we humans are created with a desire to love, we do not know how to love. We learn how to love from our parents, or whoever raises us, both good and bad. Our habits of expressing love are ingrained by their examples. Our heavenly Father wants us to look to His example of love for how to love Him and others.

> In this the children of God and the children of the devil are manifest: Whoever does not practice righteousness is not of God, nor *is* he who does not love his brother. (1 John 3:10)

> For this reason I bow my knees to the Father of our Lord Jesus Christ, from whom the whole family in heaven and earth is named, that He would grant you, according to the riches of His glory, to be strengthened with might through His Spirit in the inner man, that Christ may dwell in your hearts through *faith*; that you, being rooted and grounded in love, may be able to comprehend with all the saints what *is* the width and length and depth and height— to *know* the love of Christ which passes knowledge; that you may be *filled* with all the fullness of God. (Ephesians 3:14–19, emphasis added)

It is the change formula, knowledge of God + belief in God = changed by God. We must know and believe in Christ's love fully; then God can fill us with His fullness. The idea of fullness is complete in God. When we understand the *width and length and depth and height* of Christ's love, then we will be complete. Only after we are complete in God will we do what we are to do, love God with all our heart, soul, and mind. Then in loving God fully, we unconditionally love one another and rightly understand the love of self. In other words, we will not know how to love God and others unless we first know how Christ loves us. While it is true that we may never know fully the love of Christ which *passes knowledge*. This term *passes knowledge* in verse 19 is more of the idea that Christ love is the primary, first, and most important knowledge.

Following is my favorite illustration of God's love for us. Jesus told us that there is no greater love than when someone lays down his life for another (John 15:13). Jesus exemplified this fact by dying for us on the cross. I believe the width, length, depth, and height of Christ's love refers to the four points of the cross. We are to look to the cross as our example of the highest expression of love. We know that the chapter and verse numbers in the Bible are not inspired; they were added later. But 1 John 3:16 sure seems to be the continuation of the thought from John 3:16. "By this we know love, because He laid down His life for us. And we also ought to lay down our lives for the brethren" (1 John 3:16). God so loved the world that he gave His son to die for us as an example of how we should love by dying for one another.

Now this is the cool part. The cross is referred to in Scripture as a tree, "Cursed is everyone who hangs on a tree" (Galatians 3:13; Deuteronomy 21:22–23). That is because often, criminals were executed on actual trees rather than manmade crosses. It is interesting that when trees are studied by dendrologists, they take four key measurements (dendrology comes from the Greek word *dendron* for tree). They measure the height of trees and the width of the trunk. They estimate or measure the depth of the roots when they can. Often a tree is as large underground as it is above ground. Then they measure the length of the canopy, how far out the branches spread. The tree's roots most often go out to the far edge of the branches. God designed trees to shed water off their leaves down to where the roots are, thus, maximizing their water intake.

Therefore, I believe God intended trees to be a reminder of Christ's act of love. I learned as I traveled to Washington DC, on one of our senior trips, what the difference is between a monument and a memorial. They started building the Washington Monument while President Washington was still alive. They built the Lincoln Memorial after President Lincoln died. Therefore, a monument is to honor someone still living. I think God gave us trees as a monument to Christ's love. Every time we see a tree, it is to remind us of the greatest act of love ever expressed to mankind. Scientists estimate there are about three trillion trees in the world—that is a lot of I love yous.

As another illustration of the four steps of love, I found them in the words of an old hymn. The first stanza talks of my love of self, the second my love of others, and the third my love of God. However, in the fourth, we see it is not about "my love, what I do," but it is all about what God is doing and His love for us.

Oh, the Bitter Shame and Sorrow
by Theodore Monod

Oh, the bitter shame and sorrow.
That a time could ever be,
When I let the Saviour's pity
Plead in vain, and proudly answered,
"All of self and none of Thee."
Yet He found me; I beheld Him
Bleeding on the accursed tree;
Heard Him pray, "Forgive them, Father,"
And my wistful heart said faintly,
"Some of self, and some of Thee."
Day by day His tender mercy,
Healing, helping, full and free,
Sweet and strong, and ah! So patient,
Brought me lower while I whispered,
"Less of self, and more of Thee."
Higher than the highest heavens,
Deeper than the deepest sea,
Lord, Thy love at last hath conquered:
Grant me now my soul's petition,
"None of self, and all of Thee."

The four stanzas are also an example of the maturity levels of the Christian. Of course, the first is the unsaved who wants nothing to do with God. The second is the saved person who realizes his need for God. Unfortunately this is as far as most Christians make it, for they want to hold on to the right to run their own lives. The third is the beginning of giving up our right to run our lives and the first steps of the disciple of Christ, realizing like John the Baptist, "I must decrease, and He must increase" (John 3:30). Finally in the fourth, we see the mature Christian who understands there is nothing in self, but all is in God.

The Reward of God

Then there is the motivation of temporal and future rewards. Now some have a struggle with the idea of being obedient to God because of a reward. I fear this has come from misuse of rewards in parenting. That is when a parent tries to bribe a child to behave like before going into the store. "If you are well-behaved in the store, Daddy will buy you a toy." Yeah, probably not the best parenting method. But in adulthood, we have rewards all over the place: we get raises, bonuses, and awards for doing a good job. In sports, we have Gold Glove Awards, MVP awards, and championship trophies. Besides God is the perfect parent, and His rewards are a perfect motivator. If God wants to reward us for our faithfulness, who are we to say, "No, I don't want that?"

Actually, reward is not a full picture of what the Bible is teaching. The motivator of reward is a combination of the two previous motivators—both fear and love. The word translated *reward* in the New Testament is the Greek word *misthos* and is the idea of a wage or a payment for services done. Reward could be a payment, but *misthos* also has both a positive and negative aspect to it. So it could be a good payment or a bad payment. In Luke 10:7, Jesus is talking about a laborer being worthy of his hire (*misthos*). While most of the time, it is used in the New Testament as a positive reward/wage, it is used in a negative sense too. In 2 Peter 2:13,15, Peter warns about a reward/wage of unrighteousness that false teachers will receive.

There is nothing wrong with the Bible translators translating this word *misthos* as reward, yet it has led to some misunderstanding of the passages where it is used. Some in Christianity have come to wrongly believe all Christians will persevere to the end, doing so well that they will all receive positive rewards. These usually are the same folks that believe 1 John is teaching that real Christians will not sin in the end. However, I believe there will be two types of servants at the day of judgment: those faithful servants that have done well with the life Christ gave them and those servants who were lazy and did their own thing with the life Christ gave them. Practically we see this all the time in Christianity. When we look around our church, we see those who are excited about loving and serving God and those who only show up on Sunday mornings to warm a pew. There is an old saying in churches that 20 percent of the people do 80 percent of the work. Will they both receive the same reward?

In Old-Testament times, a father gave a double portion of inheritance to his firstborn son, and all his other sons got a single portion. However, if a firstborn did something against his father's will, he could lose his inheritance and the double portion would go to another. This didn't mean the firstborn stopped being a child of the father, just that he lost what was due him because of his disobedient behavior. In the lineage of Jesus, many were not the firstborn, for the firstborn had lost their inheritance: Seth, Isaac, Jacob, Judah, David, and Solomon. I don't think these were just interesting stories God recorded for us. No, they are reminders to us believers that it is important for us to remain faithful lest we lose out on being the firstborn.

In Jesus's time, the father of a wealthy Roman family would often adopt a man to be his firstborn and inherit control of the family's wealth. This was because his blood son would often be spoiled and incapable of running the household. Therefore, while there will be many children of Christ in the Kingdom, only the faithful will be the firstborn children.

> Now if anyone builds on this foundation *with* gold, silver, precious stones, wood, hay, straw, each one's work will become clear; for the Day will declare it, because it will be revealed by fire; and the fire will test each one's work, of what sort it is. If anyone's work which he has built on *it* endures, he will receive a reward. If anyone's work is burned, he will suffer loss; but he himself will be saved, yet so as through fire. (1 Corinthians 3:12–15)

> The Spirit Himself bears witness with our spirit that we are children of God, and if chil-

> dren, then heirs—heirs of God and joint heirs with Christ, if indeed we suffer with *Him,* that we may also be glorified together. (Romans 8:16–17)

> And we know that all things work together for good to those who love God, to those who are the called according to *His* purpose. For whom He foreknew, He also predestined *to be* conformed to the image of His Son, that He might be the firstborn among many brethren. (Romans 8:28–29)

We have seen before in 1 Corinthians 3:15 that some will suffer loss; not every Christian's work will be gold, silver, and precious stones. In Romans 8:16–17, we see that all who believe in Jesus are children of God, but only those who suffer with Him will be a joint heir. What is a joint heir? Jesus is the firstborn Son of God and receives a double inheritance; those who suffer with Him will also be firstborn sons. In Romans 8:29, Paul says Jesus will be "the firstborn among many brethren," not all brethren. But the condition of those in verse 29 which will be "conformed to the image of His Son" is in verse 28, "those who love God."

When will all this happen, when is the "Day" of 1 Corinthians 3:13? It is the Judgment Seat of Christ.

> But why do you judge your brother? Or why do you show contempt for your brother? For we shall all stand before the judgment seat of Christ. For it is written: *"As I live, says the* Lord, Every knee shall bow to Me, And every tongue shall confess to God." So then each of us shall give account of himself to God. Therefore let us not judge one another anymore, but rather resolve this, not to put a stumbling block or a cause to fall in *our* brother's way. (Romans 14:10–13)

> Therefore we make it our aim, whether present or absent, to be well pleasing to Him. For we must all appear before the judgment seat of Christ, that each one may receive the things *done* in the body, according to what he has done, whether good or bad. Knowing, therefore, the terror of the Lord, we persuade men; but we are well known to God, and I also trust are well known in your consciences. (2 Corinthians 5:9–11)

It should be obvious from just these few verses that there are both positive and negative consequences (wages) at the judgment seat of Christ. No one knows absolutely what those negative consequences are for they are future things. However, it would at the very least be a loss of rewards and most likely the loss of ruling and reigning with Christ. Why else would someone be ashamed at the appearance of Christ like we saw in our study of 1 John?

"And now, little children, abide in Him, that when He appears, we may have confidence and not be ashamed before Him at His coming" (1 John 2:28).

"Love has been perfected among us in this: that we may have boldness in the day of judgment; because as He is, so are we in this world" (1 John 4:17)

This should be a strong motivator to have that intimate relationship with Jesus Christ. For it would make sense that those who would rule and reign with Jesus would be those who have already shown that they trust Him. I see this life here on earth as a kind of on-the-job training or that probation time that some employers have. We are learning here on earth how to live by faith and be guided by the Holy Spirit. It is those that have qualified for the job that receives it. Like we saw in chapter 1 when I was talking about David's mighty men, those who showed themselves faithful were the ones who helped him rule the kingdom.

Hence the gist of this Scripture [Matthew 16:24–28, "Whoever loses his life for My sake will find it."] is to divide into two classes the disciples who have believed in the Lord and possess eternal life. One class denies self and takes up the cross; the other class does not deny self nor take up the cross. One class seeks to gain the pleasures of the world for self and is unwilling to lose the soul. A disciple of Christ is one whom the Lord has separated out from the sinners. And once again, He will separate—this time separating a self-denying disciple from the non-denying one. *We ought to know that our future position in the kingdom is decided by our deeds today.* Whatever is meant in today's gain will be the meaning of the future's gain. Whatever is meant by today's loss will be the meaning of tomorrow's loss. If today's gain means gaining the world and avoiding sufferings, then the future gain for the self-denying one will mean gaining the world without sufferings. If today's loss means forsaking the world and not following one's own will, then future loss for the non-self-denying one's own will, then future losing the world and not getting what one desires. *This is what the Lord means—that all who are gratified by the world today shall lose the position of reigning with Him in the future.* Consequently the salvation of the soul is quite different from what we commonly know as the salvation of the spirit (which means having eternal life, emphasis added).[1]

The Awards Ceremony

Unfortunately some have watered down the seriousness of the judgment seat of Christ. They think it will be just an awards ceremony, that all Christians will hear, "Well done." The reason for this is that a disobedient Christian does not fit in their theology. They believe all true Christians will persevere to the end. To them, perseverance means staying obedient to God in all things to the very end. But they are just thinking of what they believe are the big sins: adultery, murder, homosexuality, drug abuse, etc. Like we have talked about before, what about those acceptable sins that never leave the believer? There is "none righteous, no not one" (Romans 3:10). I do believe in the preservation (not perseverance) of the Christian, that once a person is saved, they can never lose that salvation. As Jesus said, those whom His Father has given Him cannot be snatched from His hand (John 10:28–29). But that doesn't mean we will always be good, obedient children. Sometimes we choose not to trust in Jesus which may have consequences at the judgment seat, but it doesn't mean we were never saved.

Because of this watering down, good believers are missing out on God's intended motivation of rewards and even more serious, the warnings of not seeking to be faithful. How sad would it be for us to meet Jesus and find our white garment all spotted and wrinkled with our unfaithfulness? I am afraid those who teach the judgment seat is an awards ceremony are doing believers a disservice. Their teaching goes something like this.

When Paul is talking about the judgment seat of Christ, he uses the Greek word *bema* which means a raised platform or step. Paul is thinking of the raised platform where athletes in those days received their awards. Like the podium we see in the Olympics where athletes receive their gold medals. For Paul used many sporting examples to illustrate the Christian life. Therefore, the judgement seat of Christ is where we will receive our rewards for being obedient Christians. There will not be negative consequences because runners don't get punished for coming in second; they may not get as nice of an award. They might get silver or bronze instead of gold. In fact, in Corinth, every two years, the Corinthians celebrated one of these ancient sporting events. So when Paul is writing to the Corinthians about the *bema,* he is obviously thinking of that event for look at what he wrote in 1 Corinthians 9.

> Do you not know that those who run in a race all run, but one receives the prize? Run in such a way that you may obtain *it.* And everyone who competes *for the prize* is temperate in all things. Now they *do it* to obtain a perishable crown, but we *for* an imperishable *crown.* (1 Corinthians 9:24–25)

There are quite a few problems with this view. Just because Paul uses sporting illustrations doesn't mean he was comparing the judgment seat of Christ to the games in Corinth. Sporting events at that time had been around for at least 800 years, 776 BC is the traditional starting date for the Olympic games. Paul could have been thinking of any of several sports events. Also the reference to sports and the reference to the judgment seat are in two different letters. Paul does not reference them together. But even if Paul was thinking of a sport, he also brings into the illustration of 1 Corinthians 9:24–25 a possible negative consequence when he is concerned himself about being disqualified in verse 27. Those arguing for an awards ceremony usually fail to mention the last verse of 1 Corinthians 9.

"But I discipline my body and bring *it* into subjection, lest, when I have preached to others, I myself should become disqualified" (1 Corinthians 9:27)

We have already seen that it was also Paul that included in his direct writings of the judgement seat, that there would be loss (1 Corinthians 3:15), both good and bad would be judged (2 Corinthians 5:10), and a warning against judging one another because we too will be judged (Romans 14:12). Also there is some question of whether the awards platform for the ancient games was ever called a *bema*. "Dr. Ken Wilson, a professor at Grace School of Theology, points out that, as far as we know, Greek literature does not directly use the term *bema* for the place where the judges at the Pan-Hellenic games sat."[2]

Also those who teach only an awards ceremony have failed to follow the very first rule of Bible interpretation. That rule is to let the Bible context define the meaning. They have assumed, without any proof, that Paul was talking about an awards platform in the ancient games. But look at what the Bible itself says about the *bema*.

> From then on Pilate sought to release Him, but the Jews cried out, saying, "If you let this Man go, you are not Caesar's friend. Whoever makes himself a king speaks against Caesar." When Pilate therefore heard that saying, he brought Jesus out and sat down in the *judgment seat* in a place that is called The Pavement, but in Hebrew, Gabbatha. (John 19:12–13, emphasis added)

> So on a set day Herod, arrayed in royal apparel, sat on his *throne* [bema] and gave an oration to them. And the people kept shouting, "The voice of a god and not of a man!" Then immediately an angel of the Lord struck him, because he did not give glory to God. And he was eaten by worms and died. (Acts 12:21–23, emphasis added)

> When Gallio was proconsul of Achaia, the Jews with one accord rose up against Paul and brought him to the *judgment seat*, saying, "This *fellow* persuades men to worship God contrary to the law." And when Paul was about to open *his* mouth, Gallio said to the Jews, "If it were a matter of wrongdoing or wicked crimes, O Jews, there would be reason why I should bear with you. But if it is a question of words and names and your own law, look *to it* yourselves; for I do not want to be a judge of such *matters.*" And he drove them from the *judgment seat*. Then all the Greeks took Sosthenes, the ruler of the synagogue, and beat *him* before the *judgment seat*. But Gallio took no notice of these things. (Acts 18:12–17, emphasis added)

> "Therefore," he said, "let those who have authority among you go down with *me* and accuse this man, to see if there is any fault in him." And when he had remained among them more than ten days, he went down to Caesarea. And the next day, sitting on the *judgment seat*, he commanded Paul to be brought. When he had come, the Jews who had come down from Jerusalem stood about and laid many serious

> complaints against Paul, which they could not prove. (Acts 25:5–7, emphasis added)
>
> So Paul said, "I stand at Caesar's *judgment seat*, where I ought to be judged. To the Jews I have done no wrong, as you very well know. For if I am an offender, or have committed anything deserving of death, I do not object to dying; but if there is nothing in these things of which these men accuse me, no one can deliver me to them. I appeal to Caesar." (Acts 25:10–11, emphasis added)
>
> To them I answered, "It is not the custom of the Romans to deliver any man to destruction before the accused meets the accusers face to face, and has opportunity to answer for himself concerning the charge against him." Therefore when they had come together, without any delay, the next day I sat on the *judgment seat* and commanded the man to be brought in. When the accusers stood up, they brought no accusation against him of such things as I supposed, but had some questions against him about their own religion and about a certain Jesus, who had died, whom Paul affirmed to be alive. (Acts 25:16–19, emphasis added)

In the context of the above Scriptures, it is quite obvious that the *bema* is correctly translated "judgment seat" for judgment is occurring in all its uses. Nowhere in Scripture is the *bema* used as an awards platform. We also see that Paul had firsthand knowledge of the judgment seat. In the Acts 18 passage, he was in Corinth (Acts 18:1) when he was brought before the judgment seat. It is far more likely that Paul had that experience in mind when he wrote to the Corinthians about the judgment seat of Christ.

The judgment seat of Christ is exactly what it says—a judgment. It is not a judgment of who is saved or not, for only believers will be there. The judgment is for what have we have done with the new life Christ died for and gave us. Those believers who gave up all, died to self, and followed Jesus will receive the rewards of a faithful disciple. Those who believed in Jesus but also believed their life remained theirs and chose to live it according to their desires are the ones who will be ashamed at the judgment. When we all stand before Jesus and clearly see the comparison of what He did for us versus what we did for Him, there will probably be a little shame for all of us. However, those who did not look for the Lord's return, by doing what He has asked them to do, will experience deep regret. As intended by God, this should be a strong motivator for us to follow after Jesus.

The Good News

Let's finish off this chapter with some good news. The word *gospel* means good news. Most of the time the Gospel is referring to the good news of Jesus's death and resurrection as a payment for our sins. But there are other uses of the word *gospel* in the New Testament, for of course there is a lot of good news in the Scriptures. The uses of the term *gospel* in the New Testament also follows our trichotomy of faith. The gospel of grace refers to the gift by faith and the salvation of the spirit. Then there is the gospel of the kingdom which is part of the walk in faith and the salvation of the soul. Finally there is the everlasting gospel which is part of the reward of faith and the salvation of the body.

> But none of these things move me; nor do I count my life dear to myself, so that I may finish my race with joy, and the ministry which I received from the Lord Jesus, to testify to the *gospel of the grace* of God. (Acts 20:24, emphasis added)

> And Jesus went about all Galilee, teaching in their synagogues, preaching the *gospel of the kingdom*, and healing all kinds of sickness and all kinds of disease among the people. (Matthew 4:23, emphasis added)

> Then I saw another angel flying in the midst of heaven, having the *everlasting gospel* to preach to those who dwell on the earth--to every nation, tribe, tongue, and people—saying with a loud voice, "Fear God and give glory to Him, for the hour of His judgment has come; and worship Him who made heaven and earth, the sea and springs of water." Revelation 14:6–7, emphasis added)

The Gospel of the kingdom is the 1,000-year reign of Jesus Christ here on earth after the tribulation. We often mistakenly think that we all go to heaven after we die or after the rapture. No, before heaven is the millennial kingdom of Jesus Christ. The end-times go like this: the New-Testament saints will meet Jesus in the sky before the tribulation (1 Thessalonians 4:13–18) and be celebrating the marriage of the Lamb during the tribulation (Revelation 19:7–9). At the end of the tribulation, Jesus returns with His bride to earth to cast Satan into the bottomless pit (Revelation 20:1–3). After that and before the start of Christ's kingdom, the Old-Testament saints will be resurrected (Matthew 24:31; Daniel 12:2). Then all believers will be in Christ's millennial kingdom (Matthew 7:21; 2 Timothy 2:12; Revelation 20:4). After 1,000 years comes Satan's last rebellion (Revelation 20:7–10), the great white throne judgment (Revelation 20:11) and after that, humanity will either spend eternity in heaven or hell (Revelation 3:12; 21:8).

As we saw in Matthew 4:23, Jesus was preaching the Gospel of the kingdom. This is seen in all the parables about the kingdom in the Gospels. They are not a comparison of who will go to heaven and who will not. They are a comparison of children of God and firstborn children of God. They are instructions on which believers will hear, "Well done, good and faithful servant" or "You wicked and lazy servant." I will not take space here to explain those parables for James Hollandsworth does a wonderful job of rightly interpreting them in his book *Keys for Inheriting the Kingdom: Unlocking the Parables of Jesus.*[3] I would only be saying what James has already said.

I believe God uses this millennial kingdom as a way of proving that Jesus truly is the Way, the Truth, and the Life. Throughout history, I believe God has been removing every excuse man might have for ruling himself. God gave mankind a chance to live in paradise in the Garden, but Adam and Eve rejected it with their sin. Then God gave mankind the opportunity to walk with Him after the fall; Enoch took advantage of it, but most of mankind rejected it. So God saved Noah and his family and started over. Then God chooses a family—the Israelites. Maybe if the world wouldn't walk with Him, a chosen family would? They too rejected a personal relationship with God and asked for a system of religion; God gave them the law. They rejected the law, and everyone did what was right in their own eyes.

The people then were not satisfied with God as their King, so they asked for a human king. The human kings ended up splitting the family; God then sent them into exile. The exile did stop them from chasing after false gods but again, the family chose the system over the relationship. Then like the parable of the landowner (Matthew 21:33–45), God sent His only Son; surely they wouldn't reject Him. Jesus came to remind the family that there was a personal relationship with their God available; they rejected and killed Him. So God gave the opportunity to a new family—the church. But we haven't done too good of a job either. Therefore, God is going to show through His Son's 1,000-year reign that Jesus has always been the answer.

Finally my friends, there is both good news and bad, but it doesn't have to be bad. As a little child, you can either choose to believe your parents love you and have your best interest in mind and obey them, or you can find out the hard way that they were right. You can either take God's loving motivation, believe it, and choose to be a dedicated disciple of Jesus Christ, or you can choose to love self more and experience the pain of running your own life. Your key to be a disciple of Jesus and experiencing the joy of living in the Promised Land here on earth is understanding and knowing Him.

---

1. Watchman Nee, The Salvation of the Soul, 11ff.
2. Dr. Ken Wilson as quoted by Joe L. Wall, Going for the Gold: Reward or Loss at the Judgment Seat of Christ (The Woodlands, Texas: Grace Theology Press, 2013), 25.
3. James S. Hollandsworth, Keys for Inheriting the Kingdom: Unlocking the Parables of Jesus (Holly Publishing, 2017).

CHAPTER 10

God's Body—the Church

From whom the whole body, joined and knit together by what every joint supplies, according to the effective working by which every part does its share, causes growth of the body for the edifying of itself in love.

—Ephesians 4:16

The final key to Christian maturity and experiencing the joy of Christ is *sharing*. One of the first principles of life we learn as kids: share your toys. It was right up there with don't hit your sister. But sharing is also an important precept of the Christian life. I call it pond theology. When I was young, we lived mostly in small towns in Oregon, and many of my friends were farm kids. I learned from them that to have a healthy pond or small lake for swimming in, they needed both an inlet and outlet. Without fresh water flowing into a pool of water, it quickly becomes scummy, stagnant, and even poisonous. In the believer's life, there is also the same danger. Remember the illustration of receiving the free flow of fellowship from our eternal spring, Jesus Christ? The thing that hindered that free flow is our sin, like throwing rocks into the creek. But on the other side of our healthy pool of fellowship with God is the danger of that fellowship becoming stagnant. A healthy fellowship pool needs both an inlet and an outlet. As we saw in 1 John, our joy is complete when there is both fellowship with God and one another.

The picture is like the Sea of Galilee and the Dead Sea in the Holy Land. The Sea of Galilee is alive and vibrant, full of fish and wildlife. However, the Dead Sea is basically dead; there are just a few organisms that can live in such a hostile environment. Both seas are fed by the same water—the Jordan River. However, the Jordan River flows both into and out of the Sea of Galilee, keeping it fresh and alive. The Dead Sea has no outlet, and therefore, its high-salt content kills the life of the Jordan River. Just like our selfishness can kill off our sweet fellowship with Jesus Christ.

We covered in chapter 1 God's simple evangelism program of parents leading their children into the same loving relationship with God that they have. Now we come to God's simple plan of discipleship or soul winning. The Scriptures say we are to "comfort those who are in any trouble, with the comfort with which we ourselves are comforted by God" (2 Corinthians 1:4). To help others grow in maturity in Christ, we simply share with them how we matured in Christ.

If you have a love relationship with God, you have come to know God through experience. He has worked in and around your life. For instance, you could not know God as the Comforter in sorrow unless you had experienced His comfort during a time of grief or sorrow. You come to know God when He reveals Himself to you. You come to know Him as you experience Him.[1]

Therefore, in this final chapter, I am going to share some additional ways we can continue to grow along with some additional resources for studying. They are, first and foremost, for you to continue your growth in Christ. But then to be a healthy pond, you need to let that growth flow into others. The simplicity of God's plan in doing this is to just share with others these same simple truths. You don't have to go off to seminary and study Hebrew and Greek to be a blessing to one another. But before doing that, there is first one more important point to the pond theology. It is that the fresh water must be from a full pool.

Another disservice some Christian leaders have done to new believers is trying to get them into services too quickly or asking the hurting believer to serve. I understand why they do this—they don't want Satan to snatch them away, drawing them back into sin. But we must be careful to allow the Holy Spirit first to fill them before they can overflow into others. Healthy lakes overflow only when they are full. The brand new believer is not yet full of the Lord's fellowship. Sometimes there is a drought in the older Christian's life, and his level of fellowship has dried up. They both are below the point of overflow. They will need to fill up first before they can pour out their lives into others. This is why many Christians and Christian leaders get burnt out; they are often trying to pour out themselves into others from their reserves rather than the overflow.

I was guilty of this myself in ministry. Part of my disappointment with serving others as I was spending a disproportionate amount of time serving over being alone with God. We think ministry is like being a coffee cup. We go to the coffee pot, which is the Holy Spirit, and fill up with coffee. After being filled from the pot, we go out to the other coffee cups and pour a little into each of them. Then we run back to the coffeepot for some more.

That ends up being a strenuous job and more dependent upon me, the cup, than the coffee. The true picture is that as a coffee cup, we go over to the coffeepot and just stay there. The coffeepot is like one of those big ones that we use at church potlucks, the ones with the little black spout that hold an unlimited amount of coffee. We then *abide* right there under the spout without moving. As long as we are abiding under the spout, it remains open and the coffee fills us. Yes, then the coffee starts to overflow and spill out all over the table; it pours off the table, filling the whole room. Eventually the coffee flows out of the room, down the hall, and into the rest of the church. After filling the church, the coffee flows out into the rest of the town, state, country, and the whole world. It becomes all about the coffee and not the cup.

Yes, one little cup, willing to abide in God and stay there in fellowship can reach the whole world. No programs, schools, churches, or organizations needed, just one person telling another person about how they came to understand and know God. Of course, I am not saying get rid of all those organizations for they serve God's purposes too. However, one person sharing their walk with one other person and teaching that person how to share their walk could reach the whole world for Jesus Christ. It is just as simple as growing yourself in a relationship with Jesus, abiding in Him, and then telling someone else how you did it. I am using that example in this book; I am telling you how I came to know and understand God, so you can too and then tell someone else how to know and understand Him. All you would have to do is buy this book again and give it to someone else then have them buy a copy and give it to someone else (smile).

Reaching the World

Some may say that that model would never work; we need organizations to reach the billions of people in the world, we don't have time to do it one-on-one. Let's try it; this next year, I will find one person to lead to the Lord, and then I will spend the next year teaching that person more about Jesus and how to do the same thing I did for them. Then the next year, the two of us will do the same thing over again, and two will become four, then four will become eight and so on. You, on the other hand, will lead, let's say, a hundred thousand people to the Lord, and not in one year but one day. Then the next day, you will lead another one hundred thousand to the Lord, and another hundred thousand the next day. In a year, you will lead 36.5 million people to the Lord, and I will have led one.

There are approximately 6 billion people in the world today. How long will it take for you to reach the whole world? That would be 6 billion divided by 36.5 million which would be a little over 164 years. By that time, there might be another billion people, so that's another twenty-seven years plus another population growth, it might be two hundred years before you reach the whole world. Now for me, it takes a little over sixteen years to do what you did in one day, and over twenty-five years to do what you did in one year. However, things start to take off after that; by year thirty, we are up to over one billion, two billion by year 31, four billion at year 32, and surpassing the population with eight billion by year 33.

If my math is correct, it means that I can reach the whole world one person at a time in less than thirty-three years. While you will never reach the whole world unless you live to be over Two hundred years old. Now you probably think, *If that were true then why hasn't someone done it?* Unfortunately as we have been learning, we humans still have free will, and not all unbelievers choose to believe. Nor do all believers choose to believe they can disciple someone else. The point is, don't think you need to come up with some grand plan to disciple others, simply share with them what has been shared with you.

This chapter is kind of the leftovers of additional resources to help fulfill that purpose. It is a hodgepodge of different ideas that you can first use yourself and then maybe teach others. Like we learned in the four T's, God loves variety. Therefore, I am trying to give you all a variety of resources so that you might find what you enjoy doing to understand and know God.

We will start with some more practical applications for the individual and then move to some suggestions for discipleship/counseling, teaching, and preaching. Then at the end of the chapter, there are some books and websites for additional study. So as promised, here are some topics and verses to get your biography of God started.

Biography of God Jumpstart

My God, My Counselor
Judges 20:23; Job 12:13; Isaiah 9:6; Hebrews 6:17–18

My God, My Creator (Maker)
Genesis 1:1; Job 33:4; Colossians 1:16–17; Revelation 4:11

My God, My Deliverer
2 Samuel 22:2; Psalms 6:4; Romans 6:17; Galatians 1:3–4

My God My Hope
Psalms 31:24, 119:74; Romans 5:5; Colossians 1:27

My God, My Life (Bread)
Psalms 42:8; Proverbs 15:24; John 8:12; Galatians 2:20

My God, My Refuge (Hiding Place, Shelter)
Ruth 2:12; Psalms 46:11; Isaiah 25:4; 2 Corinthians 4:8–10

My God, My Song
Exodus 15:2; Psalms 28:7, 118:14; Isaiah 12:2

My God Is Awesome
Deuteronomy 7:21; Psalms 66:5; Jeremiah 20:11; Daniel 9:4

My God Is Glorious (Glory)
Psalms 29:3, 76:4; Isaiah 59:19; John 17:1

My God Is Jealous
Exodus 34:14; Joshua 24:19; Psalms 79:5; 1 Corinthians 10:21–22

My God Is Just (Justice, Judgment)
Psalms 96:10; Hosea 2:19–20; John 12:48; 1 John 1:9

My God Is All-Powerful (Omnipotent, Strength)
Deuteronomy 4:37; 1 Samuel 15:29; 1 John 3:20; Jude 1:25

My God Is Wise (Omniscient, Knowledge)
Job 9:4; Proverbs 3:19–20; Romans 16:27; 1 Corinthians 3:19

My God Is with Me (Omnipresent)
Genesis 21:22; Zephaniah 3:17; Matthew 28:20; James 4:8

My God Comforts
Psalms 71:21; Isaiah 49:13; Romans 15:4; 2 Corinthians 7:6

My God Hates (Scorns)
Deuteronomy 12:31; Psalms 11:5; Proverbs 8:13; Hebrews 1:9

My God Knows me
1 Kings 8:39; Psalms 31:2, 37:18; Hebrews 4:13

My God Provides (Bountiful)
Genesis 22:14; Psalms 116:7; Matthew 5:45; Philippians 4:19

My God Gives All Things
1 Chronicles 29:14; Psalms 37:4; Matthew 7:11; James 1:17

My God Gives Grace
Exodus 33:19; Psalms 84:11; Ephesians 4:7; James 4:6

My God Gives Joy
Psalms 16:11; Ecclesiastes 2:26; Acts 13:52; Romans 15:13

My God Gives Light
Psalms 118:27; Isaiah 51:4; Ephesians 5:14; Revelation 22:5

My God Gives Peace
Psalms 4:8; Zephaniah 3:17; John 14:27; Romans 15:13

My God's Hands
Deuteronomy 33:3; Ezra 7:28; Luke 11:20; 1 Peter 5:6

My God's Loving Kindness
Psalms 26:3; Lamentations 16:5; Hosea 2:19–20; Jonah 4:2

My God's Mind
Psalms 40:5, 92:5, 144:3; Romans 11:33–34

My God's Voice
Genesis 22:18; Psalms 33:6; Matthew 12:19; 2 Thessalonians 2:8

My God's Works (Deeds, Handiwork)
Exodus 32:16; Psalms 19:1; Romans 14:20; Revelation 15:3

My God Will Not Destroy Me
Leviticus 26:44; Deuteronomy 4:30–31; 2 Chronicles 12:7; Psalms 78:38

My God Will Not Fail Me
Joshua 21:45; 1 Kings 8:56; Psalms 89:23; Lamentations 3:21–23

My God Will Not Leave Me
Deuteronomy 31:8; Psalms 27:9, 141:8; Hebrews 13:5

My God Will Not Be Silent
Psalms 28:1, 39:12, 109:1; Isaiah 65:6

My God Commands Me to Abide in Him
Psalms 91:1; John 15:4–7; 1 John 3:24, 4:13

My God Commands Me to Hear Him (Listen)
Numbers 24:16; Nehemiah 9:30; Mark 4:23–24; Mark 9:7

My God Commands Me to Obey Him (Obedient)
Genesis 22:18; Ezra 20:8; 1 Thessalonians 4:1–2; Hebrews 5:9

My God Commands Me to Rejoice in Him (Delight)
Ezra 3:11; Isaiah 58:2; Matthew 5:12; Philippians 4:4

My God Commands Me to Seek Him
Psalms 10:4; Proverbs 28:5; Amos 5:4; Acts 17:27

My God Commands Me to Walk with Him
Deuteronomy 26:17; Psalms 18:21; Ephesians 2:10; Colossians 1:9–10

My God Wants Me to Be Content
Proverbs 15:16–17; Ecclesiastes 4:6; Luke 12:15; 1 Timothy 6:6–8

My God wants me to be Happy (Blessed)
Job 5:17; Psalms 64:10; 127:3-5; Proverbs 22:4

My God Wants Me to Be Humble
Psalms 18:27, Proverbs 22:4; Matthew 18:4; James 4:10

My God Wants Me to Love and Serve Others
Proverbs 3:27–31, 18:24; Matthew 5:46; Galatians 6:2

My God Wants Me to Be at Peace
Psalms 4:8, 85:8; John 14:27; Colossians 3:15

My God Wants Me to Think Right (One Mind)
Proverbs 16:3; Isaiah 26:3–4; Romans 12:2; Philippians 2:5

My God Doesn't Want Me to Be Ashamed
Psalms 22:4–5, 25:20; Romans 1:16; 1 Peter 4:16

My God Doesn't Want Me to Be Fearful
Deuteronomy 31:8; Judges 6:10; Luke 12:32; 1 Timothy 1:7

My God Doesn't Want Me to Be Lazy
Proverbs 10:26, 19:15, 22:13, 28:19

My God Doesn't Want Me to Be Proud
2 Samuel 22:28, Psalms 31:23; Matthew 23:11–12; 1 John 2:16

My God Doesn't Want Me to Worry
Psalms 94:19; Proverbs 12:25; Matthew6:34; Luke 12:29

Perfection Summaries

Here is a simpler version of the topic study. It is a brief description of the character of God along with a description of what change will look like if believed. It is a great summary to add to the beginning of each topic in your biography.

God (title, perfections, action): is independent

Definition (a simple description): God needs nothing, He needs nothing outside Himself to be complete, He is self-generating, He is fulfilled within Himself. God created us not because He needed us but for His pleasure, that He might enjoy us and we might enjoy

Him. Like why humans have children, usually not because of need but because of love.

Change (how believing this will change you): God intends for me to live the same way; no, not to be fulfilled in myself or even another human. God wants me to need nothing outside of Himself, to need nothing other than Him to be complete, to be fulfilled within Himself. Then all the rest of creation can be enjoyed—the frosting on the cake.

I am not to find my sufficiency in any other human, goal, or thing; that is idolatry. I am, first and foremost, to find all that I need in God and God alone. A man is not to seek what he needs in a wife, his job, sex, power, money, etc. A woman is not to seek what she needs in a husband, family, children, career, security, etc.

Counseling and Discipleship

Counseling is just the secular term for discipleship; they are basically the same thing. The very first commandment God gave to us humans was to go forth and multiply. That was primarily a physical thing of populating the earth. But as we saw before, it is also a spiritual precept. Jesus reinforced this idea of evangelism in His great commission. He commanded us, His disciples, to not only give birth to new believers but to also help them grow up.

> Go therefore and make disciples of all the nations, baptizing them in the name of the Father and of the Son and of the Holy Spirit, *teaching them to observe all things that I have commanded you*; and lo, I am with you always, *even* to the end of the age. Amen. (Matthew 28:19–20, emphasis added)

Evangelism is not just leading people to the Lord, that is merely the first step. Evangelism is also helping believers mature so that they too may multiply. Like giving natural birth, we don't just have babies and then leave them alone to grow up. While our job of parenting is never fully done, it is mostly done when our children begin their own families. Thus, we are all called to discipleship/counseling. Unfortunately the church has turned over this responsibility to the professional pastor/counselor. That is because we believe that to help people with major problems in their lives, we need to have in-depth, professional solutions.

That is somewhat true when it comes to helping people with mental illness, like needing a doctor to help with cancer. But the majority of the struggles in the church are spiritual and issues of sin. Therefore, we are all qualified to help our brothers and sisters. The key is that we are not the ones making the change in others, we are to merely lead them to the *change*. We are not called to be doctors with all the answers to every problem that may present itself. We are called to be more like nurses. We are to prepare the person for seeing the Great Physician and letting Him diagnose and cure the problem. Once again, we were created by God, and only He can fix us. Our job is twofold: to find God ourselves for the change needed in our lives and to lead others to God for them to find the change in theirs.

If you are not succeeding in life, it is because you are not succeeding in the knowledge of God. What you need is not to look for life but to look for Him who can locate life for you. Many of us have never yet learned how to live. We think living is wrapped up in the things I've already mentioned—money, education, prestige, or power—when living really should be about the knowledge of God. That's why studying the Scriptures is so important.[2]

It's important to know the nature of the one you are dealing with. If you think you are getting one thing but when you get it it's not what you thought it was, you could be in trouble. That happens today with a lot of errant teaching about who God is. God has been so misdefined, tragically redefined, and even dismissed that people do not understand His true nature. Then they begin operating on this misinformation, thinking that they know the true God when in fact, they know something totally different than who and what the true God is. Knowing the nature of God as He reveals Himself rather than how we wish He were can save us from a life of confusion and defeat.[3]

In fact in this book, I have given you the answer to every spiritual problem in the church. No, it doesn't have every specific answer, but the fundamental answer to every problem starts with knowing and understanding God. When we find God, then we can hear from the Doctor the specifics for our struggle. In my counseling ministry, after a person shared their problem, I started asking them, "Did you ask God? What did He say about your problem? He has better solutions than I could ever come up with." It would bring the focus back to God, for while I could give them reasonable advice, what they needed was God. As a disciple of Christ, God does give me wisdom and insight into His ways, but it is the height of pride for me to assume I know the will of God for another person. That doesn't mean we can't give each other some practical advice; we will see how to balance these two thoughts when I talk about teaching and preaching.

Quick Reference Guide

You can help others understand and know God better in general through the things you have learned so far in this book: The four Ts of relationships, the biography of God, learning to be childlike, etc. But you can get even more specific with your guidance by applying more specific perfections of God to specific problems. I created a Quick Reference Guide where I collected a few of the more specific verses about issues and cross-referenced them to character qualities about God. You can do the same by asking yourself, "For the problem of blank, what characteristics of God need to be believed?" Following are a few pages from the guide.

Anger

1. The Problem

Anger is the unmet expectation of fairness. While anger itself is not sin, how a person responds to that anger can be sin. Probably no other emotion leads to more sin than how you choose to react to anger.

As you believe more and more that God loves you and always has your best interests in mind and how God is sovereign over the circumstances of life, you should have fewer problems with anger. As you believe that your God has allowed even unfairness into your life and sometimes even caused it, you can trust that He has done it for your good. When you are angry at the circumstances of life, you aren't angry at *them*; you are angry at *God* because He allowed it. Being angry at God is a dangerous place to be.

There are four degrees of anger:

1) Indignation—a simmering anger
2) Wrath—a burning anger
3) Fury—a fiery anger
4) Rage—a blazing violent anger

Helpful perfections:

The grace of God, love of God, holiness of God, sovereignty of God, wisdom of God

2. The Results

> "Be angry, and do not sin. Meditate within your heart on your bed and be still. Selah Offer the sacrifices of righteousness and put your trust in the Lord" (Psalms 4:4–5).

> "A soft answer turns away wrath, but a harsh word stirs up anger" (Proverbs 15:1).

> "A wrathful man stirs up strife, but *he who is* slow to anger allays contention" (Proverbs 15:18).

> "*A man of* great wrath will suffer punishment; For if you rescue *him,* you will have to do it again" (Proverbs 19:19).

"Make no friendship with an angry man, and with a furious man do not go" (Proverbs 22:24).

"A fool vents all his feelings, but a wise *man* holds them back" (Proverbs 29:11).

"Do not hasten in your spirit to be angry, For anger rests in the bosom of fools" (Ecclesiastes 7:9).

"You have heard that it was said to those of old, '*You shall not murder,* and whoever murders will be in danger of the judgment.' But I say to you that whoever is angry with his brother without a cause shall be in danger of the judgment. And whoever says to his brother, 'Raca!' shall be in danger of the council. But whoever says, 'You fool!' shall be in danger of hell fire" (Matthew 5:21–22).

"*Be angry, and do not sin:* do not let the sun go down on your wrath, nor give place to the devil" (Ephesians 4:26–27).

"Let all bitterness, wrath, anger, clamor, and evil speaking be put away from you, with all malice. And be kind to one another, tenderhearted, forgiving one another, just as God in Christ forgave you" (Ephesians 4:31–32).

"So then, my beloved brethren, let every man be swift to hear, slow to speak, slow to wrath; for the wrath of man does not produce the righteousness of God" (James 1:19–20).

Depression

1. The Problem

Depression is a sinking of the spirits; dejection; a state of sadness; want of courage. Depression also means the act of humbling; abasement; as the *depression* of pride.

Oddly the word *depression* describes both the worst and best Christian attribute. Does taking medicine for depression show a lack of faith? No! There are numerous causes of depression—some spiritual, some physical:

(1) Hormonal imbalance, (2) medications and drugs, (3) chronic illness, (4) melancholy temperament, (5) improper food or rest, (6) genetic vulnerability, (7) sin

King David was depressed but when his soul was downcast, he changed his focus to the faithfulness of His God (Psalms 42:5–6, 11, 43:5).

Helpful perfections:

The hope of God, love of God, power of God, sovereignty of God

(For depression, also a study of the "Blessed (happy) are the…" passages in Scripture are helpful.)

2. The Results

> "So the Lord said to Cain, 'Why are you angry? And why has your countenance fallen? If you do well, will you not be accepted? And if you do not do well, sin lies at the door. And its desire *is* for you, but you should rule over it'" (Genesis 4:6–7).

> "*I would have lost heart,* unless I had believed That I would see the goodness of the Lord In the land of the living. Wait on the Lord; Be of good

courage, And He shall strengthen your heart; Wait, I say, on the Lord!" (Psalms 27:13–14).

"Why are you cast down, O my soul? And *why* are you disquieted within me? Hope in God, for I shall yet praise Him *for* the help of His countenance" (Psalms 42:5).

"Anxiety in the heart of man causes depression, but a good word makes it glad" (Proverbs 12:25).

"A merry heart makes a cheerful countenance, but by sorrow of the heart the spirit is broken" (Proverbs 15:13).

"For all things *are* for your sakes, that grace, having spread through the many, may cause thanksgiving to abound to the glory of God. Therefore we do not lose heart. Even though our outward man is perishing, yet the inward *man* is being renewed day by day. For our light affliction, which is but for a moment, is working for us a far more exceeding *and* eternal weight of glory, while we do not look at the things which are seen, but at the things which are not seen. For the things which are seen *are* temporary, but the things which are not seen *are* eternal" (2 Corinthians 4:15–18).

"Rejoice in the Lord always. Again I will say, rejoice! Let your gentleness be known to all men. The Lord *is* at hand. Be anxious for nothing, but in everything by prayer and supplication, with thanksgiving, let your requests be made known to God; and the peace of God, which surpasses all understanding, will guard your hearts and minds through Christ Jesus" (Philippians 4:4–7).

The Grace of God

1. The Description

The grace of God is one of the hardest of God's perfections to explain. It is like love—it is hard to explain, but you sure know when you have it.

Webster's 1828 Dictionary says grace is "the free, unmerited love and favor of God, the spring and source of all the benefits men receive from Him; the application of Christ's righteousness to the sinner; a state of reconciliation to God; eternal life."

Grace is often confused with mercy. Mercy is *not receiving* something you deserve like punishment. Grace is *receiving* something you do not deserve like reconciliation with God.

Helps these problems:

Anger, assurance, devotion, pride

2. The Word of God

> "And the Lord passed before him and proclaimed, 'The Lord, the Lord God, merciful and gracious, longsuffering, and abounding in goodness and truth'" (Exodus 34:6).

> "They refused to obey, and they were not mindful of Your wonders that You did among them. But they hardened their necks, and in their rebellion they appointed a leader to return to their bondage. But You *are* God, ready to pardon, gracious and merciful, slow to anger, abundant in kindness, and did not forsake them" (Nehemiah 9:17).

> "He has made His wonderful works to be remembered; The Lord *is* gracious and full of compassion" (Psalms 111:4).

"So rend your heart, and not your garments; Return to the Lord your God, For He *is* gracious and merciful, slow to anger, and of great kindness; And He relents from doing harm" (Joel 2:13).

"And the Child grew and became strong in spirit, filled with wisdom; and the grace of God was upon Him" (Luke 2:40).

"And the Word became flesh and dwelt among us, and we beheld His glory, the glory as of the only begotten of the Father, full of grace and truth" (John 1:14).

"And of His fullness we have all received, and grace for grace. For the law was given through Moses, *but* grace and truth came through Jesus Christ" (John 1:16–17).

"But by the grace of God I am what I am, and His grace toward me was not in vain; but I labored more abundantly than they all, yet not I, but the grace of God *which was* with me" (1 Corinthians 15:10).

"For you know the grace of our Lord Jesus Christ, that though He was rich, yet for your sakes He became poor, that you through His poverty might become rich" (2 Corinthians 8:9).

"And He said to me, 'My grace is sufficient for you, for My strength is made perfect in weakness.' Therefore most gladly I will rather boast in my infirmities, that the power of Christ may rest upon me" (2 Corinthians 12:9).

"To the praise of the glory of His grace, by which He has made us accepted in the Beloved. In Him we have redemption through His blood, the forgiveness of sins, according to the riches of His grace which He made to abound toward us in all wisdom and prudence" (Ephesians 1:6–8).

"For by grace you have been saved through faith, and that not of yourselves; *it is* the gift of God, not of works, lest anyone should boast" (Ephesians 2:8–9).

"Therefore do not be ashamed of the testimony of our Lord, nor of me His prisoner, but share with me in the sufferings for the gospel according to the power of God, who has saved us and called *us* with a holy calling, not according to our works, but according to His own purpose and grace which was given to us in Christ Jesus before time began" (2 Timothy 1:8–9).

"But when the kindness and the love of God our Savior toward man appeared, not by works of righteousness which we have done, but according to His mercy He saved us, through the washing of regeneration and renewing of the Holy Spirit, whom He poured out on us abundantly through Jesus Christ our Savior, that having been justified by His grace we should become heirs according to the hope of eternal life" (Titus 3:4–7).

"Let us therefore come boldly to the throne of grace, that we may obtain mercy and find grace to help in time of need" (Hebrews 4:16).

> "But may the God of all grace, who called us to His eternal glory by Christ Jesus, after you have suffered a while, perfect, establish, strengthen, and settle *you*" (1 Peter 5:10).

> "The grace of our Lord Jesus Christ *be* with you all. Amen" (Revelation 22:21).

The Hope of God

1. The Description

The hope of God is not what the world considers hope to be, as in "I hope this happens." No, God's hope is a confident expectation that God will fulfill His promises.

The Scriptures are packed full of the promises of God to His children. And these you need not "hope" will come true, but with confident expectation can find hope in knowing they will come true. Many Christians who lack hope, hope in the future or hope in God, do so because they lack knowledge of the promises of God.

A wonderful way to study the Scriptures and to get to know God better is to collect the promises of God as you read through your Bible.

A belief in the promises of God leads to joy, peace, contentment, love, and happiness. Disbelief or lack of knowledge in the promises of God leads to discontentment, discouragement, depression, fear, anxiety, anger, bitterness, selfishness, brooding, and resentment.

Helps these problems:

Contentment, depression, unbelief

2. The Word of God

> "Be of good courage, and He shall strengthen your heart, all you who hope in the Lord" (Psalms 31:24).

"For in You, O Lord, I hope; You will hear, O Lord my God" (Psalms 38:15).

"And now, Lord, what do I wait for? My hope *is* in You" (Psalms 39:7).

"Why are you cast down, O my soul? And *why* are you disquieted within me? Hope in God, for I shall yet praise Him *for* the help of His countenance" (Psalms 42:5).

"Deliver me, O my God, out of the hand of the wicked, Out of the hand of the unrighteous and cruel man. For You are my hope, O Lord God; *You are* my trust from my youth" (Psalms 71:4–5).

"That they may set their hope in God, and not forget the works of God, but keep His commandments" (Psalms 78:7).

"And take not the word of truth utterly out of my mouth, for I have hoped in Your ordinances" (Psalms 119:43).

"Remember the word to Your servant, upon which You have caused me to hope" (Psalms 119:49).

"Those who fear You will be glad when they see me, because I have hoped in Your word" (Psalms 119:74).

"My soul faints for Your salvation, but I hope in Your word" (Psalms 119:81).

"Lord, I hope for Your salvation, and I do Your commandments" (Psalms 119:166).

"O Israel, hope in the Lord; for with the Lord *there is* mercy, and with Him *is* abundant redemption" (Psalms 130:7).

"O Israel, hope in the Lord from this time forth and forever" (Psalms 131:3).

"And I will wait on the Lord, who hides His face from the house of Jacob; and I will hope in Him" (Isaiah 8:17).

"Blessed *is* the man who trusts in the Lord, and whose hope is the Lord. For he shall be like a tree planted by the waters, which spreads out its roots by the river, and will not fear when heat comes; but its leaf will be green, and will not be anxious in the year of drought, nor will cease from yielding fruit" (Jeremiah 17:7–8).

"This I recall to my mind, therefore I have hope. *Through* the Lord's mercies we are not consumed, because His compassions fail not. *They are* new every morning; Great *is* Your faithfulness. 'The Lord *is* my portion,' says my soul, 'Therefore I hope in Him!'" (Lamentations 3:21–24).

"Therefore, having been justified by faith, we have peace with God through our Lord Jesus Christ, through whom also we have access by faith into this grace in which we stand, and rejoice in hope of the glory of God" (Romans 5:1–2).

> "Now may the God of hope fill you with all joy and peace in believing, that you may abound in hope by the power of the Holy Spirit" (Romans 15:13).

> "I now rejoice in my sufferings for you, and fill up in my flesh what is lacking in the afflictions of Christ, for the sake of His body, which is the church" (Colossians 1:24).

> "Thus God, determining to show more abundantly to the heirs of promise the immutability of His counsel, confirmed *it* by an oath, that by two immutable things, in which it *is* impossible for God to lie, we might have strong consolation, who have fled for refuge to lay hold of the hope set before *us*" (Hebrews 6:17–18).

> "Blessed *be* the God and Father of our Lord Jesus Christ, who according to His abundant mercy has begotten us again to a living hope through the resurrection of Jesus Christ from the dead" (1 Peter 1:3).

> "And everyone who has this hope in Him purifies himself, just as He is pure" (1 John 3:3).

Preaching and Teaching

If you get a chance to teach or preach, here are a few ideas to keep in mind. One of the weaknesses in Christian teaching/preaching today is that it is heavily weighted on the side of what people need to do. But as you have seen throughout this book, just telling people what to do does not bring about change. That is why we do not see a lot of change in the Christian community; we have missed out on God's way of change. Lasting change is about who you know, not about what you do. Now as I promised before, there is a balancing thought between knowing and doing.

The Apostle Paul in his letters to believers gave us a wonderful model for teaching and preaching. Like in Ephesians, Paul starts with who God is and then encourages the people to love the Lord their God. Only after all that understanding and knowing does he explain what that change will look like. In the second half of Ephesians, Paul gives his practical advice of what believing in God looks like. Unfortunately too often when I hear preaching on Ephesians, it starts in chapter 4 with all the things a good Christian should be doing. That message has missed out on what we first need to be knowing. Therefore, more effective teaching and preaching have more of a balance of knowing and doing. But it must begin with knowing and believing for God to make the change of heart that leads to doing. Knowledge of God + belief in God = changed by God.

Below is a sample outline of what a sermon might look like for a message on the friendship of Jesus Christ (again all the verses were easy to find because of my biography of God notebook).

What a Friend We Have in Jesus

I. A Good Friend Is There for You

> "Be strong and of good courage, do not fear nor be afraid of them; for the Lord your God, He *is* the One who goes with you. He will not leave you nor forsake you" (Deuteronomy 31:6).

> "Where can I go from Your Spirit? Or where can I flee from Your presence? If I ascend into heaven, You *are* there; If I make my bed in hell, behold, You *are there. If* I take the wings of the morning, *And* dwell in the uttermost parts of the sea, Even there Your hand shall lead me,

And Your right hand shall hold me" (Psalms 139:7–10).

"Fear not, for I *am* with you; Be not dismayed, for I *am* your God. I will strengthen you, Yes, I will help you, I will uphold you with My righteous right hand" (Isaiah 41:10).

"But the Lord *is* with me as a mighty, awesome One. Therefore my persecutors will stumble, and will not prevail. They will be greatly ashamed, for they will not prosper. *Their* everlasting confusion will never be forgotten" (Jeremiah 20:11).

"'Behold, the virgin shall be with child, and bear a Son, and they shall call His name Immanuel,' which is translated, 'God with us'" (Matthew 1:23).

"And I will pray the Father, and He will give you another Helper, that He may abide with you forever—the Spirit of truth, whom the world cannot receive, because it neither sees Him nor knows Him; but you know Him, for He dwells with you and will be in you" (John 14:16–17).

"*Let your* conduct *be* without covetousness; *be* content with such things as you have. For He Himself has said, 'I will never leave you nor forsake you'" (Hebrews 13:5).

II. A Good Friend Listens to You

"In my distress I called upon the Lord, and cried out to my God; He heard my voice from His temple, and my cry *entered* His ears" (2 Samuel 22:7).

"Depart from me, all you workers of iniquity; For the Lord has heard the voice of my weeping. The Lord has heard my supplication; The Lord will receive my prayer" (Psalms 6:8–9).

"Lord, You have heard the desire of the humble; You will prepare their heart; You will cause Your ear to hear" (Psalms 10:17).

"I sought the Lord, and He heard me, and delivered me from all my fears" (Psalms 34:4).

"As for me, I will call upon God, And the Lord shall save me. Evening and morning and at noon I will pray, and cry aloud, And He shall hear my voice" (Psalms 55:16–17).

"I love the Lord, because He has heard My voice *and* my supplications. Because He has inclined His ear to me, Therefore I will call *upon Him* as long as I live" (Psalms 116:1–2).

"Now this is the confidence that we have in Him, that if we ask anything according to His will, He hears us" (1 John 5:14).

III. A Good Friend Talks to You

"Concerning the works of men, By the word of Your lips, I have kept away from the paths of the destroyer. Uphold my steps in Your paths, *that* my footsteps may not slip" (Psalms 17:4–5).

"I will hear what God the LORD will speak, For He will speak peace to His people and to His saints; But let them not turn back to folly" (Psalms 85:8).

"*Is it* not from the mouth of the Most High That woe and well-being proceed?" (Lamentations 3:38).

"Blessed *is* the man Who walks not in the counsel of the ungodly, nor stands in the path of sinners, nor sits in the seat of the scornful; But his delight *is* in the law of the Lord, And in His law he meditates day and night. He shall be like a tree Planted by the rivers of water, that brings forth its fruit in its season, whose leaf also shall not wither; And whatever he does shall prosper" (Psalms 1:1–3).

"The words of the Lord *are* pure words, *like* silver tried in a furnace of earth, Purified seven times" (Psalms 12:6).

"The law of the Lord *is* perfect, converting the soul; The testimony of the LORD *is* sure, making wise the simple" (Psalms 19:7).

"Your word *is* a lamp to my feet and a light to my path" (Psalms 119:105).

"In the beginning was the Word, and the Word was with God, and the Word was God" (John 1:1).

"For the word of God *is* living and powerful, and sharper than any two-edged sword, piercing even to the division of soul and spirit, and of joints and marrow, and is a discerner of the thoughts and intents of the heart" (Hebrews 4:12).

IV. A Good Friend Helps Solve Your Problems

"Be anxious for nothing, but in everything by prayer and supplication, with thanksgiving, let your requests be made known to God; and the peace of God, which surpasses all understanding, will guard your hearts and minds through Christ Jesus" (Philippians 4:6–7).

"Therefore humble yourselves under the mighty hand of God, that He may exalt you in due time, casting all your care upon Him, for He cares for you" (1 Peter 5:6–7).

"Therefore do not worry, saying, 'What shall we eat?' or 'What shall we drink?' or 'What shall we wear?' For after all these things the Gentiles seek. For your heavenly Father knows that you need all these things. But seek first the kingdom of God and His righteousness, and all these things shall be added to you. Therefore do not worry about tomorrow, for tomorrow will worry about its own things. Sufficient for the day *is* its own trouble" (Matthew 6:31–34).

"Come to Me, all *you* who labor and are heavy laden, and I will give you rest. Take My yoke upon you and learn from Me, for I am gentle and lowly in heart, and you will find rest for your souls" (Matthew 11:28–29).

V. A Good Friend Forgives Your Mistakes

"If we confess our sins, He is faithful and just to forgive us *our* sins and to cleanse us from all unrighteousness" (1 John 1:9).

"I, *even* I, *am* He who blots out your transgressions for My own sake; And I will not remember your sins" (Isaiah 43:25).

"And be kind to one another, tenderhearted, forgiving one another, just as God in Christ forgave you" (Ephesians 4:32).

"For if you forgive men their trespasses, your heavenly Father will also forgive you" (Matthew 6:14).

"For You, Lord, *are* good, and ready to forgive, and abundant in mercy to all those who call upon You" (Psalms 86:5).

Additional

A Good Friend Avenges	Romans 12:18–19
A Good Friend Guides	Luke 1:78–79
A Good Friend Comforts	Psalms 94:19
A Good Friend Corrects	Proverbs 3:11–12
A Good Friend Knows	Psalms 31:7
A Good Friend Protects	Psalms 62:7–8
A Good Friend Uplifts	Psalms 145:14
A Good Friend Is Loyal	Deuteronomy 7:9
A Good Friend Is Faithful	Psalms 37:3
A Good Friend Is Compassionate	Psalms 111:4

A Good Friend Is Gracious	Psalms 145:8
A Good Friend Is Merciful	Psalms 145:8
A Good Friend Is Wise	Proverbs 3:19

Application

How would believing Jesus is your best friend change your life?

It would help remove loneliness, fear, discouragement, anger, and depression.

It would be an example of how to be a good friend to others.

What a Friend We Have in Jesus
Joseph M. Scriven

What a Friend we have in Jesus,
All our sins and griefs to bear!
What a privilege to carry,
Everything to God in prayer!
O what peace we often forfeit,
O what needless pain we bear,
All because we do not carry,
Everything to God in prayer.
Have we trials and temptations!
Is there trouble anywhere?
We should never be discouraged,
Take it to the Lord in prayer.
Can we find a friend so faithful,
Who will all our sorrows share?
Jesus knows our every weakness,
Take it to the Lord in prayer.
Are we weak and heavyladen,
Cumbered with a load of care?
Precious Savior, still our refuge—
Take it to the Lord in prayer.
Do thy friends despise, forsake thee?

Take it to the Lord in prayer,
In His arms He'll take and shield thee,
Thou wilt find a solace there.

Additional Study

As I told you before, continuing to grow in your knowledge of God is vital to you continuing in His joy. While your priority should be God's Word, it is also good for you to read what others have written. Like me, you will not necessarily agree with all that others have written; but if you are first grounded in God's Word and trusting the Holy Spirit, you need not worry about error. Below are some excellent books and websites to help you continue in your study. Once you read all these, you will be as smart as me, probably even smarter (smile). After you read all of them, give me a call, and I will give you a few more to read. Also each of these books speaks of other good books too, the reading of books is endless.

Knowing God

These books are directly related to knowing God. Tony's is my favorite and the one I recommend the most. I used it as our textbook for the college class I taught. Not only does Tony do a great job explaining the importance of knowing God, in the middle of his book, he has sixteen chapters on the different attributes of God. Dan's book I recommend over J.I. Packer's *Knowing God* because it is a little more up-to-date. But Packer's book is a good possibility for when you run out of books to read.

Mardi's is another one of my favorites; while not as large as others, she does a great job of making it very practical. She has a whole section in the book of how different character qualities of God help her in everyday life. Mardi's book is also good because it is a lady's point of view on knowing God. Sam's book is a devotional workbook, it doesn't have a lot of reading. If you are interested in doing a biography of God but not sure you can organize it yourself, get this workbook. Also it can be a good homework devotional for those you might be discipling.

Tony Evans, *Our God Is Awesome: Encountering the Greatness of Our God* (Chicago: Moody Press, 1994).

Dan DeHaan, *The God You Can Know* (Chicago: Moody Press, 1982).

Mardi Collier, *What Do I Know About My God?* (Greenville: Journeyforth, 2006).

Sam Brock, *My Biography of God: Discovering the Excellency of the Knowledge of Christ* (Newberry Springs: Iron Sharpeneth Iron Publications, 2008).

Henry T. Blackaby and Claude V. King, *Experiencing God: How to Live the Full Adventure of Knowing and Doing the Will of God* (Nashville, Broadman & Holman Publishers, 1994).

Herbert Lockyer, D.D., *All The Divine Names and Titles in the Bible* (Grand Rapids: Zondervan, 1988).

Paul E. Miller, *A Praying Life: Connecting with God in a Distracting World* (Colorado Springs: NavPress, 2009).

First John and Hebrews

If you enjoyed the study on 1 John and wanted to dig deeper yourself, here are three good books to get started. I have put them in order of easiest to hardest so you can work your way into some good studying. I also include M.R. DeHaan's study on Hebrews because it is my favorite commentary on Hebrews. M.R. makes understanding some of the toughest passages in the Scriptures as easy as they were intended.

J. Dwight Pentecost, *The Joy of Fellowship: A Study of First John* (Grand Rapids: Kregel Publications, 1977).

David R. Anderson, *Maximum Joy: First John—Relationship or Fellowship?* (The Woodlands, Texas: Grace Theology Press, 2013).

Zane C. Hodges, *The Epistles of John: Walking in the Light of God's Love* (Denton, Texas: Grace Evangelical Society, 1999).

M.R. DeHaan, *Studies in Hebrews* (Grand Rapids: Kregel Publications, 1996).

Kingdom

Like I mentioned before, the study on the kingdom by James Hollandsworth and others has been a major influence on my spiritual life. Most Christians think we all go to heaven when we die but no! Jesus still has some important work for us to do in His coming kingdom. Your faithfulness here and now will greatly influence your reward and position in the coming kingdom. A good place to start is the website by James Hollandsworth, *Kingdom Preparation.* There you can find out more about his books and listen to his series of sermons (http://kingdompreparation.com/).

Then James's books are a great introduction to the subject along with Thomas's book. They are well-written and easy to understand. For those of you who want to dig into it even deeper, Joseph's (Jody) book *Final Destiny* is a classic and should be read by everyone. But it will take you a while to get through the one thousand-plus pages.

James Hollandsworth, *The End of the Pilgrimage: Your Judgment Seat Verdict and How it Determines Your Place in His Kingdom* (Holly Publishing, 2015).

_____. *Christ Magnified: Glorifying Jesus by Your Life* (Holly Publishing, 2016).

_____. *Keys for Inheriting the Kingdom: Unlocking the Parables of Jesus* (Holly Publishing, 2017).

Thomas M. Lancaster, *Improving the Quality of Your Eternal Life: A Primer on New Testament Exhortations to the Believer* (The Woodlands, Texas: Grace Theology Press, 2016).

Joseph Dillow, *Final Destiny: The Future Reign of the Servant Kings* (Houston: Grace Theology Press, 2012).

The Salvation of the Soul

For those of you who would like to study more on the salvation of the soul or those who are not too sure I know what I am talking about, here are some books for your consideration. The term *salvation of the soul* is not heard very often in our churches but as we saw, the Bible makes an important distinction between it and the salvation of the spirit.

Watchman Nee, *The Salvation of the Soul* (Richmond: Christian Fellowship Publishers, 2009).

Arlen L. Chitwood, *Salvation of the Soul Saving of the Life: A Study About the Salvation to be Revealed at the Time of Christ's Return* (Norman, Oklahoma: The Lamp Broadcast, Inc., 2011).

Dennis M. Rokser, *Salvation in Three Time Zones: Do You Understand the Three Tenses of Salvation?* (Duluth: Grace Gospel Press, 2013).

Bible

If you don't already have a Bible or you have been thinking of getting a new one, I recommend *The Blackaby Study Bible.* While there are many wonderful Bibles available nowadays, if you want to stay in the theme of knowing God, the Blackaby Bible does a wonderful job. The little "Encounter [God]" notes are all about having a deeper relationship with God and are very encouraging. I have quoted from it numerous times in this book. Unfortunately the Bible is not widely available anymore, so if you find one, grab it.

Richard Blackaby, M.Div., PhD, general editor, *The Blackaby Study Bible: Personal Encounters with God Through His Word* (Nashville: Nelson Bibles, 2006).

Conclusion

As we come to the end of the book, do you remember in the preface when I had you write out your purpose of life? Has it changed? What is your purpose in life now? So as you start your journey of walking with our Savior, I leave you with this last thought. All of life, both spiritual and natural, is founded on a personal, intimate, knowledge of our God!

> Grace and peace be multiplied to you in the *knowledge of God and of Jesus our Lord*, as His

divine power has given to us *all things that pertain to life and godliness*, through *the knowledge of Him* who called us by glory and virtue, by which have been given to us exceedingly great and precious promises, that through these *you may be partakers of the divine nature,* having escaped the corruption *that is* in the world through lust. (2 Peter 1:2–4, emphasis added)

---

1. Blackaby and King, 12.
2. Evans, 24.
3. Ibid., 37ff.

Scripture Index

Proverbs

Ecclesiastes

Isaiah

Jeremiah

Lamentations

Daniel

Hosea

Joel

Jonah

Amos

Zephaniah

Matthew

Mark

Luke

John

Acts

Romans

1 Corinthians

2 Corinthians

Galatians

Ephesians

Philippians

Colossians

1 Thessalonians

2 Thessalonians

1 Timothy

2 Timothy

Titus

Hebrews

James

1 Peter

2 Peter

1 John

Jude

Revelation

About the Author

Todd J. Tjepkema (pronounced Chep-ka-ma) has been serving as a discipleship and counseling pastor for more than twenty-five years. He has counseled hundreds of families through the struggles of life. Todd's strong desire is to see God's children have a deeper and passionate relationship with their Savior. Todd and his lovely wife, Barbara, have been married for over thirty years and live in the Phoenix, Arizona area. They have six grown children (two by marriage), all who love their God.

CPSIA information can be obtained
at www.ICGtesting.com
Printed in the USA
FSHW021938230719
60340FS

9 781645 159797